I0810588

IMAGES
of America

NEW WINDSOR

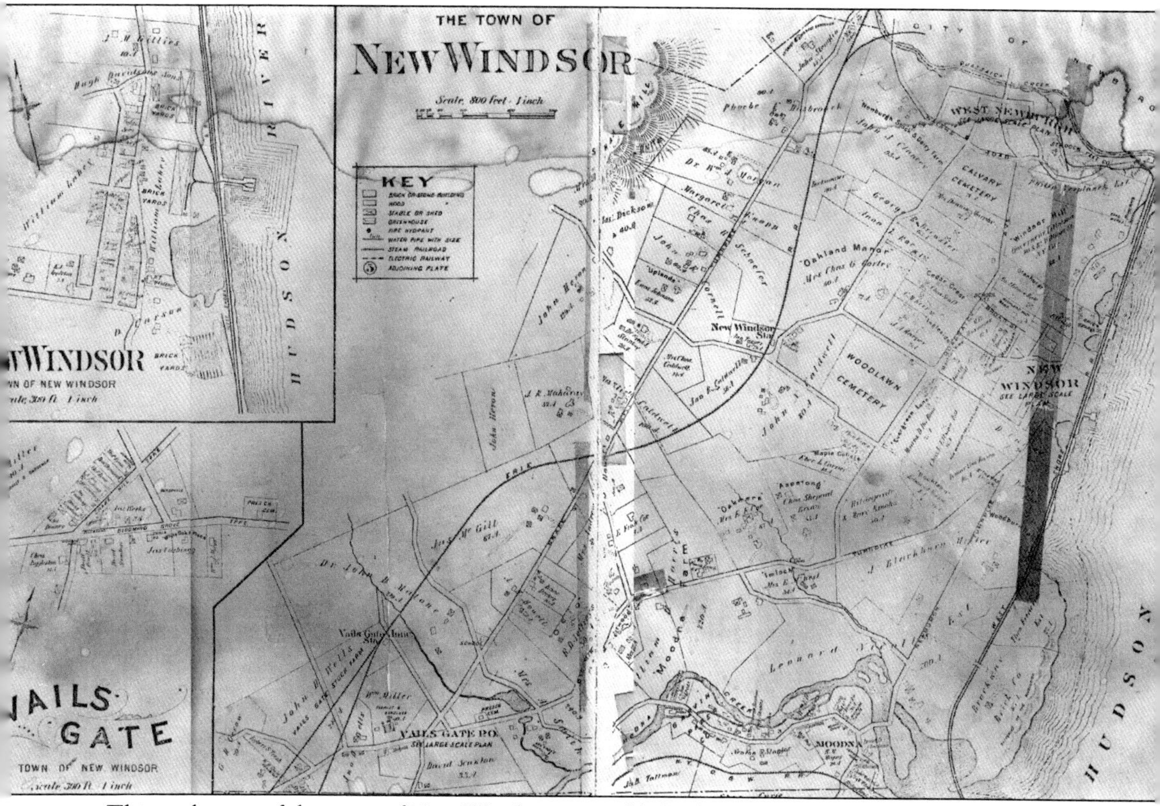

This early map of the town of New Windsor was published around 1903 by H.A. Mueller. It shows the eastern side of the town and is labeled with the names of landowners, buildings, and roads, and even discerns steam railroads from electric railways. Insets show the hamlets of New Windsor and Vails Gate. (Courtesy of James Pullar.)

On the Cover: The 1950 Victory Parade enters John Street from Quassaick Avenue. Seen from left to right are New Windsor Super-Market, Gus's Tailor Shop, and private residences, including the Brennan homestead. The original Gus's Tavern was taken down (see foundation at bottom right) to make way for the new Route 9W bridge from New Windsor to Newburgh. (Courtesy of the Quassaick Fire Engine Company.)

IMAGES
of America

NEW WINDSOR

Barbara Stotesbury Dabroski
and Donna Barker Pullar

ARCADIA
PUBLISHING

ISBN 978-0-7385-9943-4

Published by Arcadia Publishing
Charleston, South Carolina

Printed in the United States of America

Library of Congress Control Number: 2012956239

For all general information, please contact Arcadia Publishing:
Telephone 843-853-2070
Fax 843-853-0044
E-mail sales@arcadiapublishing.com
For customer service and orders:
Toll-Free 1-888-313-2665

Visit us on the Internet at www.arcadiapublishing.com

This book is dedicated to our husbands, James Pullar and William Dabroski.

Contents

ACKNOWLEDGMENTS

The completion of this book depended on many people who gave us access to their personal records, helped us to find the public records we needed, and told us stories that made this project possible.

First, our husbands—Donna's husband, James, spent many hours suggesting, gathering, copying, and returning contributors' information; and Barbara's husband, William, listened, offered suggestions, and gave support.

Our greatest help came from Patricia Favata, volunteer librarian/archivist for the Historical Society of Newburgh Bay and the Highlands; Walter Whitehill, who shared his knowledge and postcard collection; John T. Babcock, who shared his meticulously kept photographs; and Matthew Colon, historic interpreter for Washington's Headquarters State Historic Site.

The following people contributed in a most meaningful and supportive way: Ralph Aiello, the Robert Babcock family, Barbara Bedell, Ethel Coleman, Joseph J. Bux, Michael Crudele, the Cummings family, William Dabroski Jr., Carmine Damario, Ronna Dixson with the New York State Peebles Island Resource Center, the Drennan family, Mary Jane Lahey Dybas, Gregory Gaetano, Robert Gould, Deborah and George Green, Marilyn Hearns, Joan Henderson, Richard Hovey, Jerry Huddleston, Ray Kelly with the Ontario & Western Railway Historical Society, Kathleen Kissel, Anthony Lentini, Anthony Mancinelli, William Martin, Bob McCue with the Ontario & Western Railway Historical Society, Michael S. McGurty with the New York State Parks Educational Program, Robert McKnight, Mary Jane Miller, Patricia Mullarkey, Eugene Murphy, Catherine Molloy Nugent, Robert Overbey, Jeri Paffendorf, Frank Pierri, Joseph C. Primavera, Scott Pryne of American Felt & Filter Company, Irene Pullar, William Pullar, William Shorter, Dr. William Small, Everett Smith, John Smith, Michael Smith, Margaret Spignardo, Edward Stent, Sandra Lewis Terwilliger, Joanne Swanson Versusky, Bruce Williams, and Charles Zgrodek. A special thank-you goes to Remy Louis Thurston, our Arcadia acquisitions editor.

The only thing more rewarding than going back in time to produce this book was to connect with so many wonderful old and new friends.

INTRODUCTION

One cannot find two people born and brought up in New Windsor who will not soon be talking about the "old days." So it was after being married for over 50 years to New Windsor natives James Pullar and William Dabroski and listening to them so joyfully reminisce that we decided to document such stories and introduce the New Windsor area to others.

One of the earliest settlers to the area was Colonel McGregorie in 1685. He established a settlement and trading post at Plum Point, a place of importance during the Revolutionary War. McGregorie's family retained ownership of the property until about 1720, when Dr. John Nicoll purchased the land and subsequently erected a house.

Very early hamlets were New Windsor Village, Orangeville (or Moodna), Mortonville (or Tooker's Gate), Hunting Grove, Quassaick Valley, Ragville, and the Square, also known as Liberty Square. Those areas are now known as Little Britain, Rock Tavern, Vails Gate, and New Windsor.

The thoughts of freedom from British rule began early in this country. The people were upset at the restrictions placed upon them after they had left their native lands to seek various freedoms. The mood spread quickly, eventually coming to the little hamlet of New Windsor. The Revolutionary War, which sought independence from British rule, began in 1775. It went on for eight years, with many of the soldiers who fought in the war finding themselves at what became the New Windsor Cantonment. It was during this time that many historical buildings and sites we see here today were established.

For decades, winters made life difficult. The only heat available came from a fireplace, and the only light at night came from candles or oil lamps. Summers were not much better. Escaping the heat of the Hudson River valley's summer days came only from jumping into a local lake or stream.

Early residents, with their religious convictions, began to gather in halls, stores, and homes to share their thoughts and goals for their families and lives. Churches of a variety of denominations began to dot the landscape. An increased number of children, originally taught at home or in other private settings, generated a greater need for both private and public schools. The danger of fires created a need for organized firehouses.

New Windsor was never able to develop like its northern neighbor Newburgh as its limited waterfront was owned by only one or two individuals who were not interested in further developing their property. This forced many businesses to be established in other areas. Eventually, many more immigrants of all nationalities came. Some came through New York City but identified the New Windsor area as a better place for their families to live and work. Population growth caused factories, stores, schools, and churches to spring up in both New Windsor and Vails Gate. Little Britain and Rock Tavern developed into farmlands and have remained more rural.

From the 1940s to the late 1980s, population expanded. Changes began just outside of Newburgh along Route 94, in the area known as Estate Road. Many of the mansions became apartment buildings, and the land sold. The greatest change came when housing developments began to spring up. Lacey Field was one of the first subdivisions, followed by a development on what was the Cameron Estate, across from the New Windsor School. Farther down Route 94 was Willow Acres, where homes were built by the Schoonmaker Brothers firm. Near Vails Gate, they also built the next large housing development, Forge Hill Development, on land where Forge Hill Farm once stood. About the same time, Kingswood Gardens was built, offering condominiums. Local people were astonished that anyone would buy anything looking like an apartment. The influx of people into these homes only created demand for additional services. The addition of fast food restaurants, banks, stores, and infrastructure that supported these trends would continue.

New Windsor as a governing entity also grew. As early as 1763, the town created a constabulary. These early constables patrolled the town, served warrants, and provided security at annual town meetings and elections. One of the early constables was also the poormaster, responsible for checking on local families to make sure they had food, water, and shelter. In 1909, the constables recovered their first stolen car, which had been abandoned on the Moodna Creek Bridge. In the 1960s, the town board recognized the need to establish a full-time police department.

While subsequent years brought many good things to the area, they did not remain free from the effects of war. One way or another, citizens became involved in conflicts like the Civil War, World War I, World War II, Korea, Vietnam, and more recent engagements in the Middle East. Stewart Airport was established on farmlands donated by the Archie Stewart family during the Great Depression. Because of its national strategic location, proximity to West Point, and distinction of having one of the largest and longest runways in the nation, it became a most important military asset. Fighter pilots were trained there, and a defensive tracking facility for NORAD (North American Air [later Aerospace] Defense Command) was established. Today, Stewart serves as an international airport.

The area's history laid the foundation for what followed. Over the years, families, organizations, schools, churches, and businesses have all played a vital role in the town's growth. When we approached local families and friends to explain that we had decided to memorialize New Windsor with this book, they went to their attics and dressers to find long-stored-away family pictures of the very people who so early on were the core of the community. They have shared those pictures with us, and now, we can share them and their stories with you. Our hope is that each of you, whether from New Windsor or not, will have as much fun reading this exploration of New Windsor's history as we did putting it together.

One

Early Revolutionary Times

In 1609, Henry Hudson was chosen by the Dutch East India Company to lead its effort to discover a water passage to the Far East. Hudson sailed from Amsterdam up what would later be named the Hudson River. He anchored in a broad bay located above the Highlands to trade with the aboriginal inhabitants of the forests along the shoreline. In 1685, twenty-five families of Scottish and Irish immigrants settled on 80 acres at the mouth of Moodna Creek. New Windsor was granted in a patent to Capt. John Evans between 1694 and 1699. Captain Evans vacated his patent after 1699. The number of settlers grew, and houses began to spring up.

Later, a committee was formed to regulate prices of merchant goods. The Ellisons of New Windsor became the victims of a riot when a large crowd came to William Ellison's store accusing him of price gouging and engrossment. They seized all the salt, leaving just one bushel for the use of his family.

Tea caused more trouble than salt. One night, when a tea vendor stopped at Isaac Schultz's tavern, the establishment was mobbed by locals. The people wanted to purchase tea that had been selling for six schillings, and when the vendor demanded more, they seized the load and sold it themselves.

Soon, the settlers began to reject Great Britain's authority and all its restrictions and taxation without representation. Thoughts turned to freedom, and the political upheaval known as the Revolutionary War ensued in 1775. George Washington, after the 1781 American victory at Yorktown, Virginia, moved his army to New Windsor to winter at the cantonment.

It was here that a rebellion nearly erupted over the army's grievances regarding pensions, land bounties, and back pay that had been promised; ultimately, though, army discipline prevailed. News of a provisional peace treaty allowed Washington to issue cease-fire orders, effective April 19, 1783. The eight-year war ended, and the men were furloughed home.

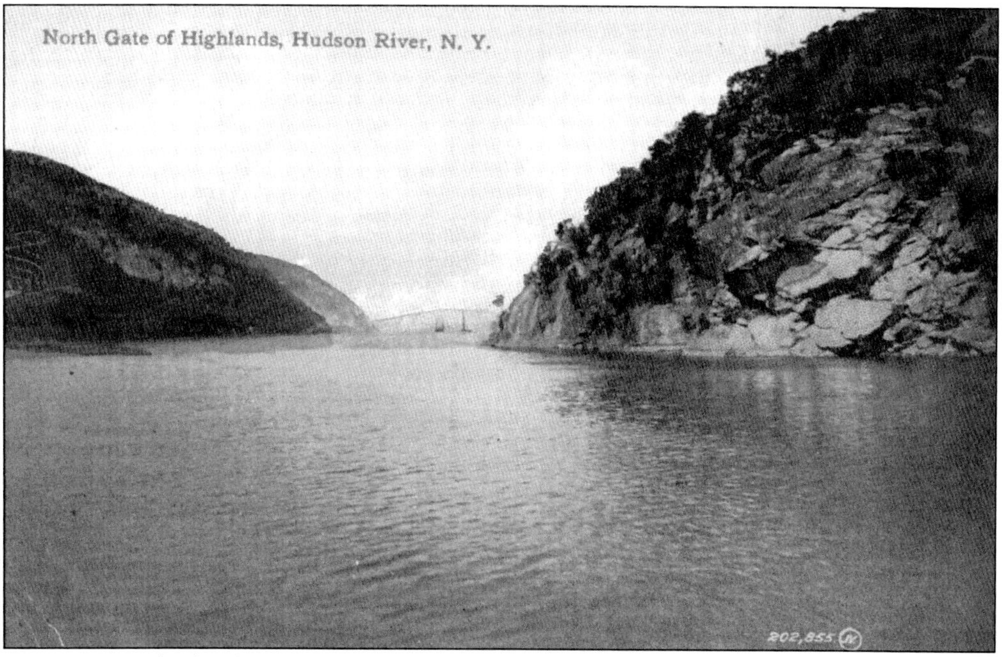

Mountains on both sides of the Hudson River form the Hudson Highlands. Stony Point lies to the south, New Windsor to the north. The name North Gate was coined by early Dutch explorers using the term *wey gat*, or "wind gate," later interpreted as "North Gate." The Hudson River and Highlands played a significant role in early America's cultural and military history. (Courtesy of the Dabroski family.)

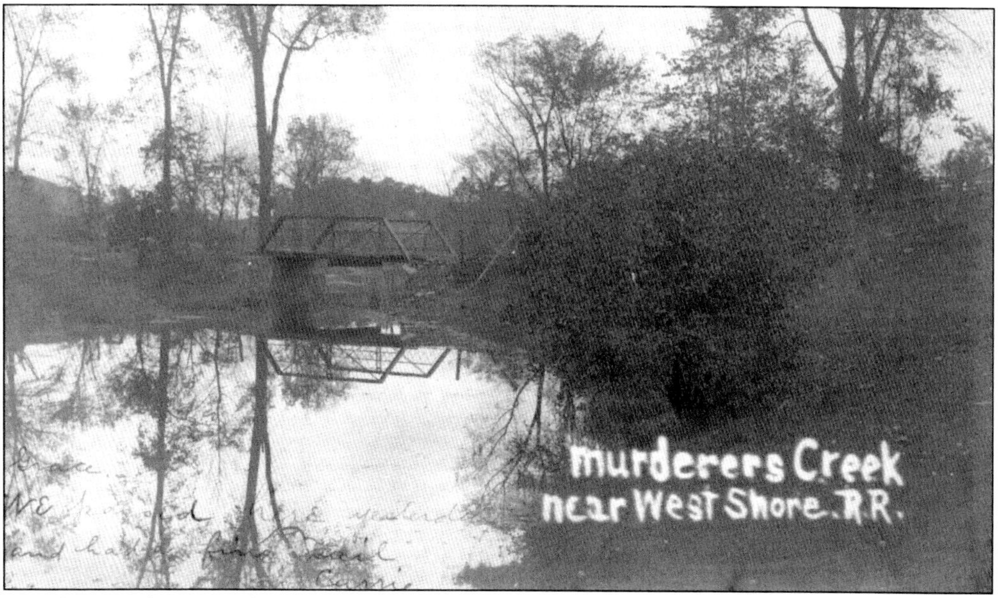

Moodna Creek is a Hudson River tributary that marks the southern boundary of the town of New Windsor. Moodna comes from a Dutch word *moordenaars* ("killers") and evolved from the creek's original name, Murderers' Creek. The latter name originated with the massacre of the Stacy family, early settlers along its banks. By the 20th century, Murderers' Creek became known as Moodna. (Courtesy of the Whitehill Collection.)

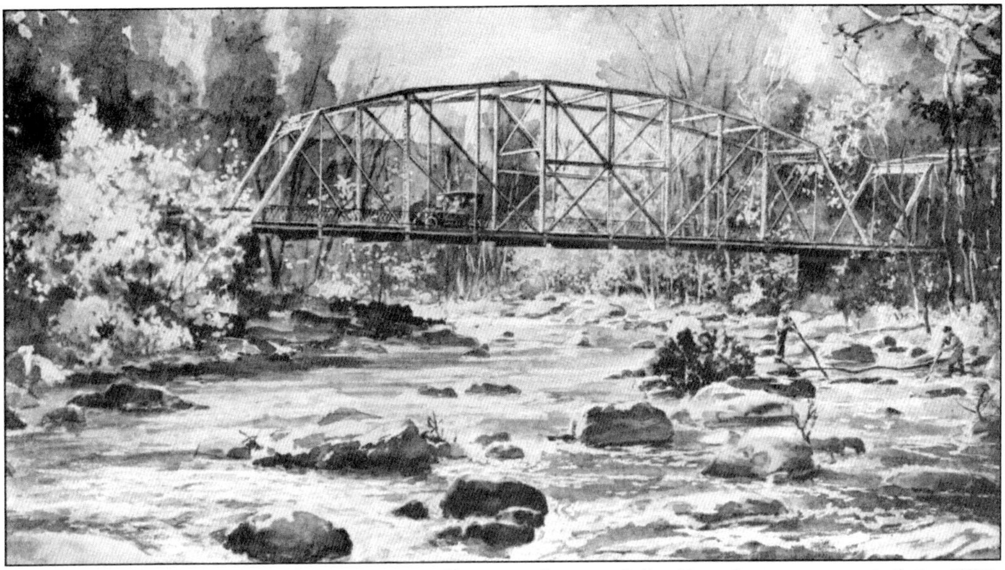

Forge Hill Road was named for Brewster Forge, a figure of the Revolutionary period. In 1750, Nathaniel Hazard used manual labor to built the road, which included a timber bridge over Moodna Creek. Soldiers marching to the New Windsor Cantonment in 1782 passed over this road. Around 1870, a single-span iron bridge (pictured) replaced the original. (Courtesy of the Legacy of Artist John F. Gould.)

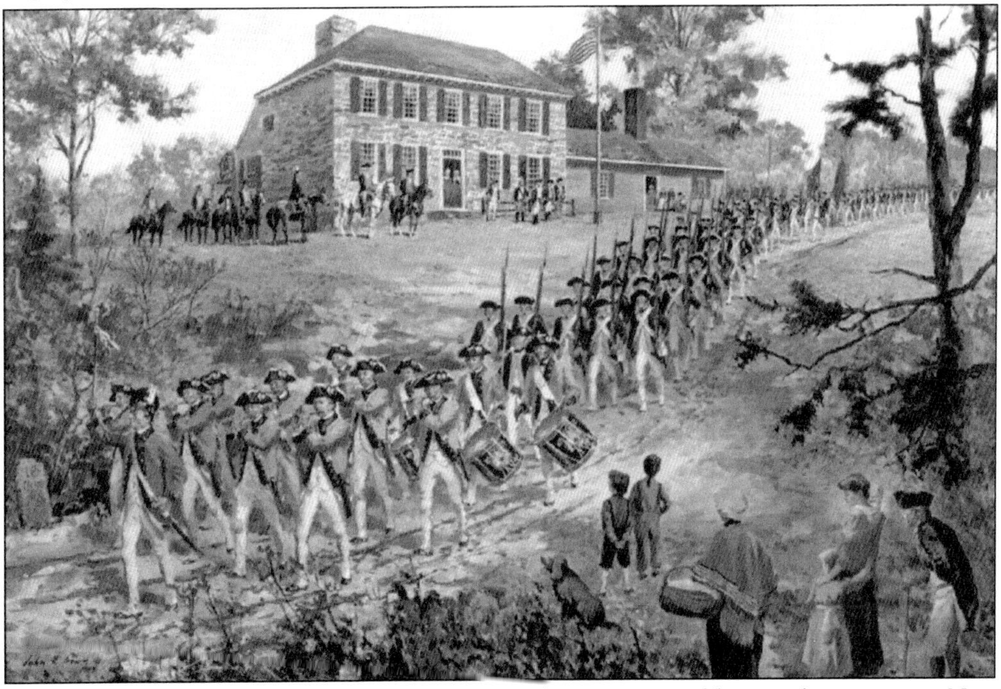

After the British defeat at Yorktown in 1781, Washington moved his northern army to New Windsor to build a winter encampment. The Last Great March saw 7,500 soldiers and 500 wives and children travel through the Hudson Highlands, passing Knox's Headquarters. They built adequate living quarters for the winter and continued training as they awaited news of a peace treaty. (Courtesy of the Legacy of Artist John F. Gould.)

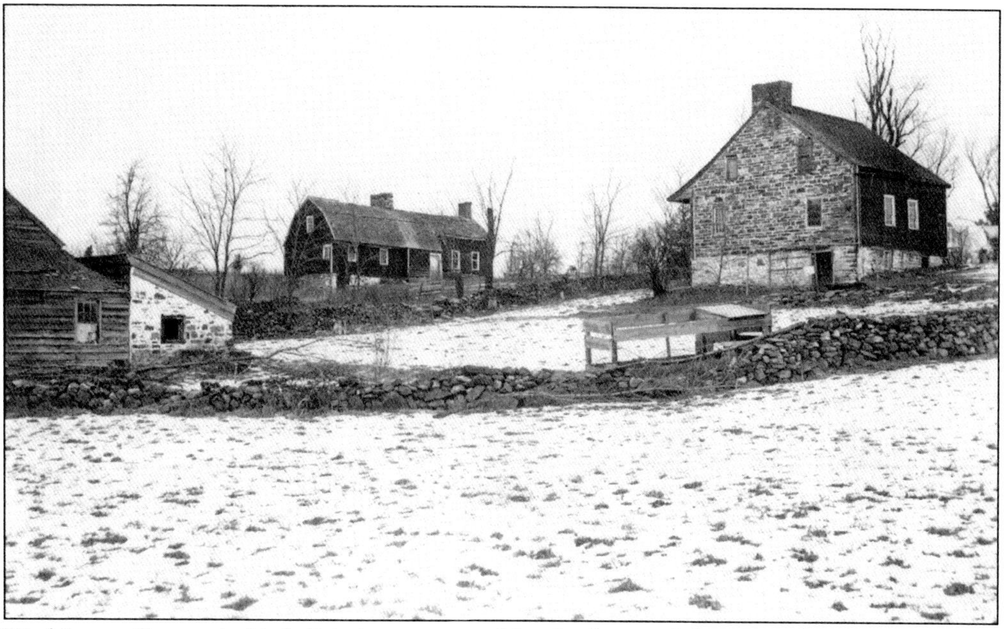

Washington Square, in Little Britain, was named for the diamond-shaped enclosure formed by its public roads. At the outbreak of the American Revolution, it was renamed Liberty Square because not one person living on any of the four roads was of questionable loyalty. When Washington arrived here with his army, Liberty Square became their camp. (Courtesy of the Historical Society of Newburgh Bay and the Highlands.)

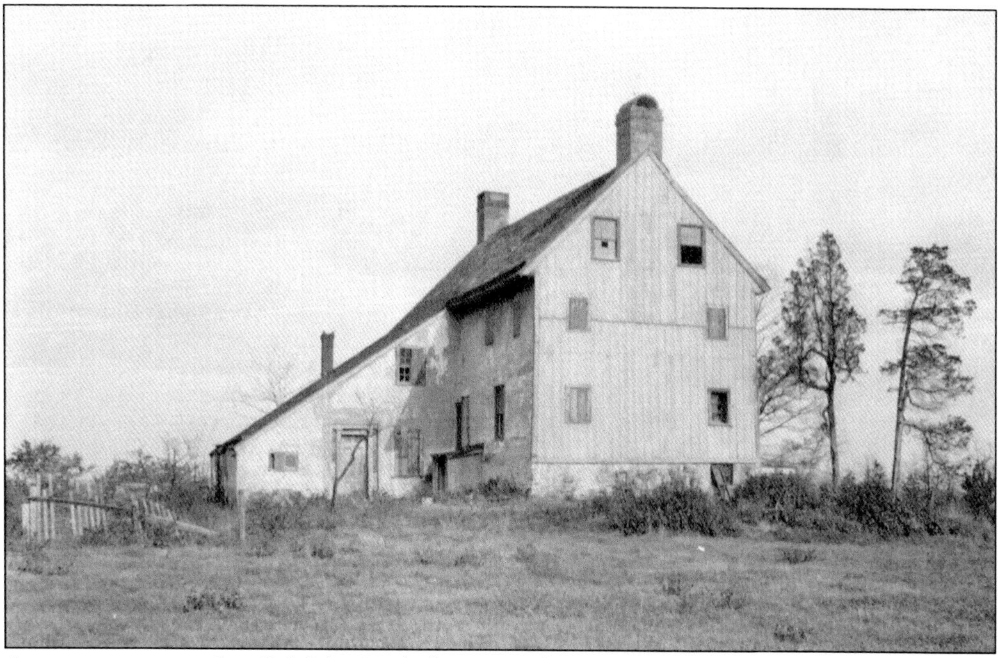

A patent was granted to Col. John Haskell in 1719 of 2,000 acres, with an additional 2,000 acres added in 1721. Around 1729, Haskell erected a home on the slopes of Snake Hill, adjacent to what is now St. Joseph's School. On April 19, 1964, fire destroyed the Haskell homestead. (Courtesy of the Historical Society of Newburgh Bay and the Highlands.)

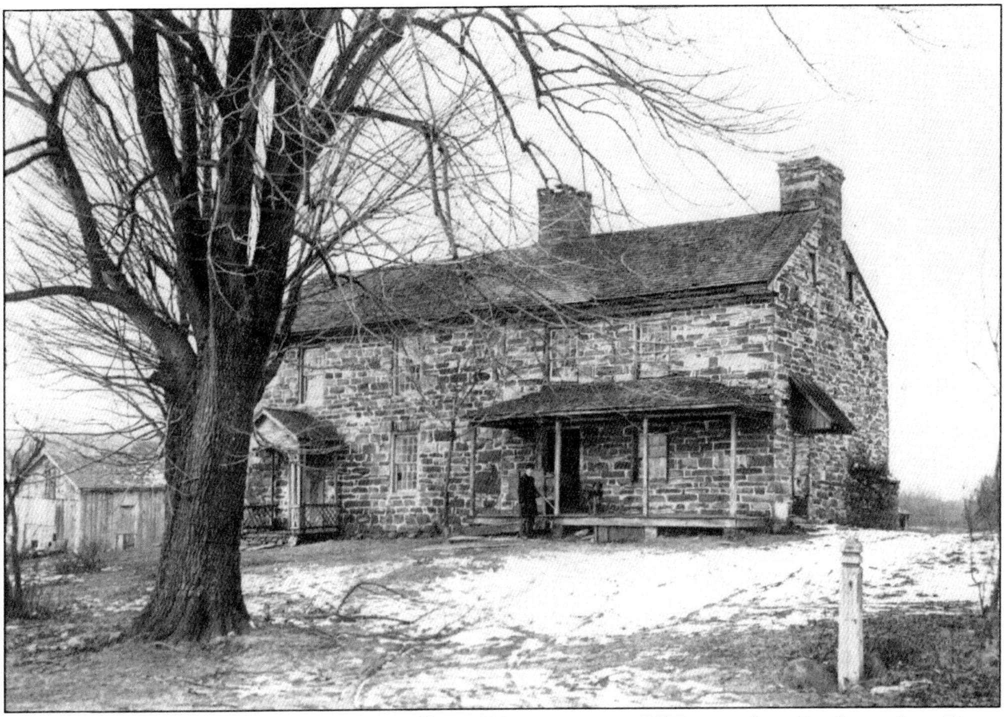

The Edmonston House was built by William Edmonston in 1755 to replace his log cabin. From 1782 to 1783, it served as headquarters for Continental generals Arthur St. Clair and Horatio Gates. Medical staff used it as a base for the Continental army because of its proximity to their encampment. (Courtesy of the Historical Society of Newburgh Bay and the Highlands.)

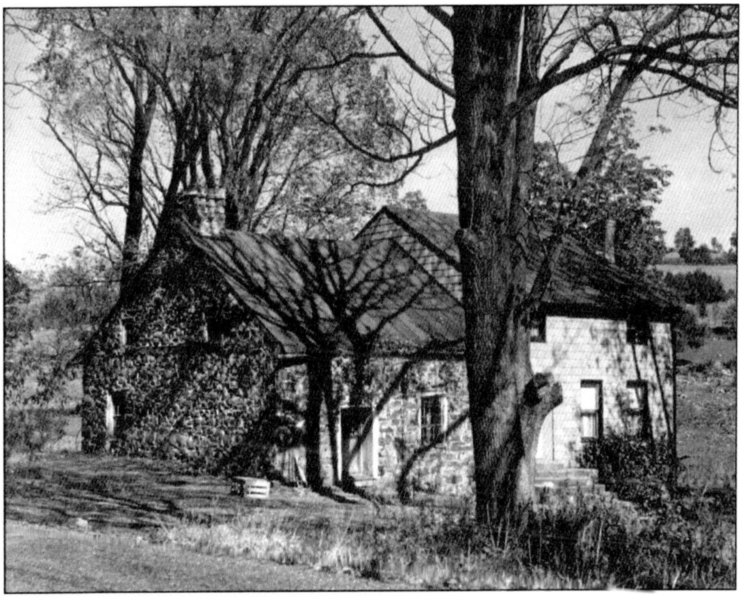

The Young-Welling House is located on Toleman Road. John Young purchased the site in 1730 and lived there in a log cabin. As an associate of Samuel Adams, Young led the disguised "Indians" at the Boston Tea Party. The Wellings built this house on the site in 1764; it remained there into the 20th century. (Courtesy of the Historical Society of Newburgh Bay and the Highlands.)

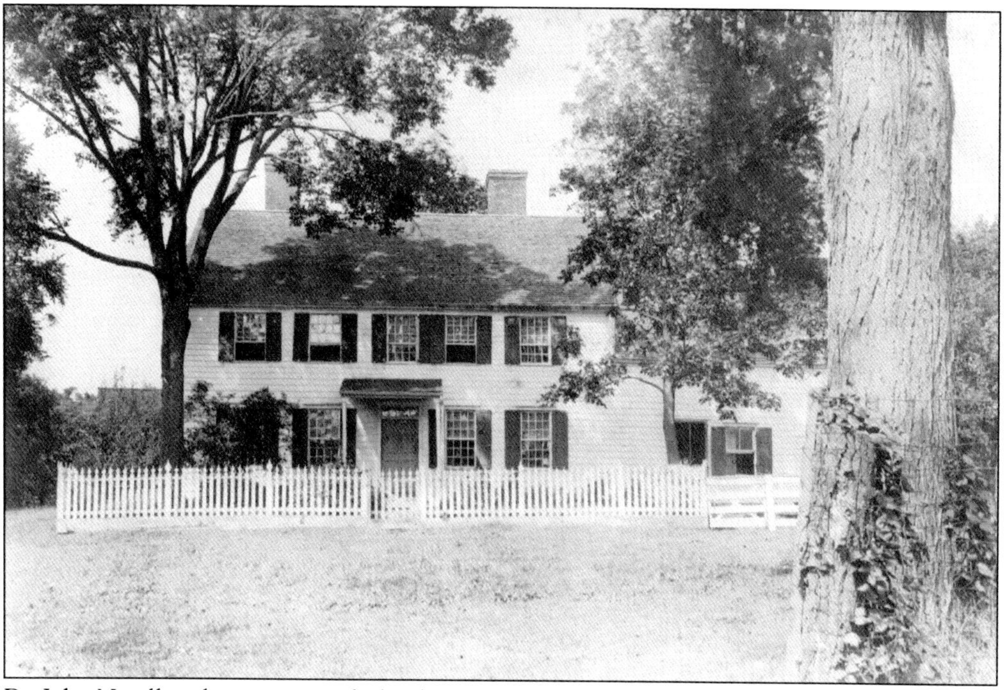

Dr. John Nicoll took possession of a land tract—extending from New Windsor Village to Snake Hill—around 1730. Shortly thereafter, Nicoll House was built overlooking Storm King Mountain. During the Revolution, General Washington's headquarters, located two miles north, conveniently used the Nicoll House's front yard as a supply drop-off point. (Courtesy of the Historical Society of Newburgh Bay and the Highlands.)

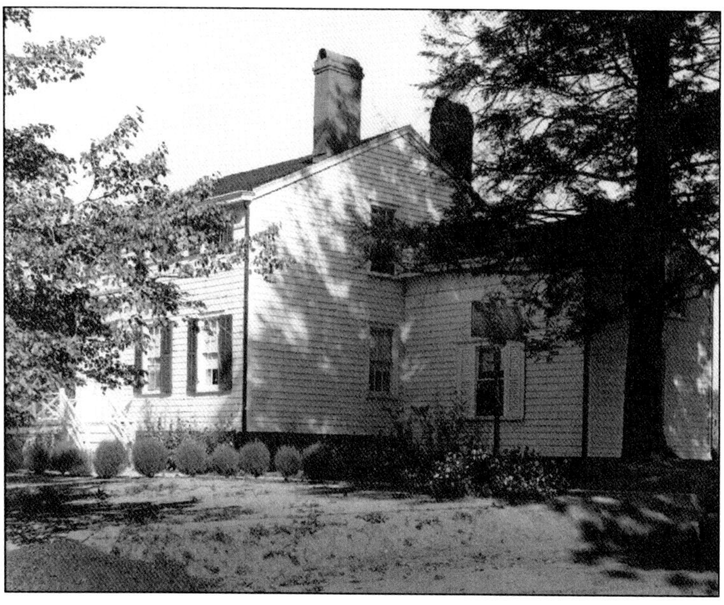

Dr. Moses Higby occupied this house during the Revolution. Following a 1778 smallpox outbreak, he inoculated troops, thus saving lives. He was also known to have removed a silver bullet from the stomach of British spy Daniel Taylor that contained a message from Sir Henry Clinton to British general John Burgoyne. (Courtesy of the Hudson Society of Newburgh Bay and the Highlands.)

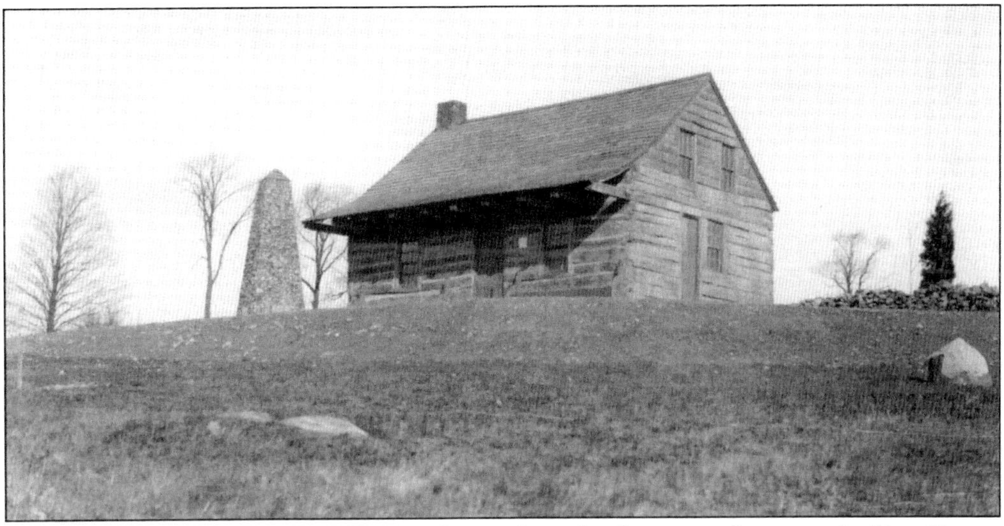

New Windsor Cantonment State Historic Site is where the Continental army, under Gen. George Washington, spent the last winter and spring of the Revolutionary War (1782–1783). Mountainville Hut, the only surviving example of original timber construction by the Continental army, stands front right of the reconstructed Temple of Virtue, which served as a chapel and office. (Courtesy of the Whitehill Collection.)

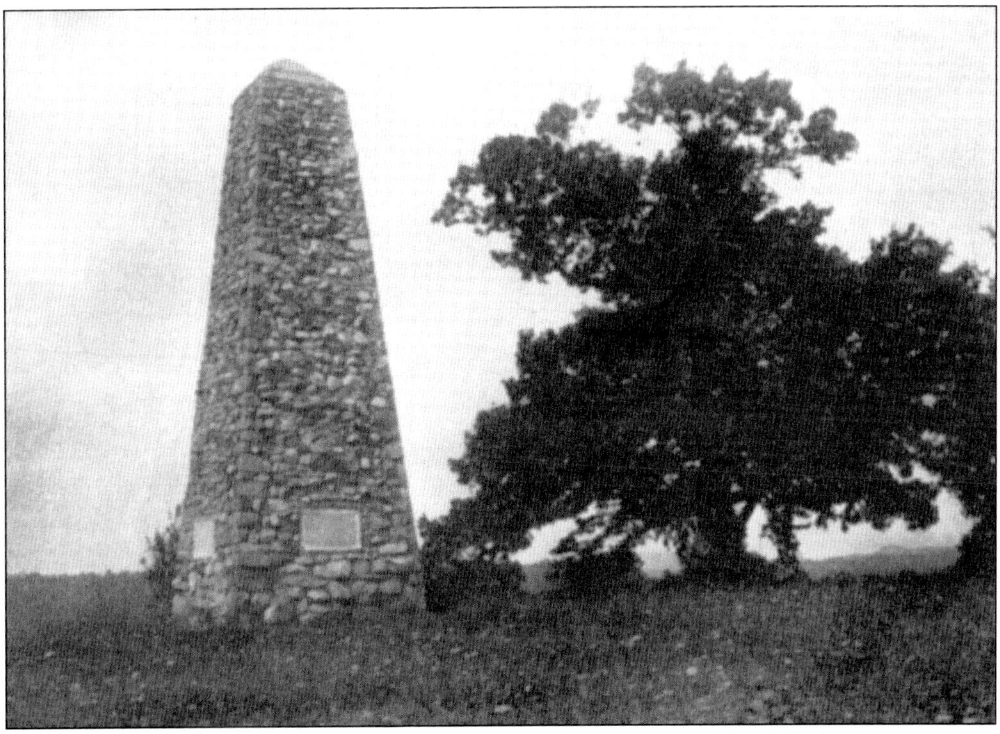

The Temple Hill monument, a massive stone centennial monument at New Windsor Cantonment, was completed in 1891. The location, the final encampment of the Continental army, has been called the "birthplace of the Republic." After eight years of fighting, on April 19, 1783, orders for the cessation of hostilities were publically proclaimed, and the Revolutionary War ended. (Courtesy of the Dabroski family.)

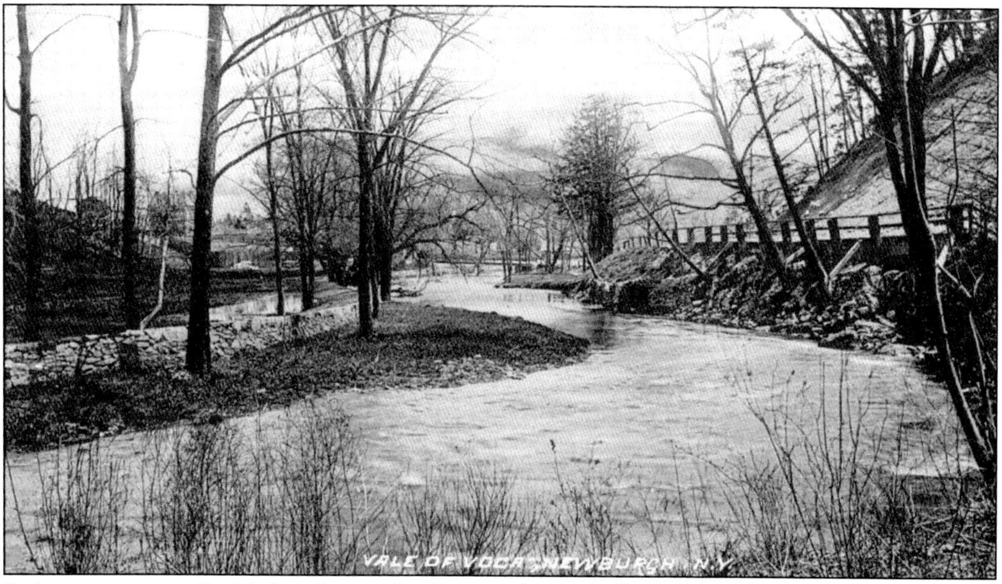

Before it runs into the Hudson River, the Quassaick Creek flows through a deep valley called the Vale of Avoca. In this area, the creek bed is narrow, and the banks are 100 feet high. There was a plot to capture Gen. George Washington here, but it failed when his daughter overheard the plan and warned her father, who then captured the culprits. (Courtesy of Mary Jane Miller.)

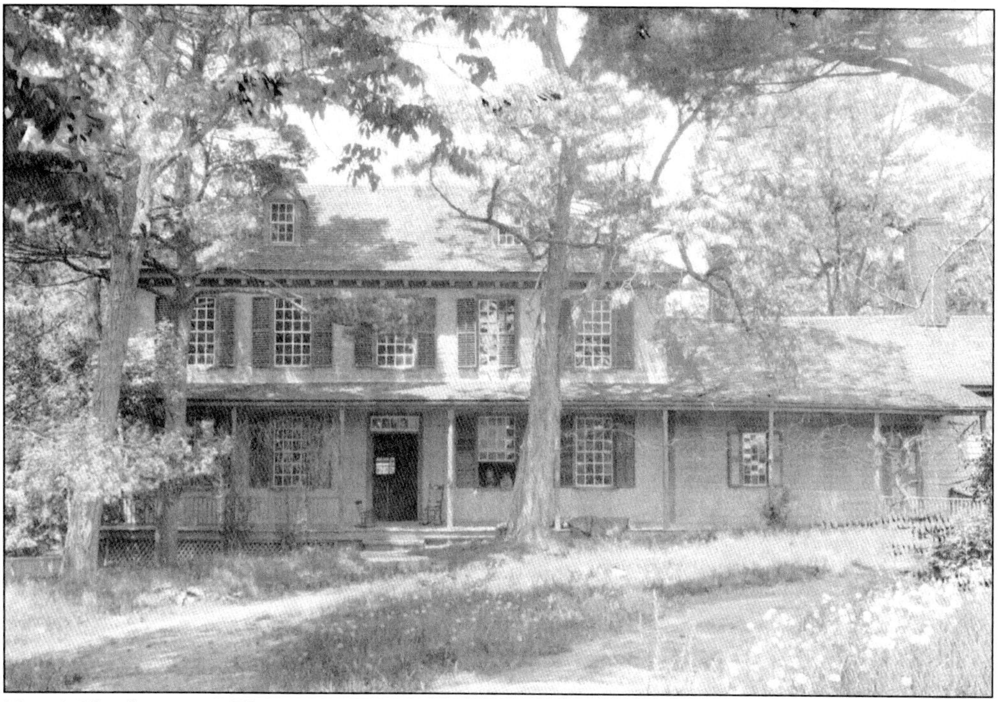

Knox's Headquarters, Blooming Grove Turnpike, was erected by Col. Thomas Ellison in 1754. Revolutionary War general Henry Knox occupied the house in 1780. It was headquarters for Maj. Gen. Horatio Gates, cantonment commander in 1783. Diamond scratches on the parlor window reveal the names of Revolutionary War–era belles Sally Jansen, Gitty Wynkoop, and Maria Colden. (Courtesy of the Historical Society of Newburgh Bay and the Highlands.)

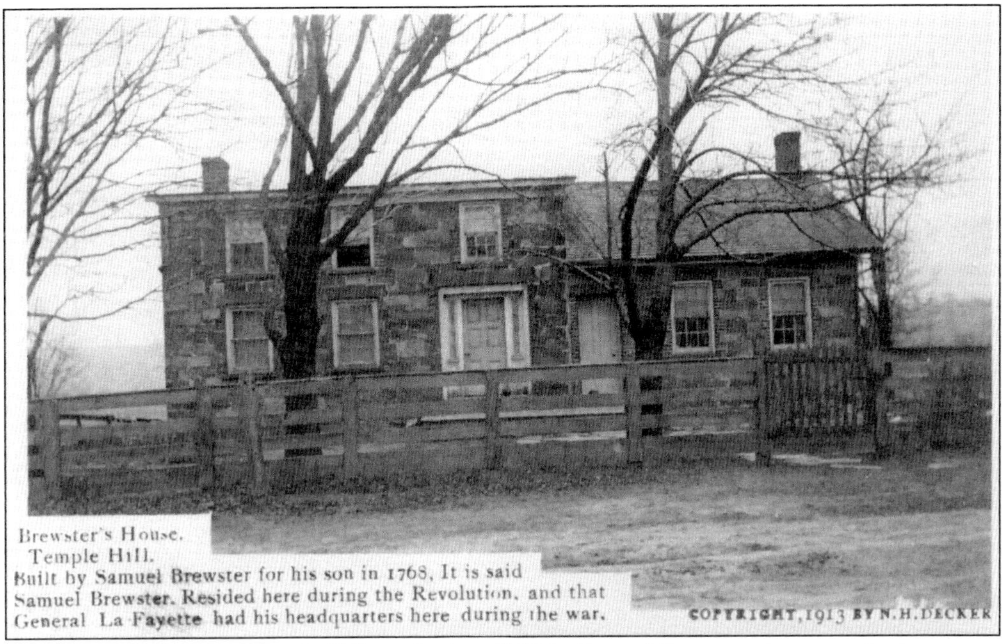

The Brewster House in Temple Hill was built in 1768 by Samuel Brewster. An astute businessman, he was mainly known for owning a forge that made some of the chain links that were used across the Hudson River in an effort to stop the impending invasion of the British during the Revolution. (Courtesy of the Historical Society of Newburgh Bay and the Highlands.)

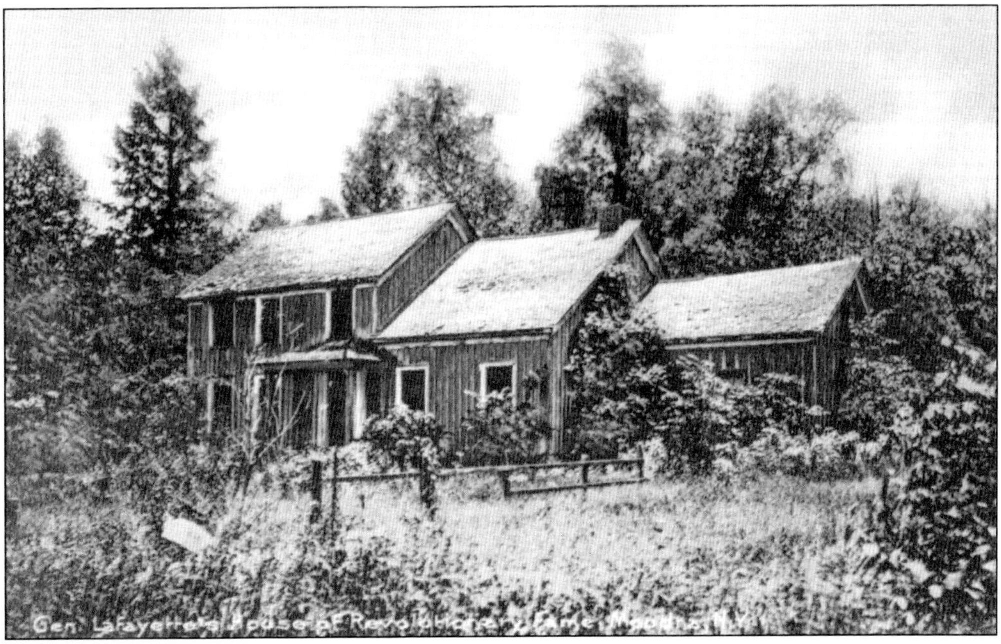

General Lafayette of Revolutionary fame lived in this Moodna home. On one occasion, General Knox and wife planned to give a party in Lafayette's honor, which would require Lafayette to cross the creek. There was no bridge, so dressed in his best, the general chose an Irishman's back as his mode of transportation. Somehow, he ended up in the creek and had to return home drenched, missing the dance entirely. (Courtesy of the Whitehill Collection.)

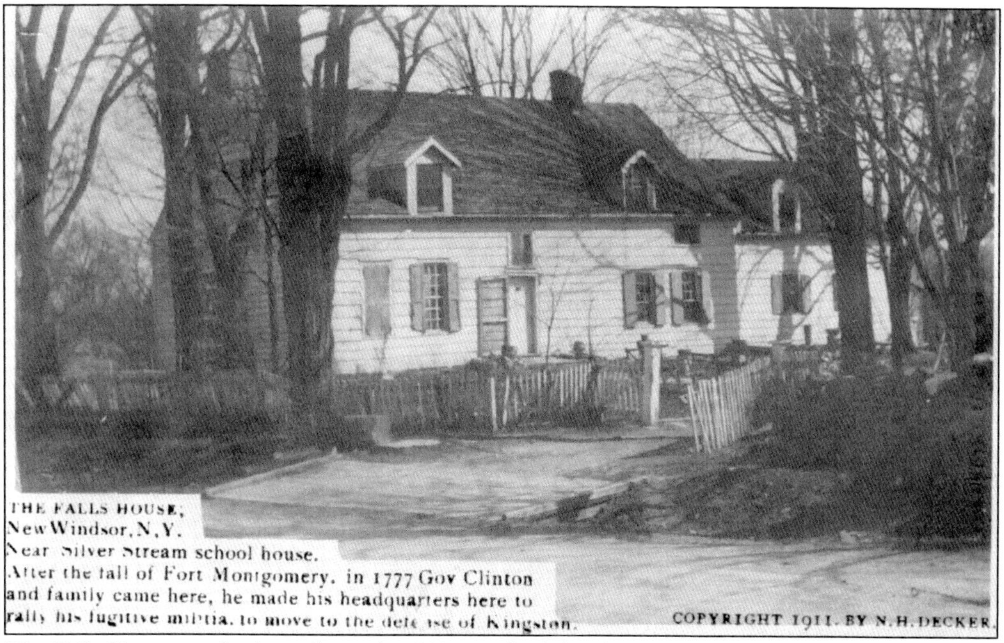

The Falls House was built in the early 1700s on the left side of Route 207 under what is now the New York State Thruway overpass. Gov. George Clinton, a brigadier general in charge of the militia, had his headquarters there in 1777. The building also served as one of several inns, or "stopping places," for thirsty travelers. (Courtesy of the Historical Society of the Newburgh Bay and the Highlands.)

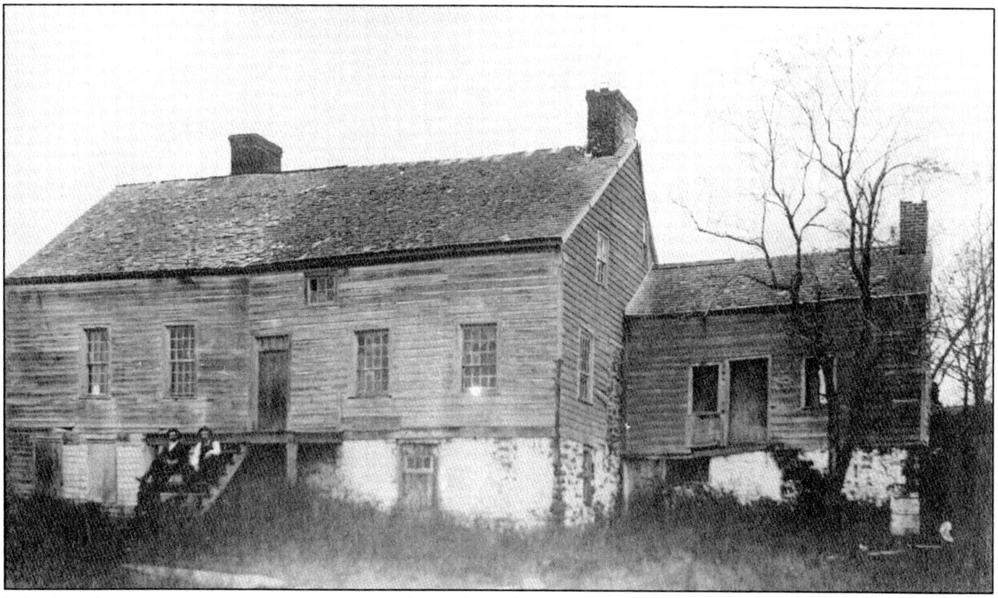

The Rock Tavern was built on a very large boulder, hence its name. In 1740, John Humphrey owned and operated the establishment, which was located near the present-day intersection of Forrester Road and Route 207. During the Revolutionary War and beyond, it was the scene of important historic events. Here, plans were made for the organization of the present Orange County. (Courtesy of the Historical Society of Newburgh Bay and the Highlands.)

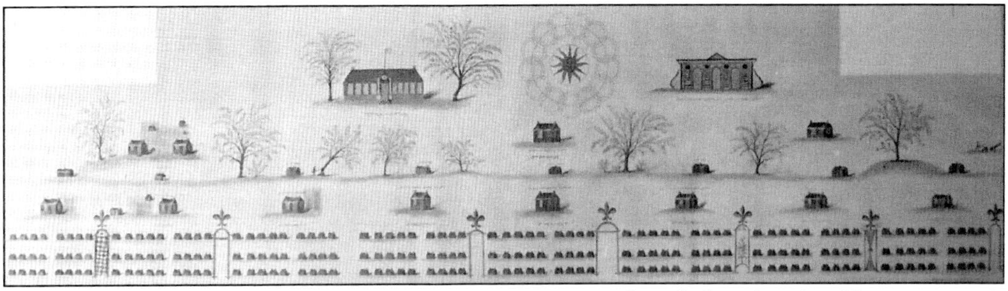

Pvt. William Tarbell, 7th Massachusetts Regiment, produced this sketch of his regiment's encampment areas. The Temple, a soldier-built meetinghouse, is at the upper center of the drawing. The huts of generals and field officers occupy the ground below, and three lines replicate battle formation—two bottom rows of huts for soldiers and a third inhabited by company officers. (Courtesy of Washington's Headquarters State Historic Site, New York State Office of Parks, Recreation and Historic Preservation.)

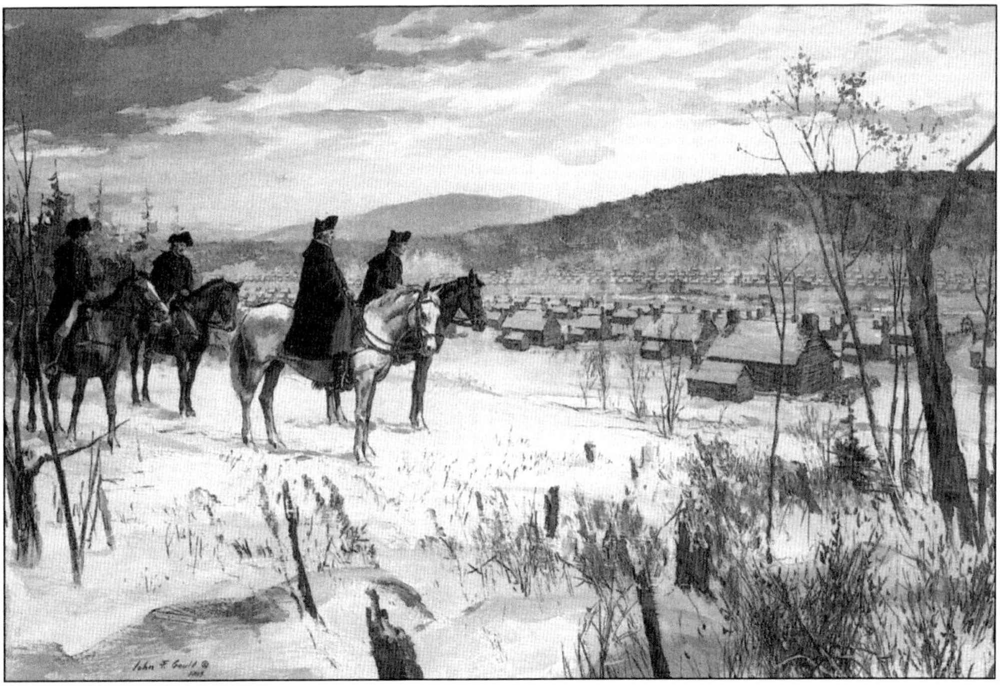

George Washington is depicted in 1783, overlooking the Temple Hill encampment, the last cantonment of the Revolutionary War. There, soldiers from Massachusetts, New York, New Jersey, New Hampshire, and Maryland lived in log huts with their wives and children. They drilled in preparation for a spring campaign should the peace negotiations taking place in France prove unsuccessful. (Courtesy of the Legacy of Artist John F. Gould.)

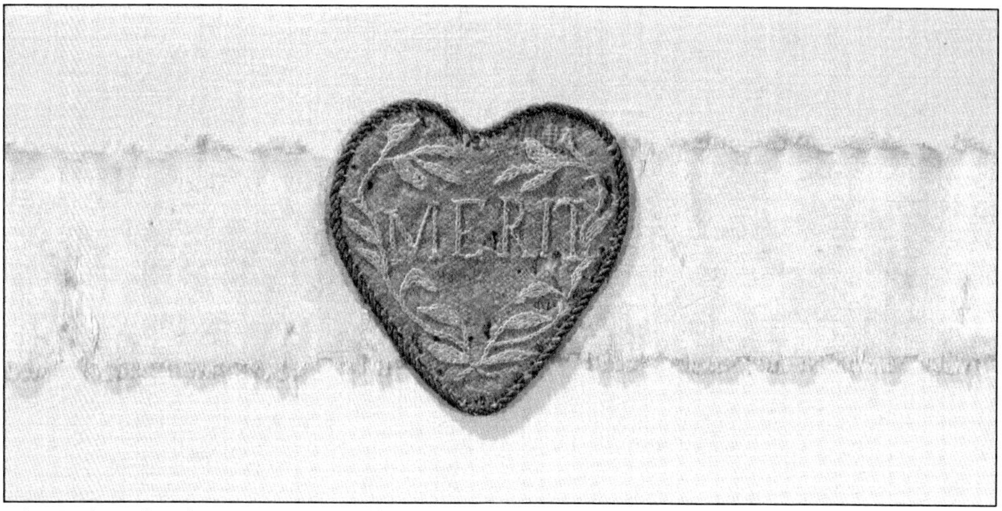

The Badge of Military Merit, established in August 1782 and personally designed by George Washington in the form of a purple heart, was the general's way of honoring soldiers' merit. Only three people received the badge during the war, and after the Revolution's end, it was forgotten. (Courtesy of the New Windsor Cantonment State Historic Site.)

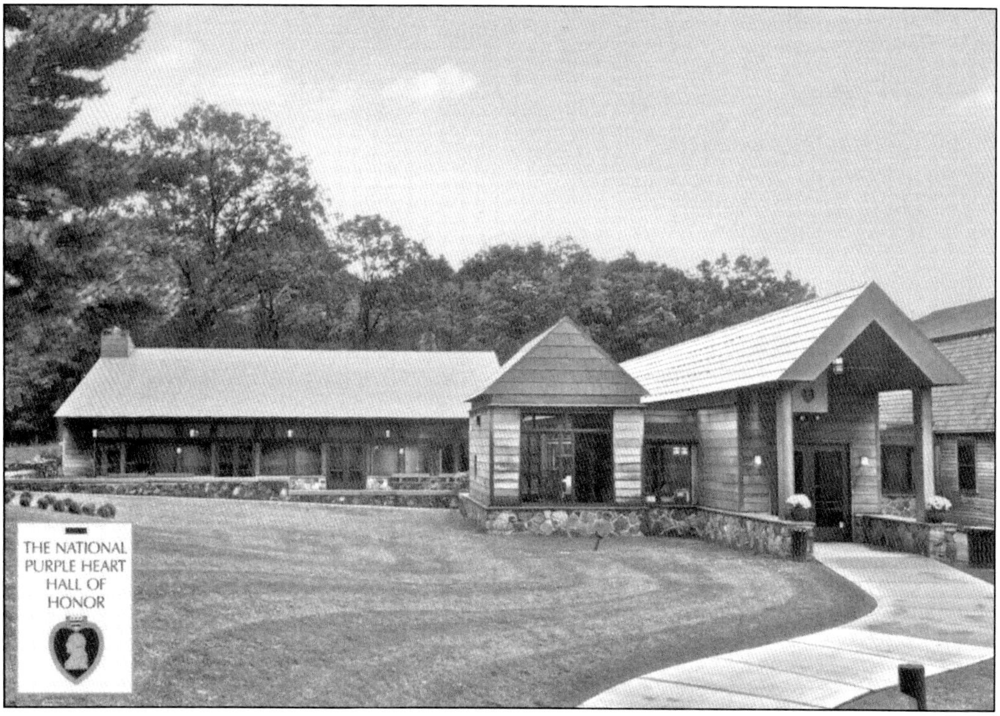

In January 1931, Gen. Douglas MacArthur resurrected the Purple Heart idea. Elizabeth Will, an Army heraldic specialist, designed the medal. The War Department announced the establishment of the Purple Heart on February 22, 1932, the bicentennial of Washington's birthday. The New Windsor Cantonment is home to the National Purple Heart Hall of Honor, preserving the stories of America's combat-wounded veterans. Some individuals featured never came back, but all were recipients of the Purple Heart. Starting with World War I veterans, over 1.7 million military personnel have earned the Purple Heart. (Courtesy of the Pullar family.)

Two

Churches and Cemeteries

The religious persecution imposed in many countries led to an influx of immigrants who practiced a variety of faiths. The most well known of the New Windsor churches are included in this chapter, although it is fair to mention that many more were formed—though some no longer exist. Still in existence is the King of Kings Lutheran Church on Union Avenue. The Little Britain Presbyterian Church was organized in 1760 by Scottish and Irish immigrants. In 1765, land was acquired from a part of the Andrew Johnston patent, owned by Patrick McClaughry, for the purpose of erecting a meetinghouse for public worship. The original building was occupied by the congregation until 1826.

Many churches had their own cemeteries, as did several families, still visible from the road. The Congregation Agudas Israel Cemetery is the result of the merger of two congregations, Agudas Achim and Sons of Israel. The St. Francis Cemetery is overseen by St. Francis of Assisi Catholic Church in Newburgh.

The remains of many Revolutionary and Civil War veterans are buried in New Windsor. Among them are members of Clinton family, whose most famous son, James Clinton, was born in Little Britain. Well-educated and inclined toward the military life, he entered early into the Revolutionary War. Upon leaving the service, he became a member of the legislature, aided in the adoption of the Constitution of the United States, and became a state senator. He was an able soldier, an incorruptible patriot, and a truehearted man.

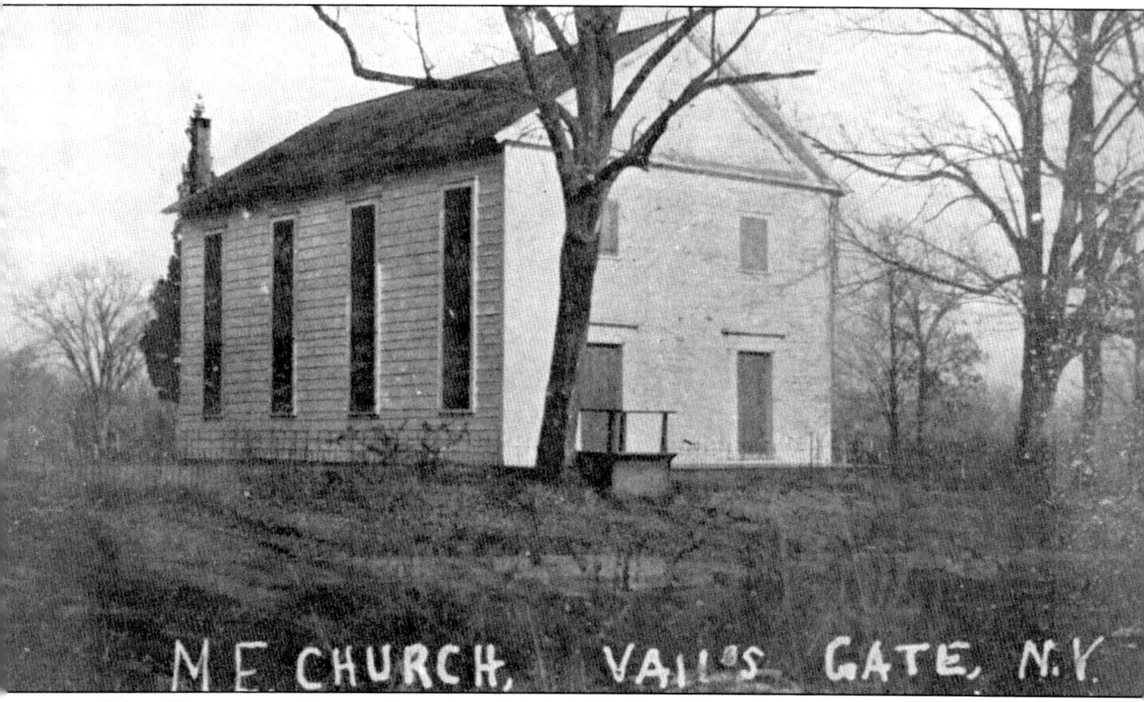

John Ellison, a wealthy merchant, founded the Vails Gate United Methodist Church in 1789. Early meetings were held in the upper floor of his store, and later, a barn. While itinerant preachers of all denominations were permitted to occupy the hall, it was specifically reserved for those of the Methodist faith. The church was built in 1807 on land donated by Ellison, and the meeting room behind the sanctuary was added in 1950. An educational wing was built in 1962, also in keeping with the original architecture. It is thought to be the oldest United Methodist church west of the Hudson River offering continuous service. There are also 12 veterans of the Civil War buried in the cemetery on the church property. (Courtesy of the Whitehill Collection.)

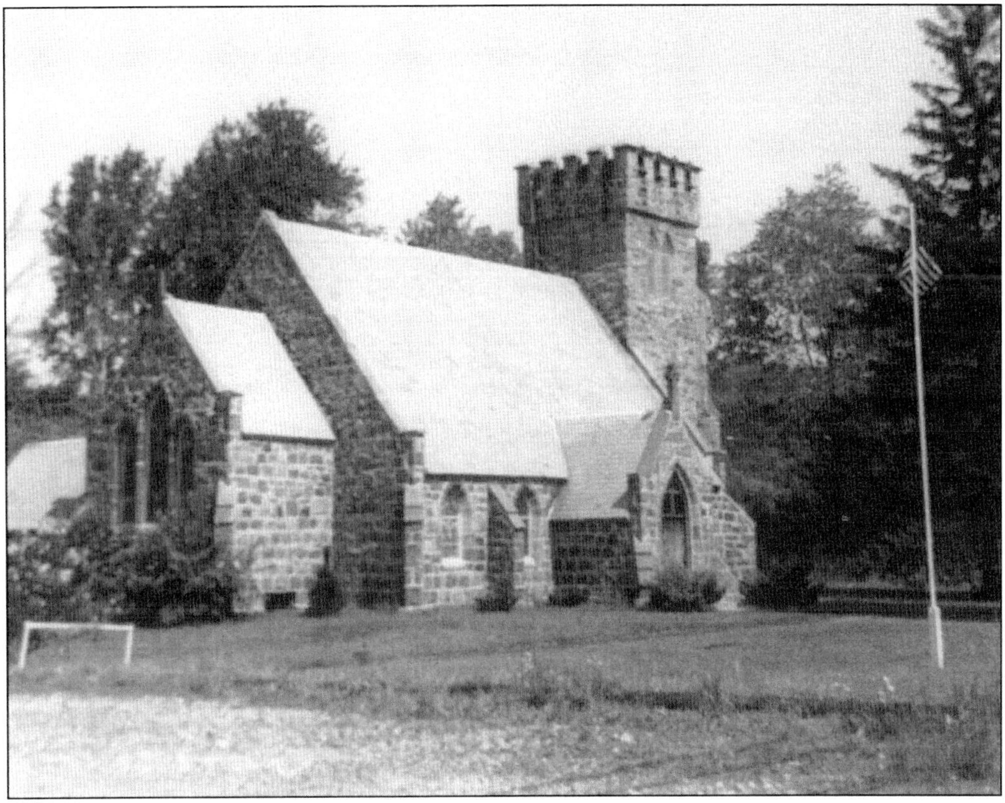

In trust, Thomas Ellison willed money and 56 acres of land to his brother and nephew for the purpose of a religious organization. St. Thomas Episcopal Church, on River Road, was established on April 18, 1818. Interest from the trust was to be paid annually to any active servicing minister. New Windsor resident Rev. John Brown was rector from 1818 through 1847. (Courtesy of the Historical Society of Newburgh Bay and the Highlands.)

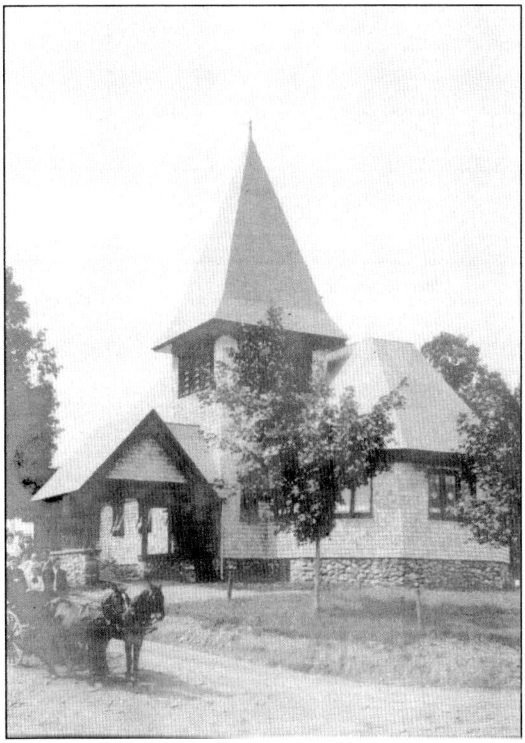

Little Britain Presbyterian Church was organized by Scottish and Irish immigrants as an Associated Reformed parish. The first edifice was erected in 1765 and was rebuilt in 1826. The church's first pastor, Robert Annan, was installed in 1768 and served until 1783. Rev. Thomas J. Smith was his successor, serving from 1791 until 1812. The Scottish Rev. James Schringeour, was then installed, serving until his death in 1825. (Courtesy of the Whitehill Collection.)

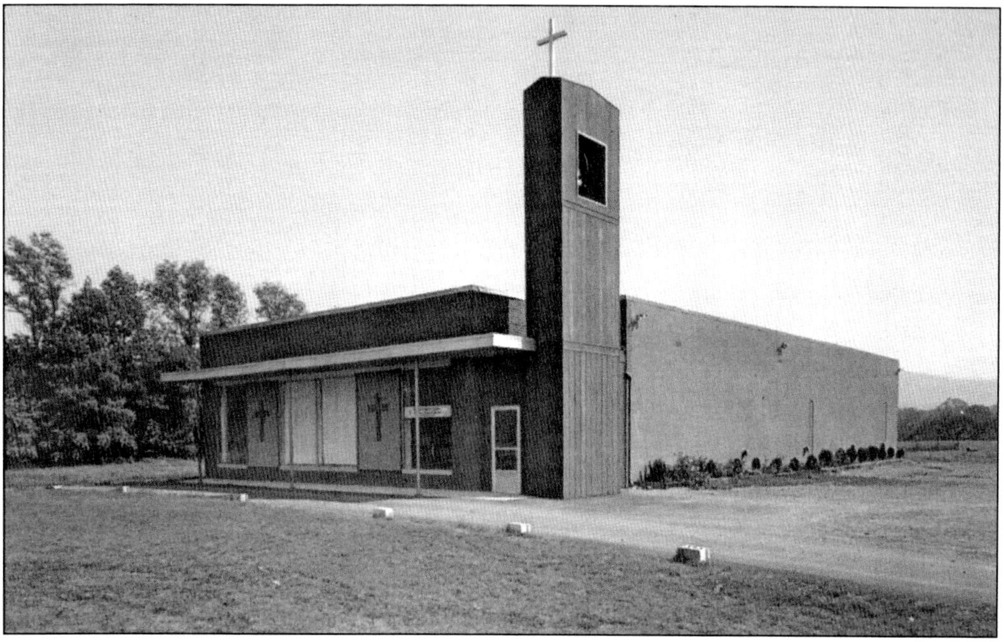

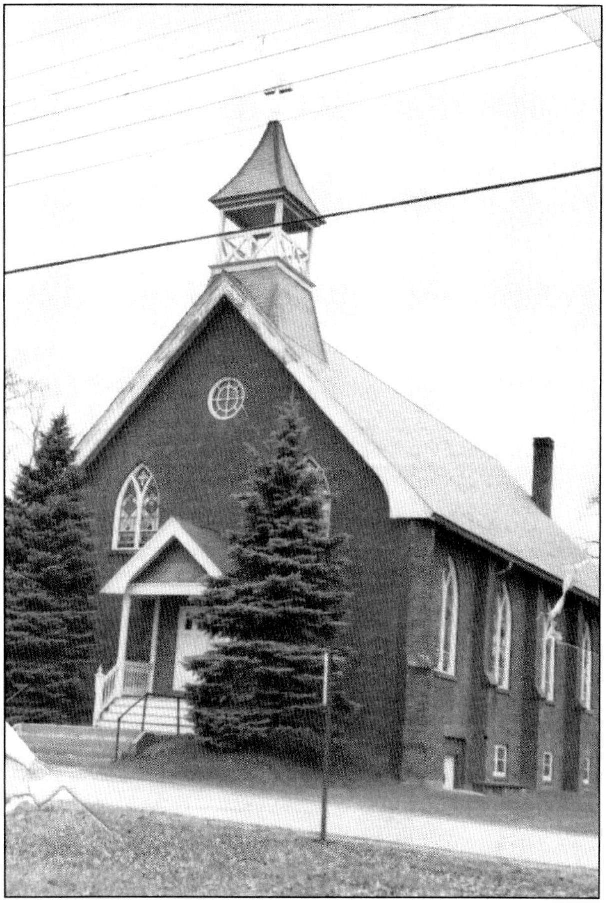

Ridgecrest Baptist Church on Blooming Grove Turnpike was begun in 1962. The diverse congregation includes families, students, and retirees. They gather from countries around the world, seeking community and friendship. (Courtesy of the Whitehill Collection.)

St. Joseph's Church began as a mission chapel in 1880. By 1911, the population growth warranted a new, larger church. The new building was constructed on Route 9W using donated land and donated bricks made in local brickyards. Many improvements have been made through the years, but the church maintains its original look and size. (Courtesy of St. Joseph's Church.)

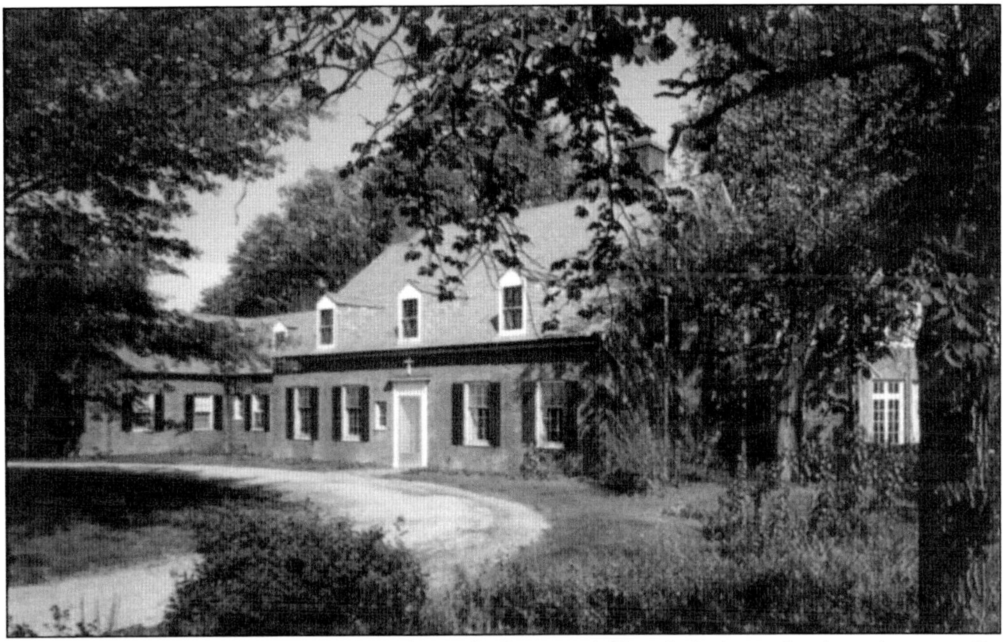

The Order of St. Helena is a religious order in the Episcopal Church for lay and ordained women. St. Helena's Convent had been in New Windsor since 1954. In 2009, the 51 acres at Blooming Grove Turnpike and Forge Hill Road were sold to an Orthodox Jewish congregation, and all the sisters were then moved to a convent in Atlanta, Georgia. (Courtesy of the Whitehill Collection.)

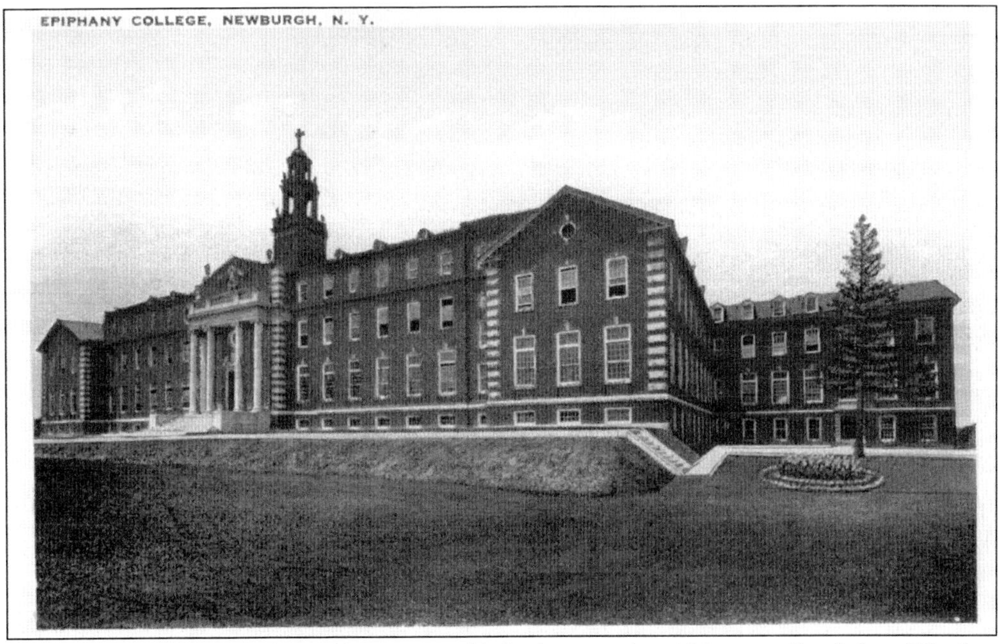

In 1925, Epiphany Apostolic College was established, situated on 156 acres of land along Windsor Highway and overlooking the Hudson River. The main building contained classrooms, a chapel, and administrative offices; the gymnasium was separate. A preparatory seminary for students entering St. Joseph's Society of the Sacred Heart, it also housed a Brothers' training school. It is now owned by the Newburgh Enlarged City School District. (Courtesy of Mary Jane Miller.)

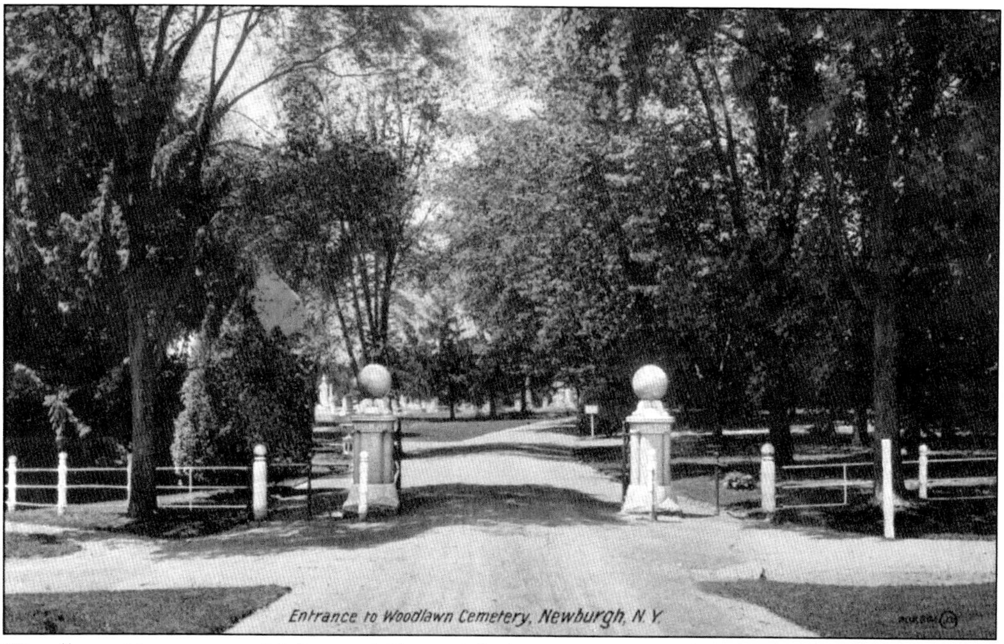

Woodlawn Cemetery, at Union and Quassaick Avenues, is one of two principal New Windsor burial sites. French and Indian War colonel Charles Clinton, born in Ireland in 1690, settled in New Windsor in 1731. He died November 19, 1778, and is among the many famous people interred in Woodlawn Cemetery. (Courtesy of the Whitehill Collection.)

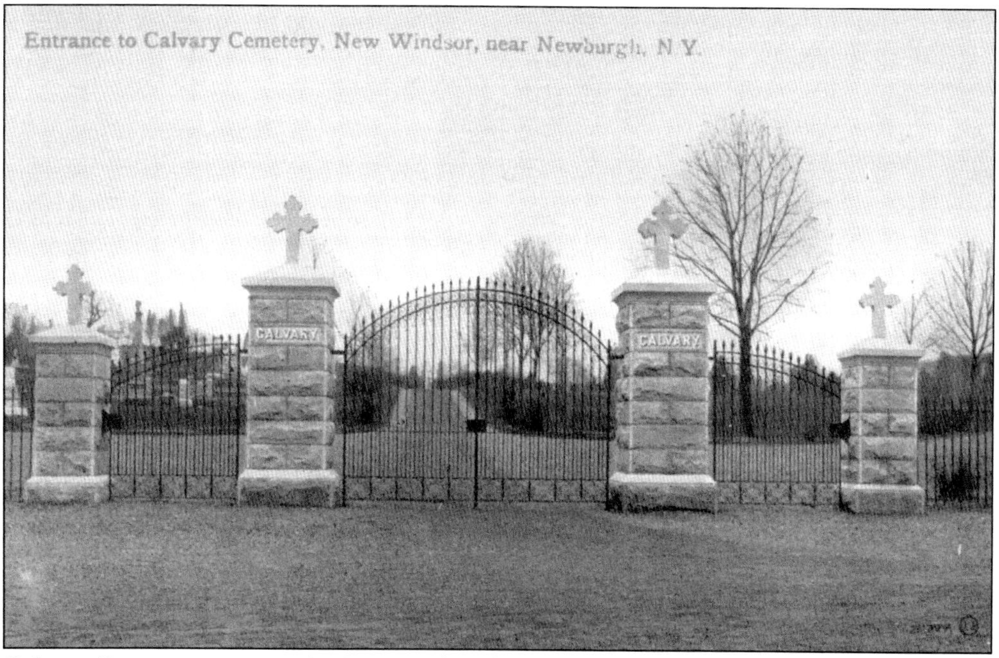

Calvary Cemetery, overseen by St. Patrick's Church in Newburgh, is located at the junction of Quassaick Avenue and Walsh Road in New Windsor. It was opened in 1888 for those of the Catholic faith and is one of two principal New Windsor cemeteries. (Courtesy of the Whitehill Collection.)

Three

Schools in Transition

With the 1796 New Windsor annual election of commissioners came the first entry regarding public schools. On September 18, 1814, the town was divided into nine school districts—No. 1, Village of New Windsor; No. 2, Murder's Creek; No. 3, Good Hope; No. 4, Center; No. 5, Square; No. 6, Little Britain Meeting House; No. 7, Union; No. 8, Good-Will; and No. 9, Hunting-Grove. Schools and district numbering changed many times over the following years.

New Windsor School District trustees leased land located on Quassaick Avenue from Leonard Lee to erect their first one-room frame building on December 20, 1841. B.B. Foley became principal in 1888, serving for the next 40 years at an annual salary of $700. In the 1850s, furniture and supplies for the schools were nearly nonexistent, as were teacher's salaries. Schools were closed from November to February because of a lack of funds available to pay teachers. By 1866, records show teachers by name and annual salary. Administrators at Little Britain, known for years as Mount Airy School, decided in 1867 that classes would continue through the winter. A stove was purchased, which satisfied the chill in fall and spring but failed during the cold winter. The following year, Mary Frances Fulton got chilblains so badly from the cold floor that she never fully recovered. The school baseball team of 1909 included Fred Fayo, Nick Farina, and Russell Baxter. In 1911, Pearl Fennel, a teacher at Silver Stream School, taught students including Kenneth Sloan, Robert Glassey, Kenneth Lockwood, and Ruth E. Clark.

In 1963, the voters agreed to consolidate certain schools in the towns of Newburgh and New Windsor with those in the city of Newburgh, forming the current Newburgh Enlarged City School District.

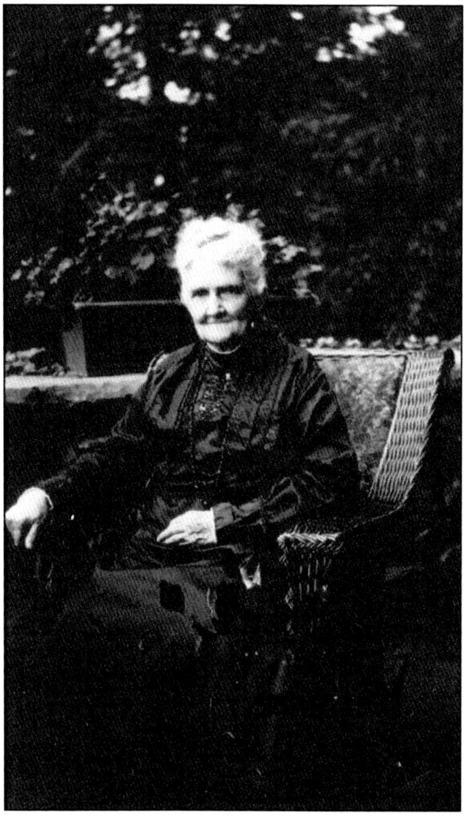

Mary Flynn Brennan, great-grandmother of James and Jerome Pullar, is shown in 1922 at her home on Quassaick Avenue. In 1886, New Windsor School presented Brennan with the Sands Medal Award, one of the country's oldest awards for students. Since 1865, it has been presented to those students in the New Windsor and Cornwall schools who exhibit outstanding scholastic achievement, deportment, and citizenship. In 1861, Abraham Sands had set aside a sum of money to be invested in real estate, stipulating that the interest be used to procure the Sands Medal. The medals are cast each year by Tiffany & Company in New York City. Other recipients have included Alice Ryan (1879) and Shirley Babcock (1943 and 1944), the aunt and sister of John T. Babcock, respectively. (Both, courtesy of the Pullar family.)

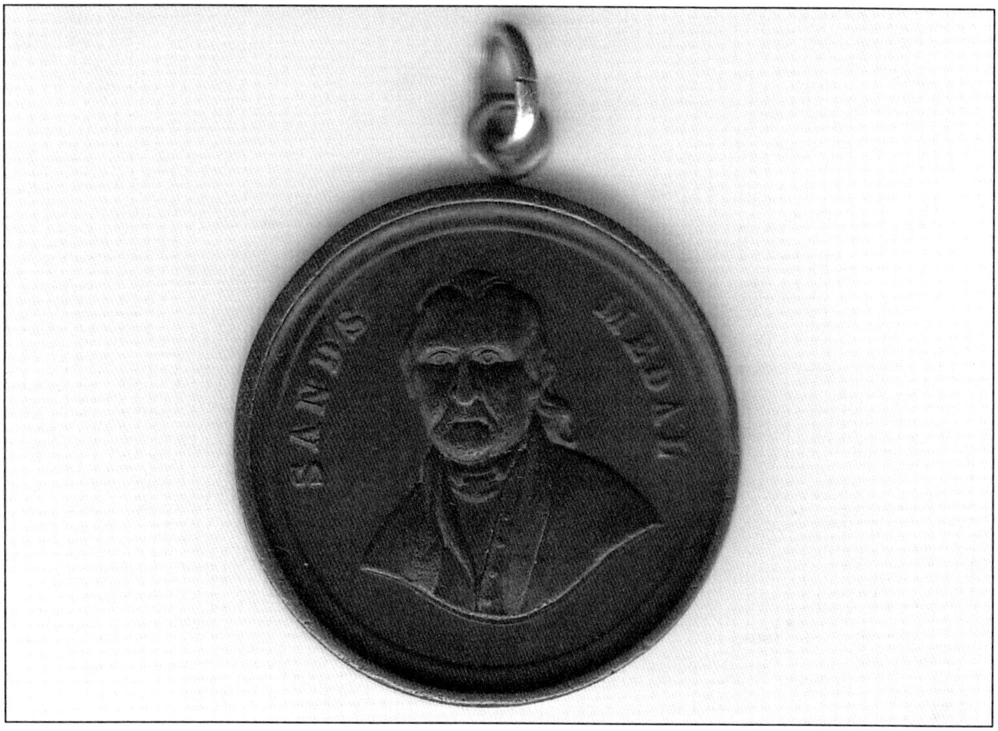

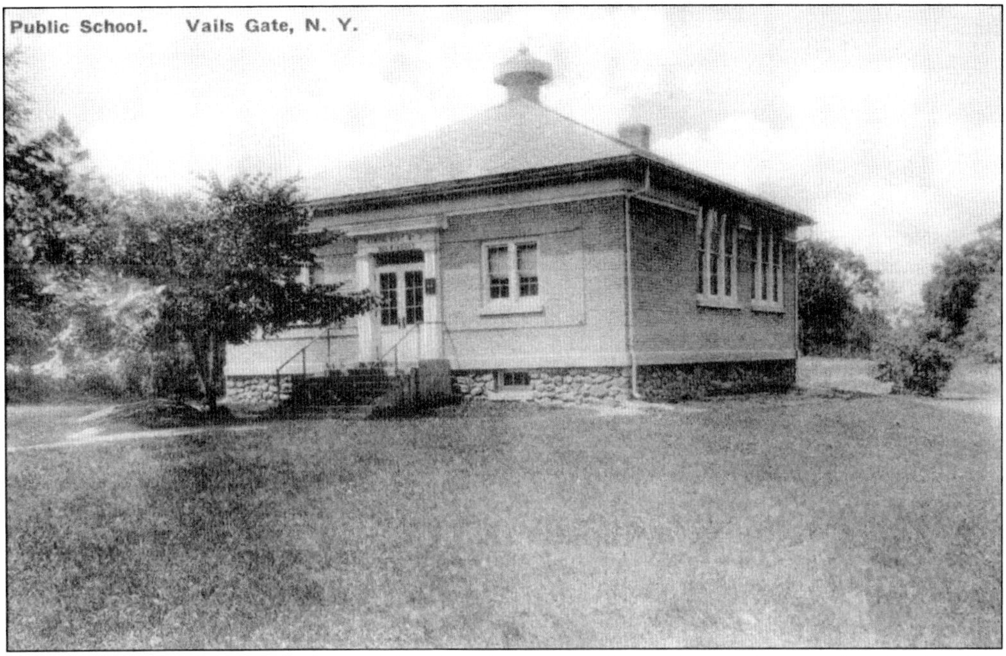

Above, the two-room Vails Gate School on Blooming Grove Turnpike was the third public school in District No. 3, New Windsor School District. The first school was torn down when the viaduct was constructed; the second, near the site of the present Vails Gate Elementary School, was replaced by this two-room school. Because of the ongoing population growth and the goal of ensuring quality education, it became clear that expansion was necessary. Below, a new, larger school opened in 1958. (Above, courtesy of the Whitehill Collection; below, courtesy of the Pullar family.)

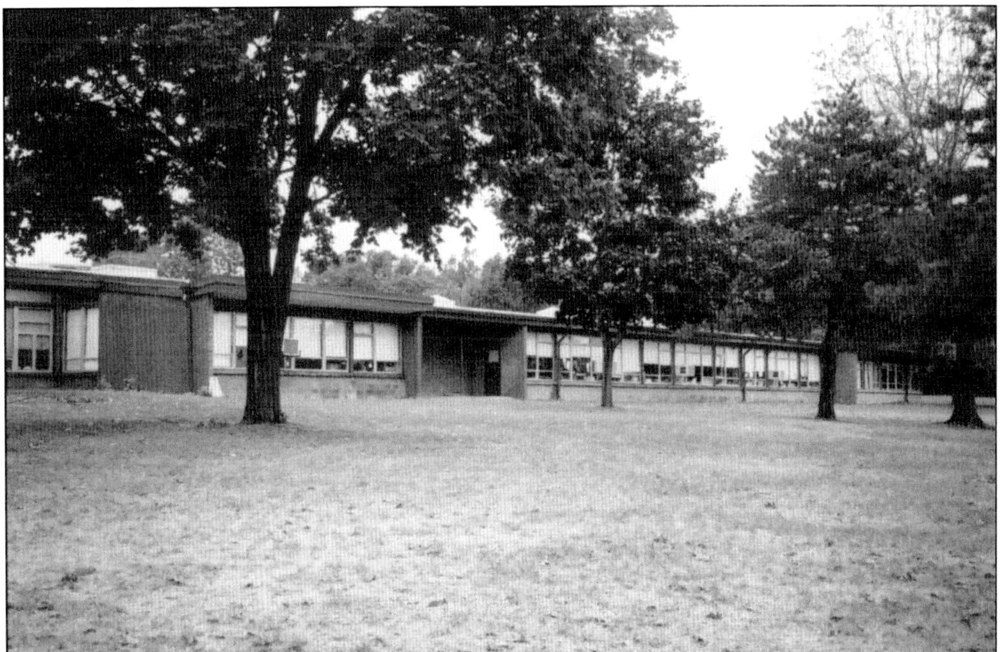

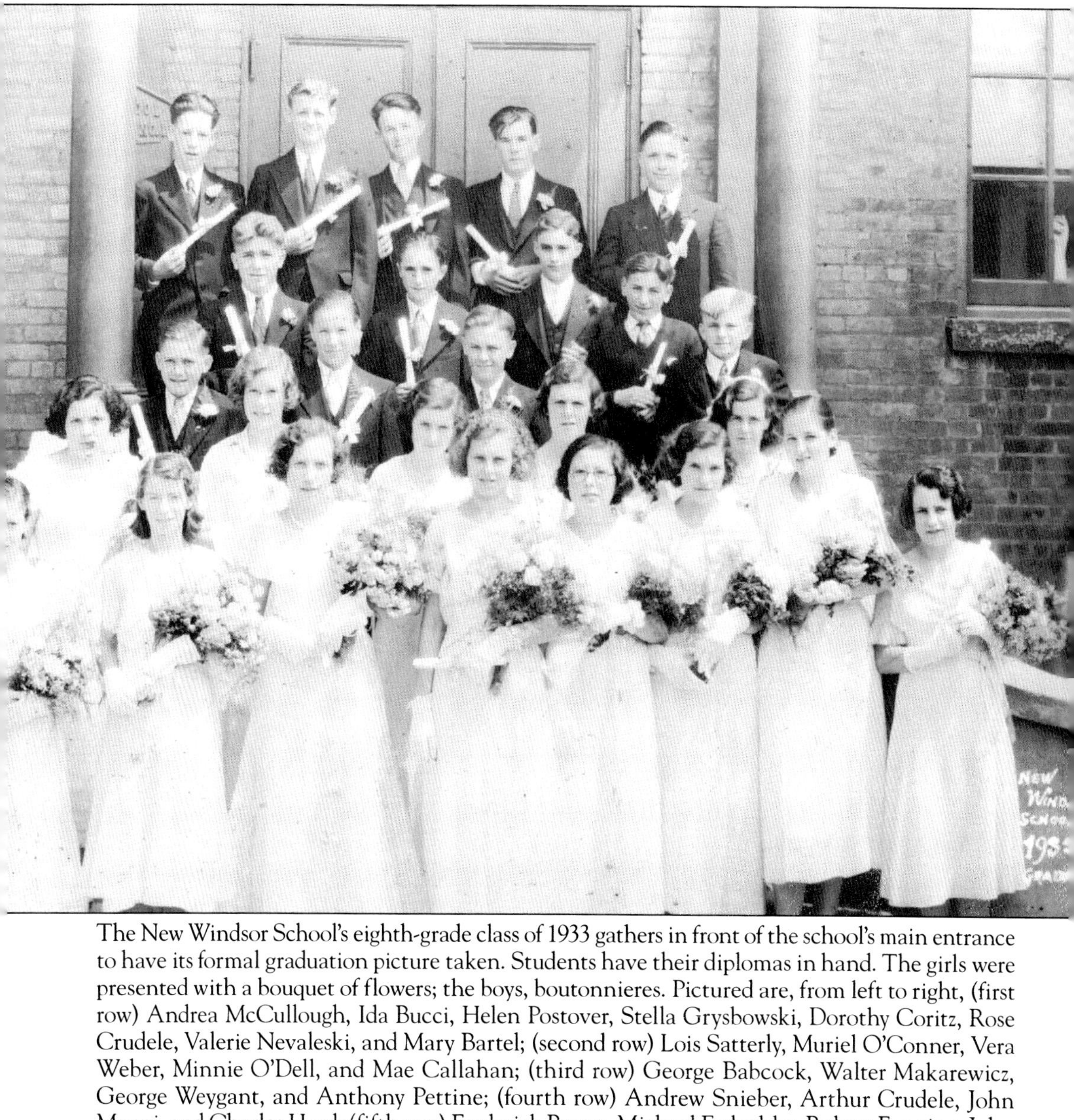

The New Windsor School's eighth-grade class of 1933 gathers in front of the school's main entrance to have its formal graduation picture taken. Students have their diplomas in hand. The girls were presented with a bouquet of flowers; the boys, boutonnieres. Pictured are, from left to right, (first row) Andrea McCullough, Ida Bucci, Helen Postover, Stella Grysbowski, Dorothy Coritz, Rose Crudele, Valerie Nevaleski, and Mary Bartel; (second row) Lois Satterly, Muriel O'Conner, Vera Weber, Minnie O'Dell, and Mae Callahan; (third row) George Babcock, Walter Makarewicz, George Weygant, and Anthony Pettine; (fourth row) Andrew Snieber, Arthur Crudele, John Mangi, and Charles Hurd; (fifth row) Frederick Brune, Michael Feduchka, Robert Fanning, John Snieber, and Peter Fornal. To the right, ? White, their teacher, peaks out the window to observe the class in which she had taken so much pride. (Courtesy of John T. Babcock.)

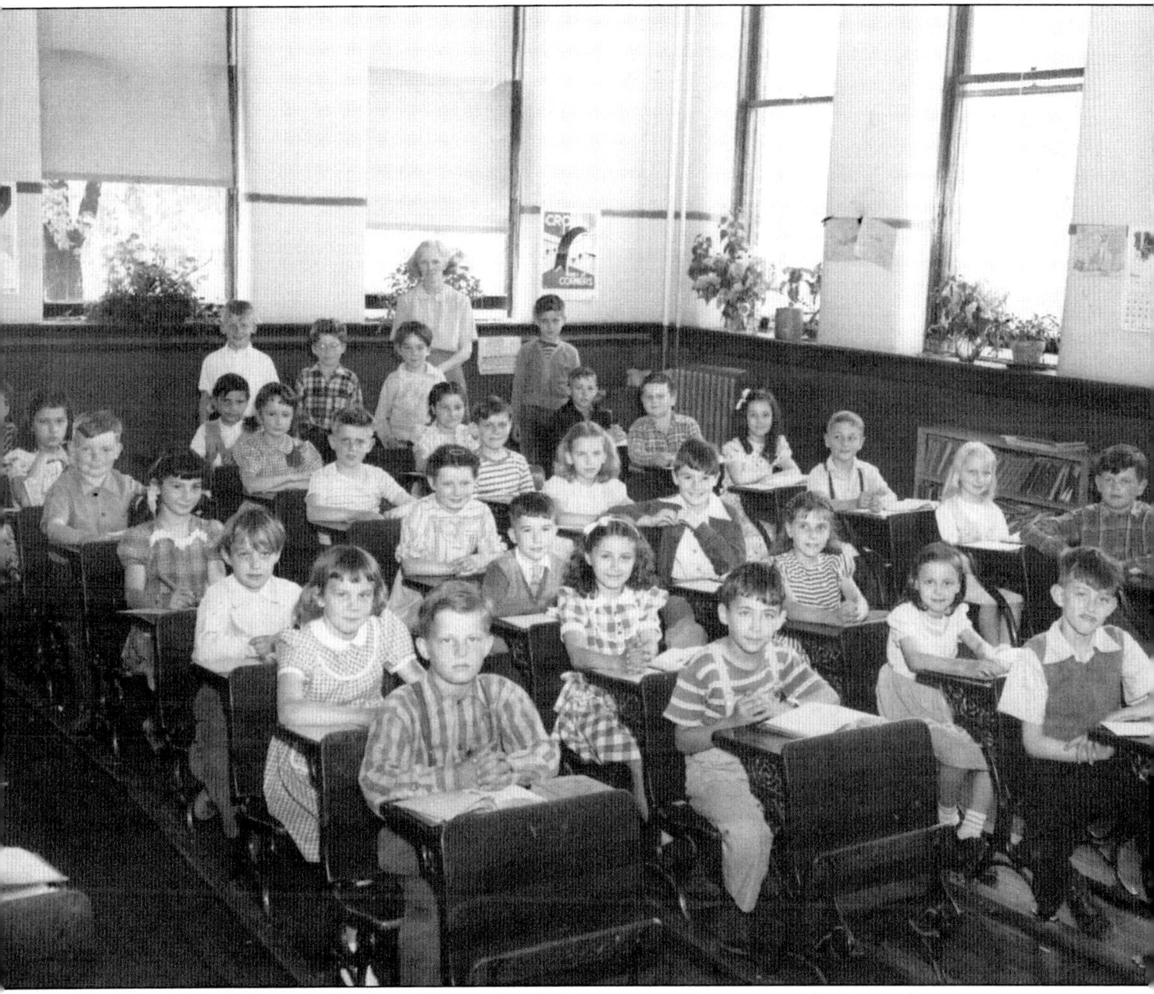

Inside teacher ? Tierney's New Windsor School classroom, students pose for their class picture in May 1947. Seated are, from front to back, (far left column) Gordon Scott, Karen Smith, Richard Hotaling, Elizabeth Inglima, Kirk McQuiston, Elizabeth Jane Shelly, and Lloyd Post; (second from left) Paul Tibby, Donna Coritz, Peter Ralph, unidentified, James Pullar, Judith Bard, and Edward Makarewicz; (third from left) Kenneth Corwin, Francis Brander, unidentified, Kenneth Davis, Rosalie Masloski, Robert Gaydos, Mary Cervoni; (fourth from left) John Babcock, Patricia Lucy, Robert Schebesta, Barbara Radiker, Frank Hacunda, and Robert Jaczko. Standing with their teacher at the back of the room are, from left to right, John Dabroski, Ronald Sadler, Maurice Dayton, and Robert Radulski. The posters on the classroom wall remind students to "stay to the left, facing traffic," and to "cross only at corners." (Courtesy of the Babcock family.)

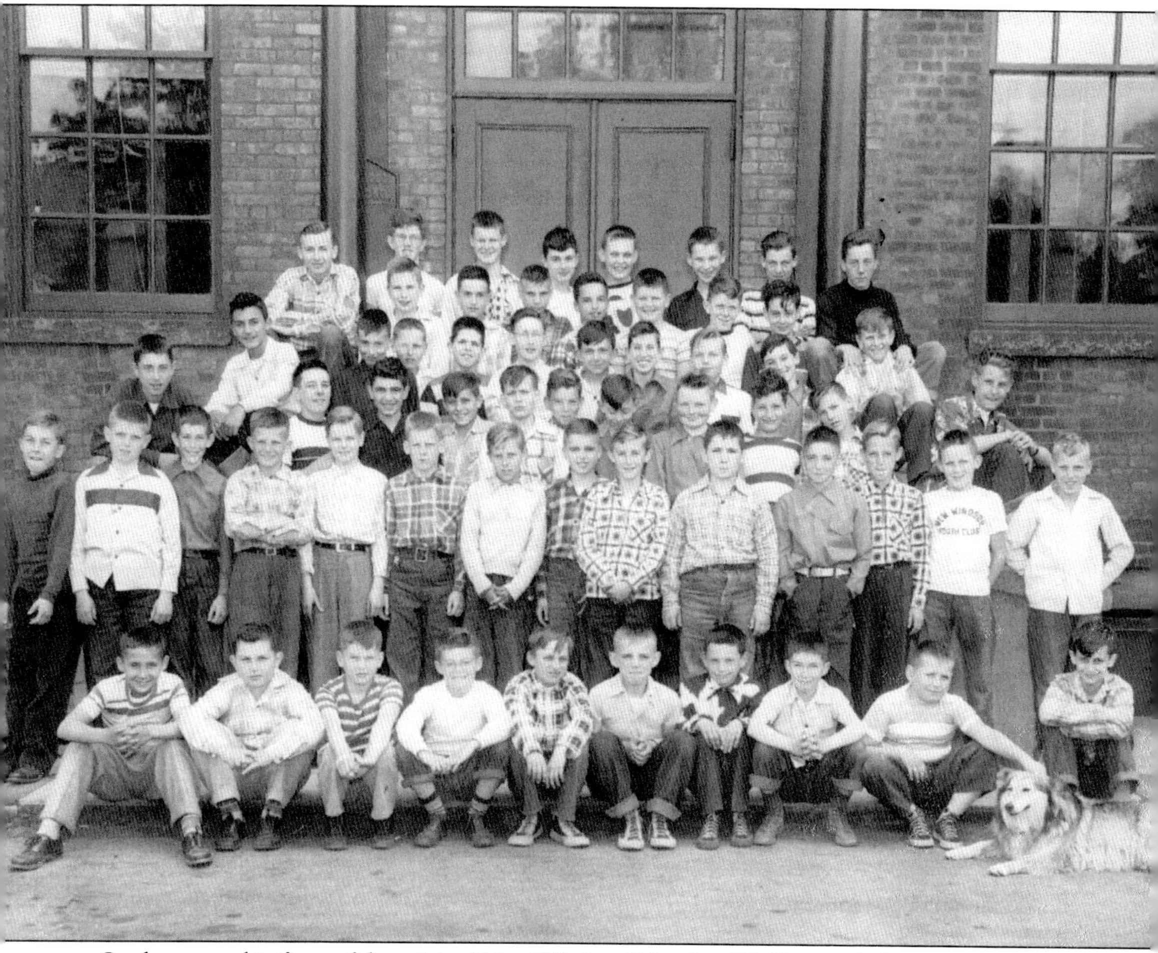

Students stand in front of the original New Windsor School at 175 Quassaick Avenue in 1951. They are, from left to right, (first row) Paul Tibby, Edward Sloboda, Donald Babcock, Ronald Sadler, Richard Hotaling, Daniel Riley, John DelPup, Peter Ralph, Robert Forsyth, and Alfred Crudele; (second row) Lawrence Delerose, James Pullar, John Cavanaugh, Gordon Scott, unidentified, John Dabroski, Thomas Flagler, John Scott, Robert Jaczko, Franklin O'Dell, Dante Musco, unidentified, Edward Coykendal, and Joseph Masloski; (third row) John Nunnley, Richard Forsyth, unidentified, Robert Radulski, Robert Gaydos, unidentified, Kenneth Corwin, Kirk McQuiston, John Bento, unidentified, and Kenneth Bolduc; (fourth row) Leon Commandi, unidentified, Robert Lewis, Chet Hayes, William Laddick, Clarence Ferguson, Fritz DeKay, Joseph Caesar, Kenneth Davis, and Michael McCarthy; (fifth row) James Hammer, Joseph Krum, unidentified, Edward Makarewicz, Robert Hamel, John Babcock, unidentified, and Robert Welsh; (sixth row) Charles Riser, Robert Scott, Al Kniffen, Joseph Rogowicz, John Remisheski, Herbert Walker, and Charles McClure. (Courtesy of the Babcock family.)

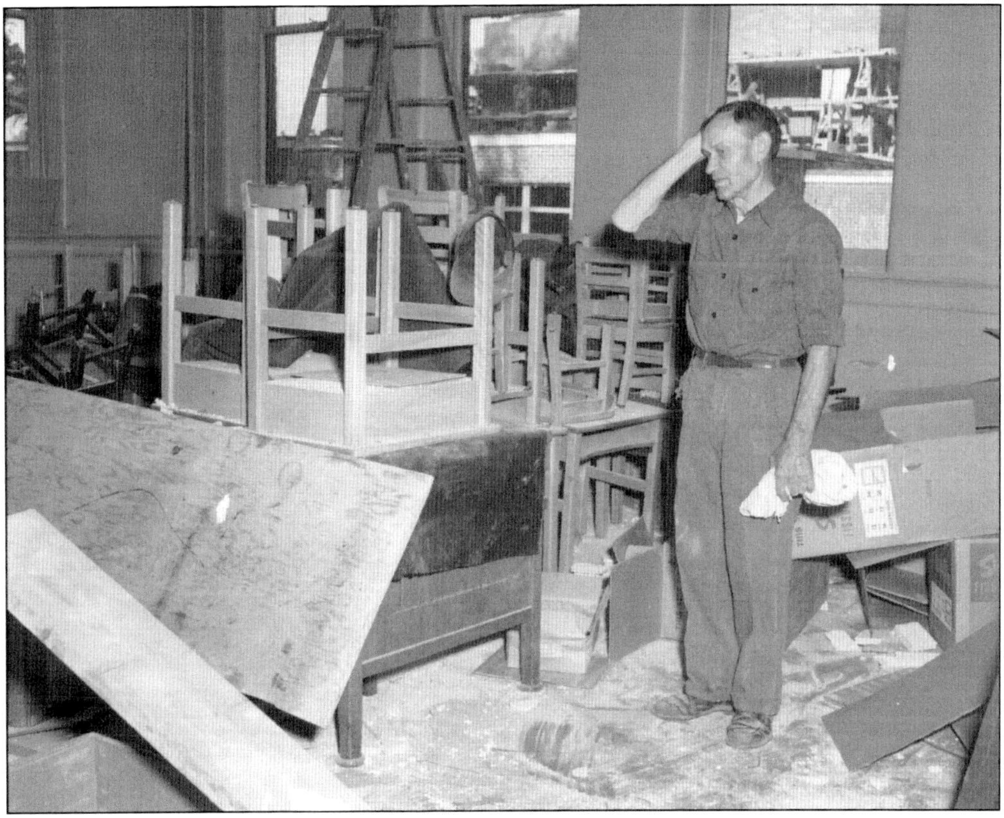

School custodian Fred C. Swanson Sr. prepares to get this New Windsor School classroom ready to begin classes in September 1955. Tables, chairs, teachers' desks, and maps all had to be placed in their proper positions. Swanson, who also owned a grocery and meat market, was very popular and highly respected by the faculty and students. (Courtesy of Joanne Swanson Versusky.)

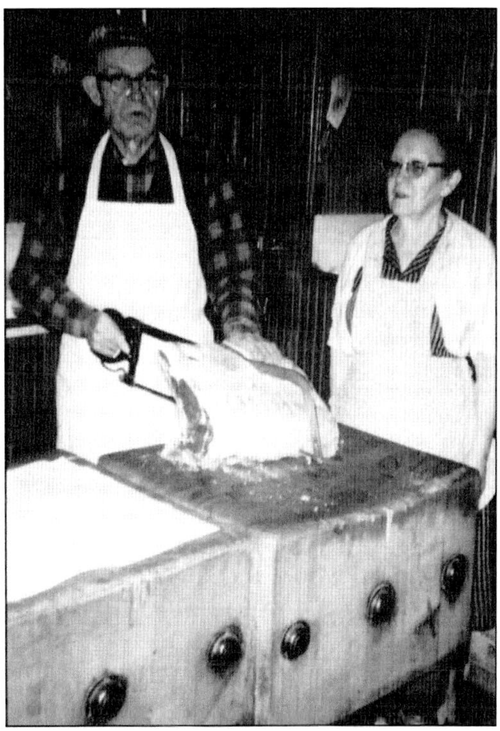

Fred C. Swanson Sr. and his wife, Julia, are shown here just before they closed their business, Fred C. Swanson Grocery & Meat Market, in the early 1960s. They had owned the store, located on Walsh Avenue in Ducktown, since 1919. Julia ran the operation while Fred was working at his other job as custodian of New Windsor School. (Courtesy of Joanne Swanson Versusky.)

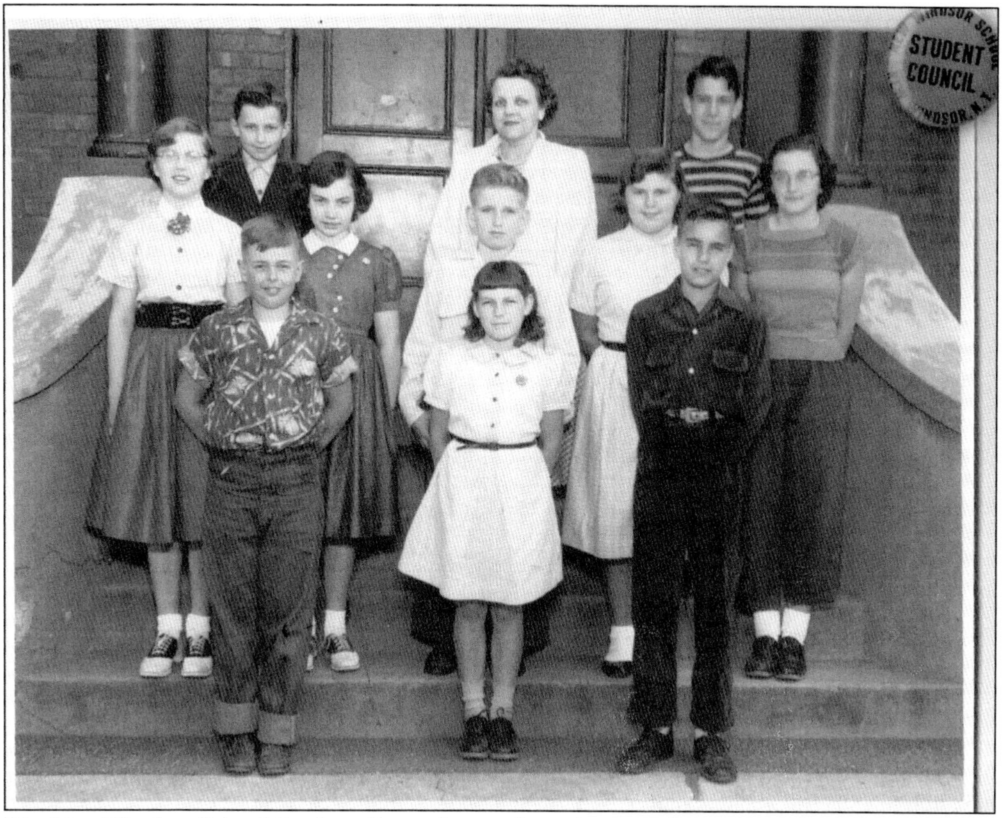

The New Windsor School Student Council poses for a photograph on May 26, 1957. Pictured are, from left to right, (first row) John Glassey, Joyce Maute, and Paul Zamenick; (second row) Joan Stortecky, Diane Williams, Jerome Pullar, Marie Simanoski, and Kathleen Popowick; (third row) Lynn Pyle, teacher ? Wells, and George Mocko. (Courtesy of Irene Pullar.)

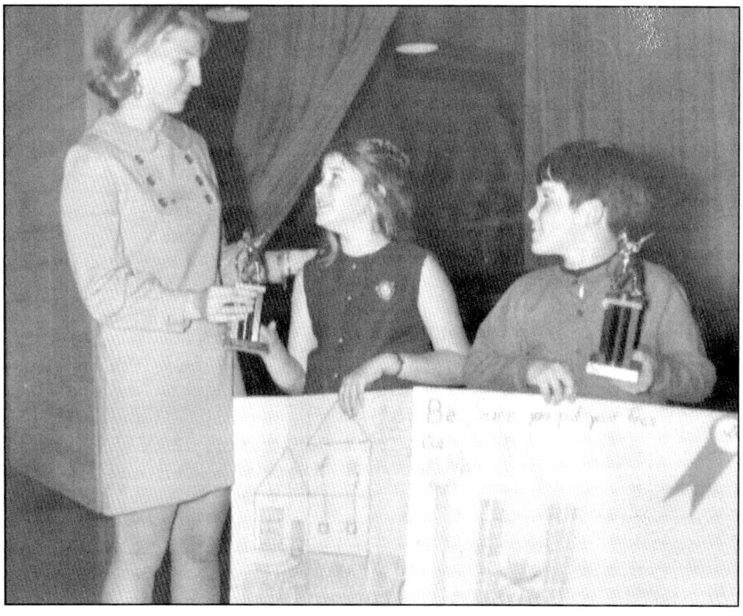

In this image from November 1970, Vails Gate Elementary School art teacher Carolyn Ruff presents individual trophies to Barbara Biggio and Douglas Hovey, winners of the Fire Prevention Week poster contest. Each year, these prized trophies were donated by the Vails Gate Fire Company. (Courtesy of the Vails Gate Fire Company.)

Four

FACES OF FAMILIES

New Windsor has seen an influx of people of many different nationalities, including those of Polish, English, Italian, Irish, and German origins. They came for different reasons, bringing their families as well as their ideas, skill sets, goals, and desires to contribute to the common good. These newcomers took pride in looking out for one another, and as more and more new families arrived, they went to local churches and schools, started businesses, and joined a variety of organizations.

These families represented the fiber of life throughout New Windsor, living in places with names like Vails Gate, Rock Tavern, Little Britain, and those lovingly referred to as Clancyville or Ducktown. An early settling place was the farm of John J. Clancy, which would become known as Clancyville. Small houses were built and subsequently enlarged as families grew in numbers or affluence. Ducktown got its name as the MacArthur Avenue settlers arrived, bringing with them a number of ducks. The story goes that, when it rained, the ducks would congregate in the mud puddles formed in the dirt streets.

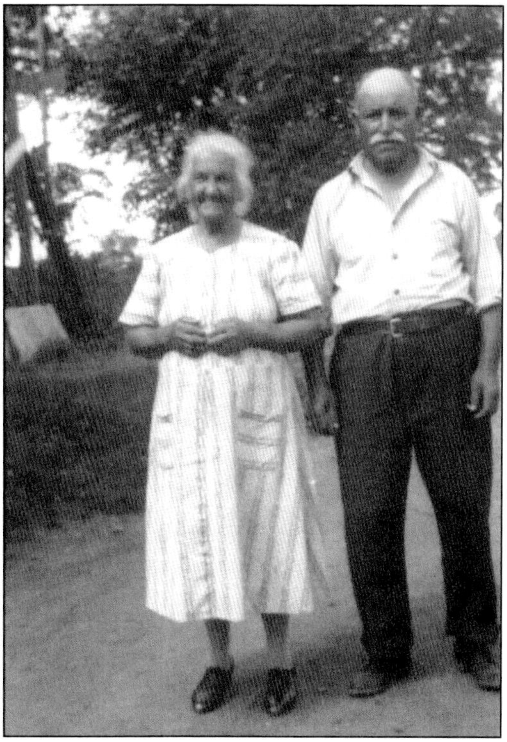

Destino and Mary Faricelli emigrated from Italy (he, in 1911; she, in 1914) and had three children. In 1946, Destino, who worked at Trap Rock, purchased property on Walsh Avenue, where he grew vegetables and raised cows, goats, and 150 chickens. He later rented more property to farm across the street. (Courtesy of Carmine Damario.)

Friends and family gather at a 1957 wedding reception. Everyone is dressed to the nines, with ladies always wearing hats on such special occasions. Pictured are, clockwise from front left, Carmine Damario, Frank Asaro, Nora Asaro, Susan Monarchie Dabroski, Helen and Michael Crudele, Alfred Crudele, and Margaret and Ralph Faricelli. (Courtesy of the Crudele family.)

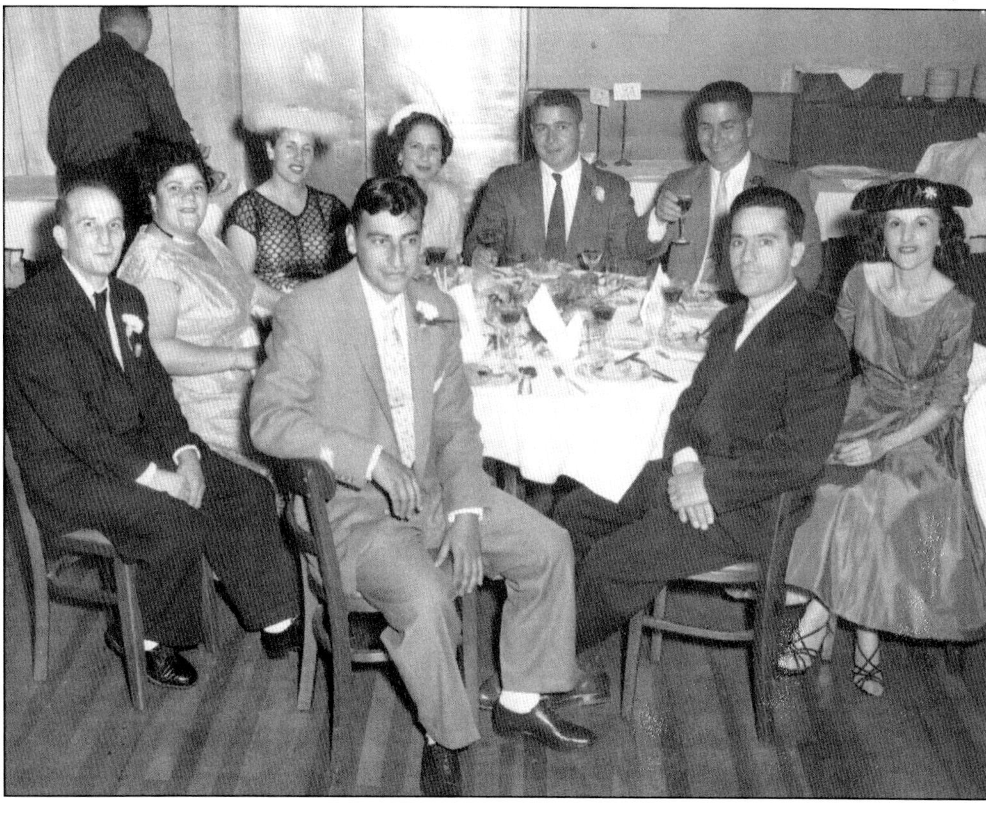

Three generations of Crudeles, all named Michael, stand together for a family portrait. The elder Crudele (left) was an Italian immigrant who worked in construction. His son, Michael A. Crudele (center) worked at the Little Falls Paper Mill until it closed and then went to work at Texaco. His son (right) served in the Air Force. (Courtesy of the Crudele family.)

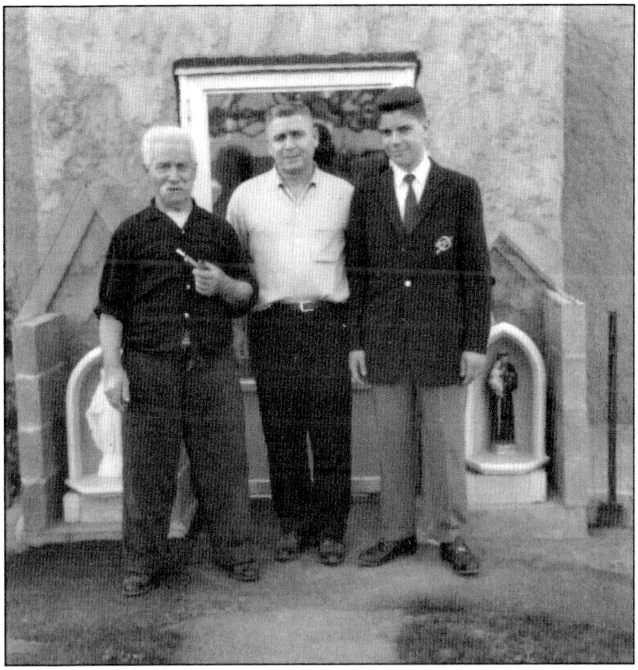

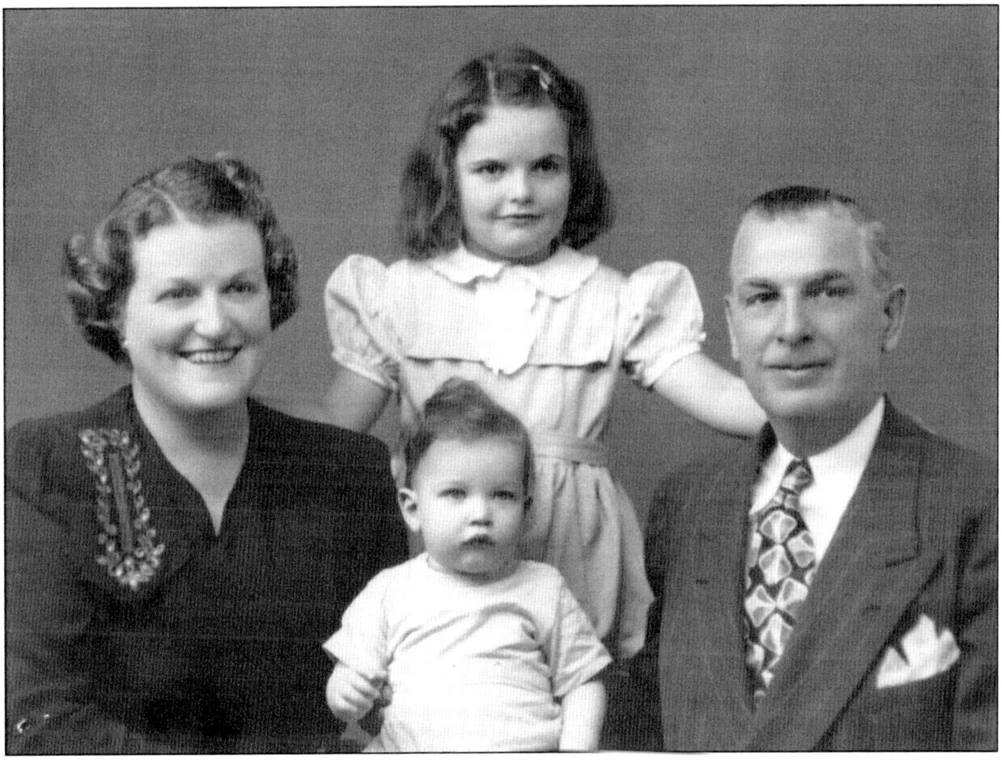

James H. Molloy poses with his family prior to his 1952 death. The son of Irish immigrants, Molloy put himself through Columbia University and became vice president of Burroughs Adding Machine Company in New York City. The family's 1880 Colonial home was torn down to make way for the Squire Village Cinema. (Courtesy of Catherine Molloy Nugent.)

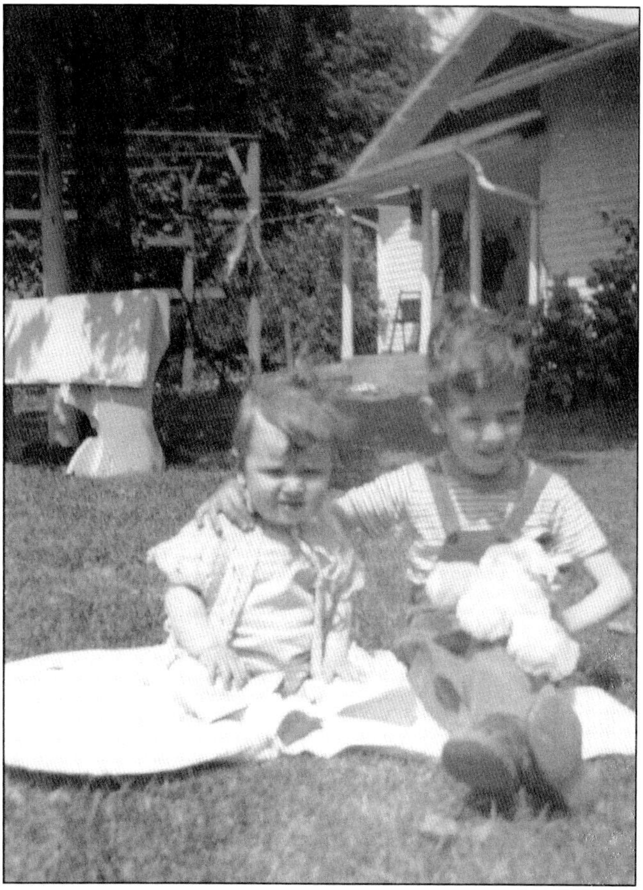

Arthur (left) and James Nugent are shown on their back lawn at 194 Quassaick Avenue. James currently resides in this same house with his wife, Catherine Molloy Nugent; both are New Windsor townies. Arthur also remained in the area. (Courtesy of Catherine Molloy Nugent.)

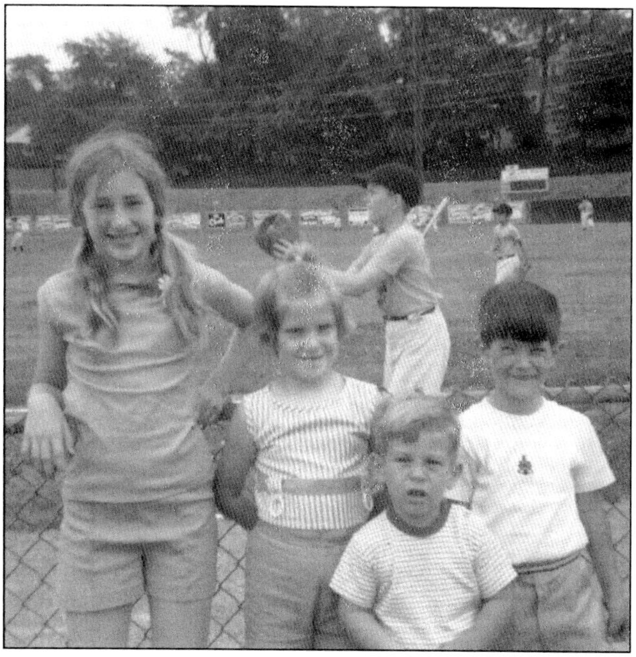

These children are pictured on June 5, 1971, cheering on their brothers at a New Windsor Little League baseball game. They are, from left to right, Jane Pavlik, Nancy Pullar, James Pavlik, and Mark Pavlik. Big brothers William Pullar and Richard Pavlik, along with their team, won the game that day. (Courtesy of the Pullar family.)

Michael Popowick and William Lewis are taking a boat ride to Nutty Grove on Beaver Dam Lake, where a tent on a foundation would already be set up for them. At the location of the tent, there was a small building with cooking facilities for campers' use. (Courtesy of Sandra Lewis Terwilliger.)

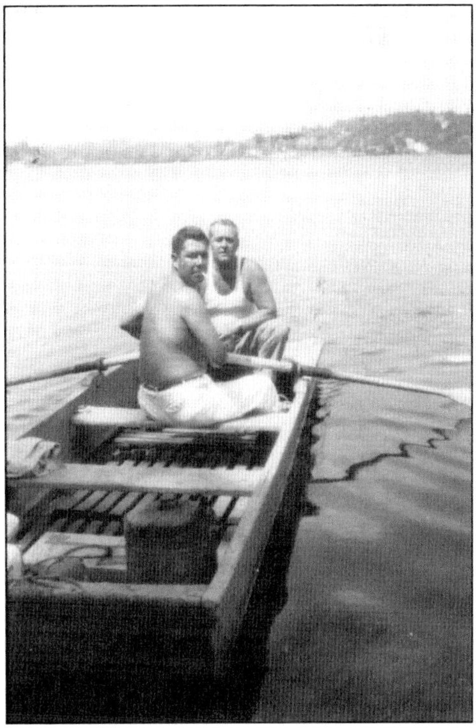

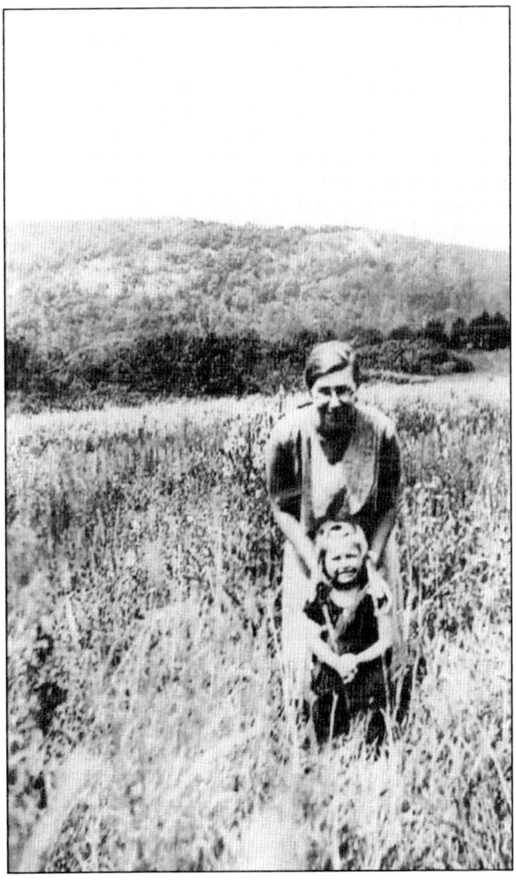

Rose Weygant stands in a hayfield with her mother, Pauline Weygant, around 1933. Rose's father, James Anderson Weygant, worked the Myrtle Avenue farm for years and raised his family there. In the background is Snake Hill, also known as Spy Rock, which was used as a watch site by Continental soldiers during the Revolutionary War. (Courtesy of Charles Zgrodek.)

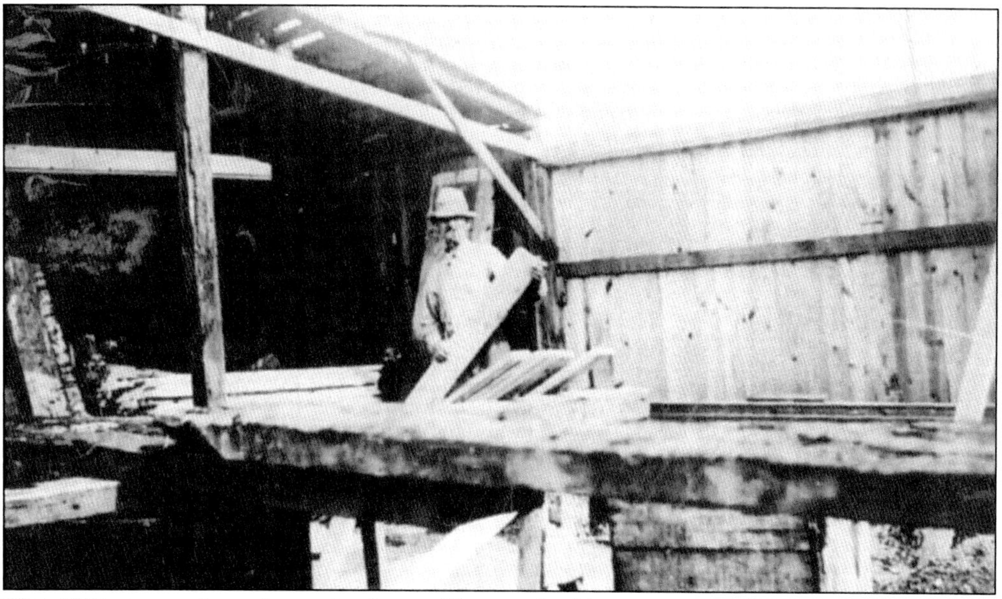

This 1940s image shows James Anderson Weygant building a new chicken coop on his Myrtle Avenue farm. The lumber was cut at his own sawmill, located on the property where Susan and Edward Wein's house was located, next to local favorite hangout Crudele's Bar & Restaurant. (Courtesy of Charles Zgrodek.)

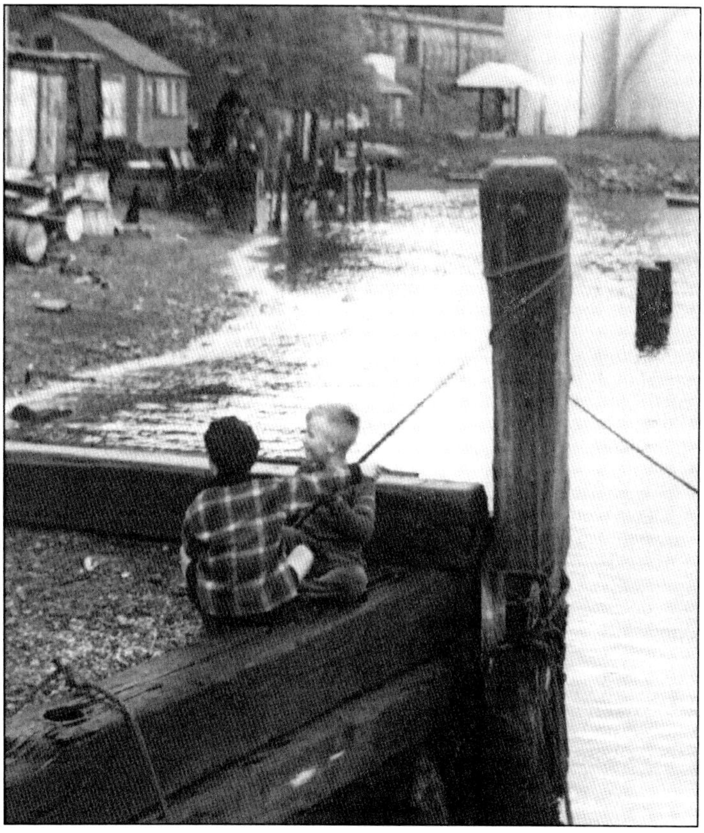

These two young New Windsor boys have found a wonderful way to spend a summer in the early 1940s, fishing off a dock at Steel Style along River Road. Many a lad caught dinner for his family in the bountiful Hudson River. (Courtesy of the Historical Society of Newburgh Bay and the Highlands.)

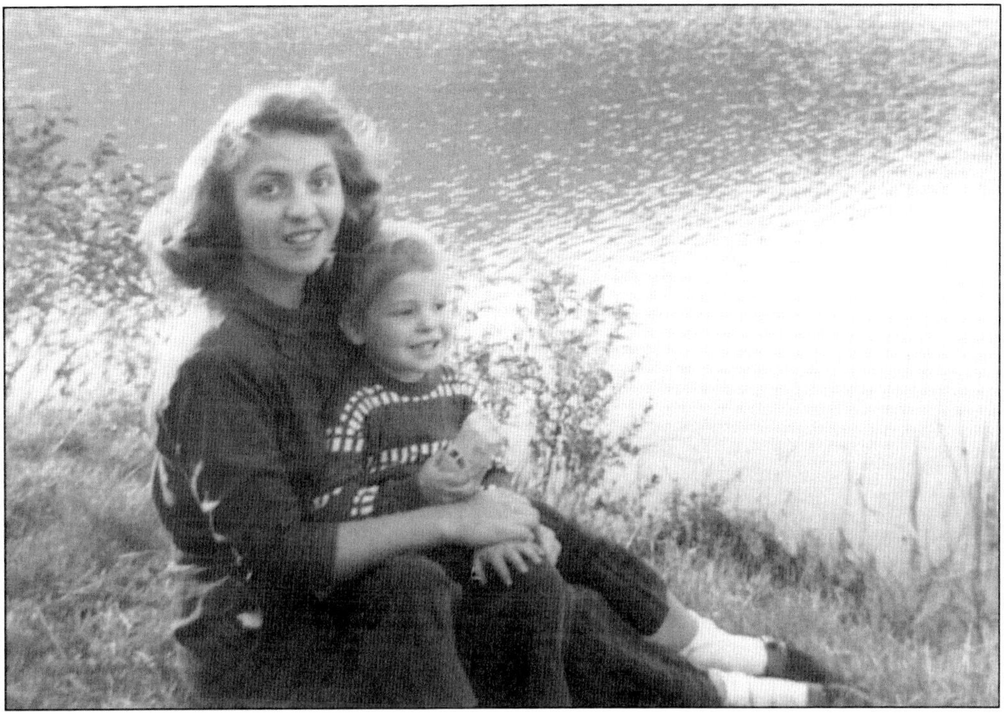

Catherine De Luca Babcock and son Paul Jr. are pictured in early 1953 at Seaman's Beach, enjoying the lake. They could go there often because of its proximity to the Paul Babcock Sr. Dairy Farm in Little Britain, where they lived. Little Paul enjoyed skipping stones over the water, watching for fish, and running around the banks of the lake. (Courtesy of the Robert Babcock family.)

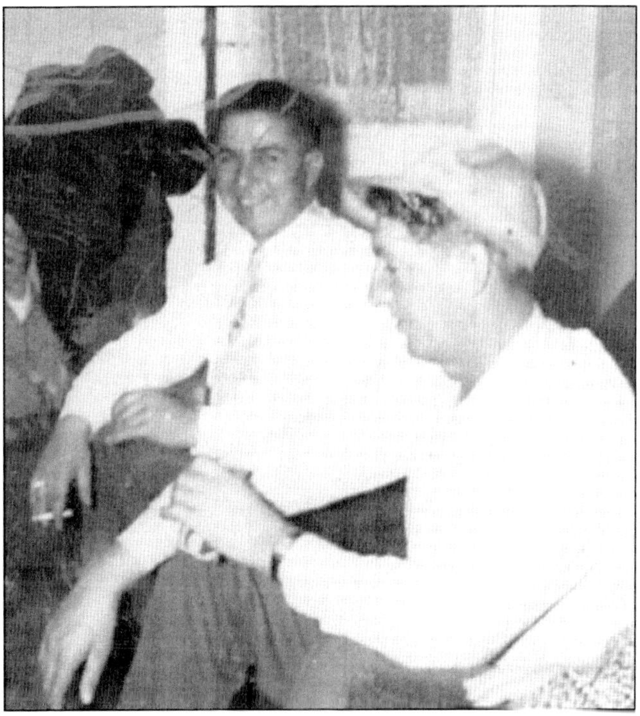

Alfred Crudele (left) and John Zgrodek enjoyed a few beers and talked about life in Ducktown as it was in the 1950s. They were all good neighbors and loved getting together whenever possible. John, Charles, and Anthony Zgrodek worked with Alfred Crudele at the National Gypsum Paper Mill on John Street. (Courtesy of Charles Zgrodek.)

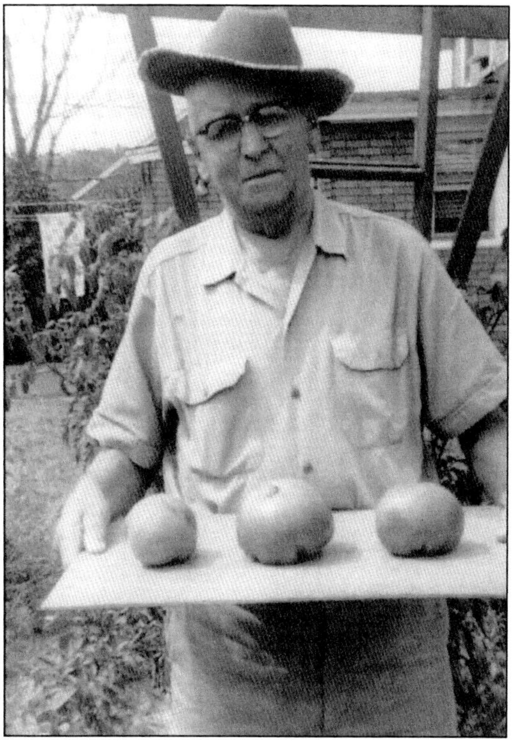

Peter Duda displays the fruits of his labor at the corner of Clancy and Cherry Avenues. A friendly neighborhood rivalry existed as to who could grow the finest tomatoes, and some grew so big that one slice would cover a piece of bread. Duda is representative of many locals who were not of wealthy means and resorted to growing their vegetables, and keeping chickens, ducks, and the like, all of which they shared with neighbors. (Courtesy of Charles Zgrodek.)

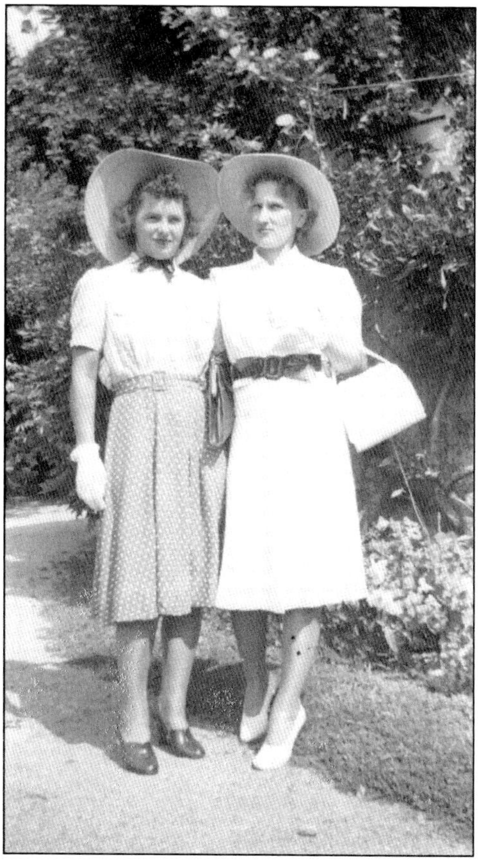

Victoria Gastka (left) and her friend Blanche ? are pictured on a 1935 visit to New Windsor. It was not uncommon for ladies to don hats, gloves, and high heels for the slightest occasion. Victoria planned to spend the day with her parents, Mary and George Gatska. (Courtesy of Irene Pullar.)

Arthur Smith (seated) is pictured at age 20 with good friend Thomas Waite in 1889. Both men had crossed the many miles from England to America as teenagers. Smith was but 17 years old when he arrived in New Windsor from Yorkshire, England, in 1885. (Courtesy of Sandra Lewis Terwilliger.)

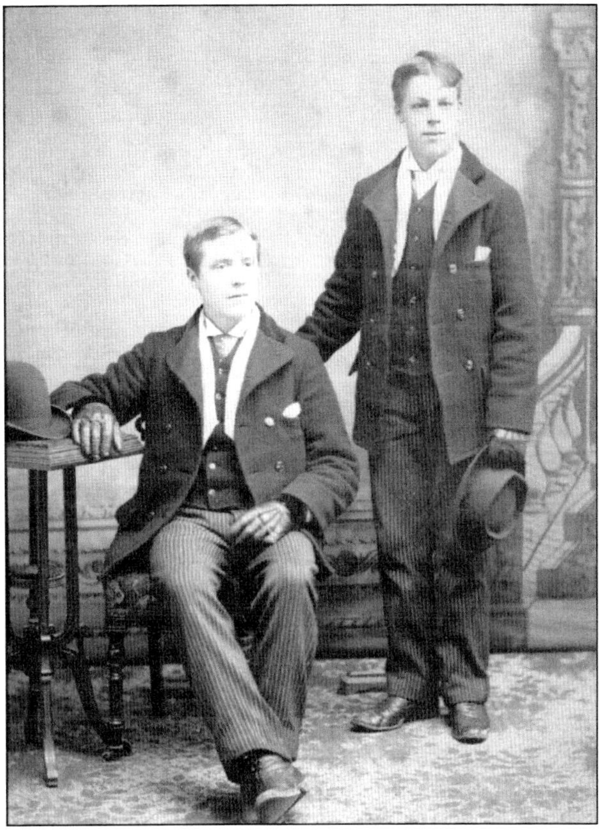

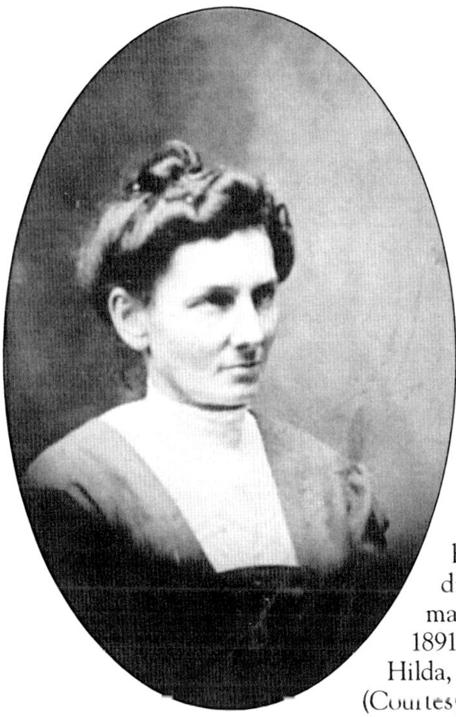

Hilda Loulla VanKeuren Smith was the daughter of Tjisick and Susan Kettle Van Keuren. Hilda and her twin sister, Ina, were born March 24, 1874. Ina died around age 21, while Hilda lived to age 94. She married Arthur Smith and settled in New Windsor in 1891. The couple had nine children—William, Sidney, Hilda, Arthur, Jennifer, Harry, Ann, Winifred, and Leslie. (Courtesy of Sandra Lewis Terwilliger.)

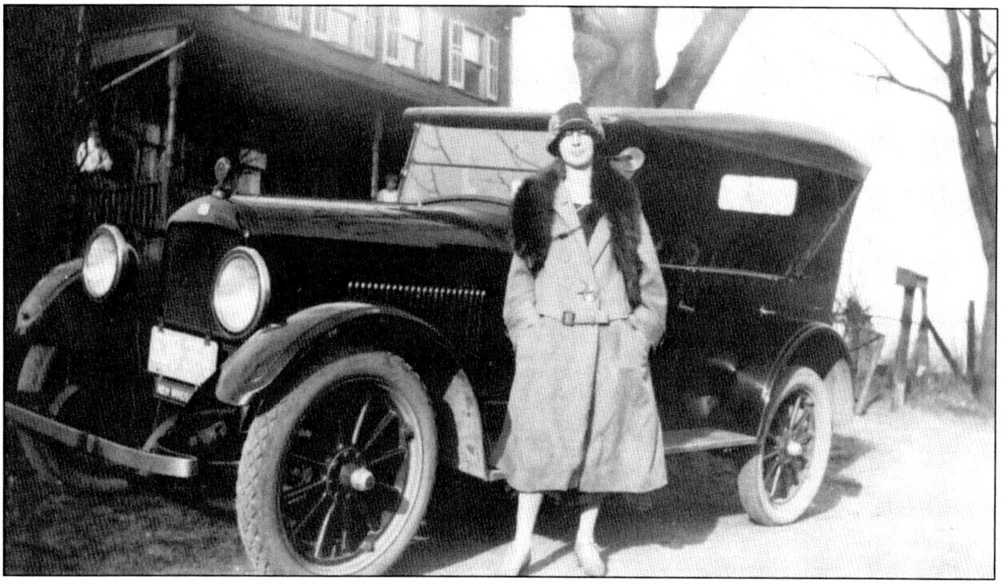

Hilda May Smith, wife of Harry Rockafellow, stands in her parents' front yard. Parked beside her is a new touring car won by her sister Jennifer in a popularity contest around 1927. The car's roof could be removed on sunny days. (Courtesy of Sandra Lewis Terwilliger.)

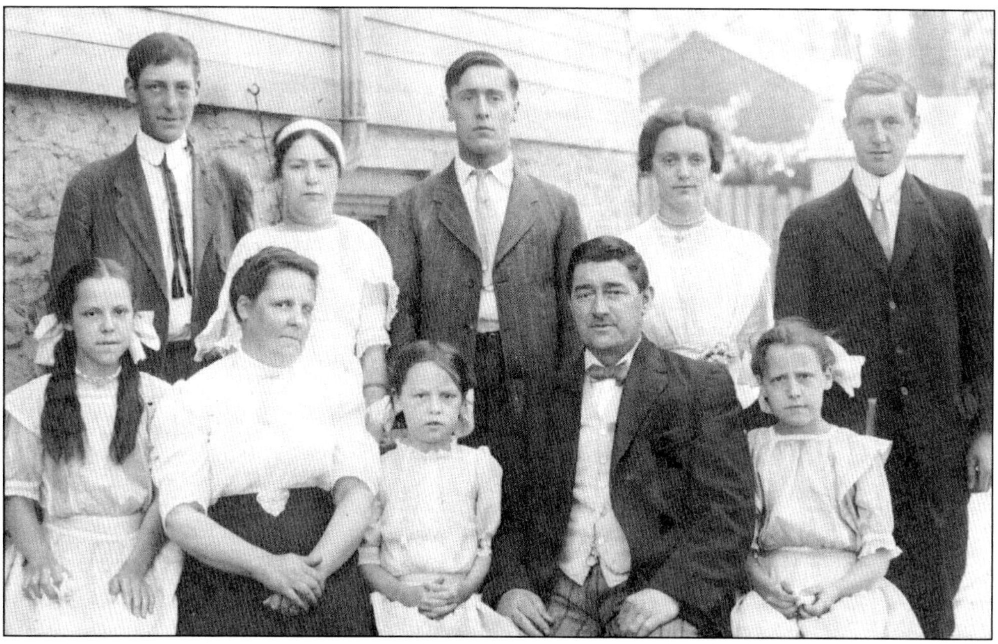

Ramsden Smith and his wife, Mary Jane Waite Smith, came from England. Their family includes, from left to right, (first row) Julia, Mary Jane, Edna, Ramsden, and Grace; (second row) Lorenzo, Ada, Arthur, Alice, and Delbert. Mary Jane, born in 1866, was a sister of Thomas Waite; Ramsden was a brother of Arthur Smith. Mary Jane and Ada both died in 1918. (Courtesy of Sandra Lewis Terwilliger.)

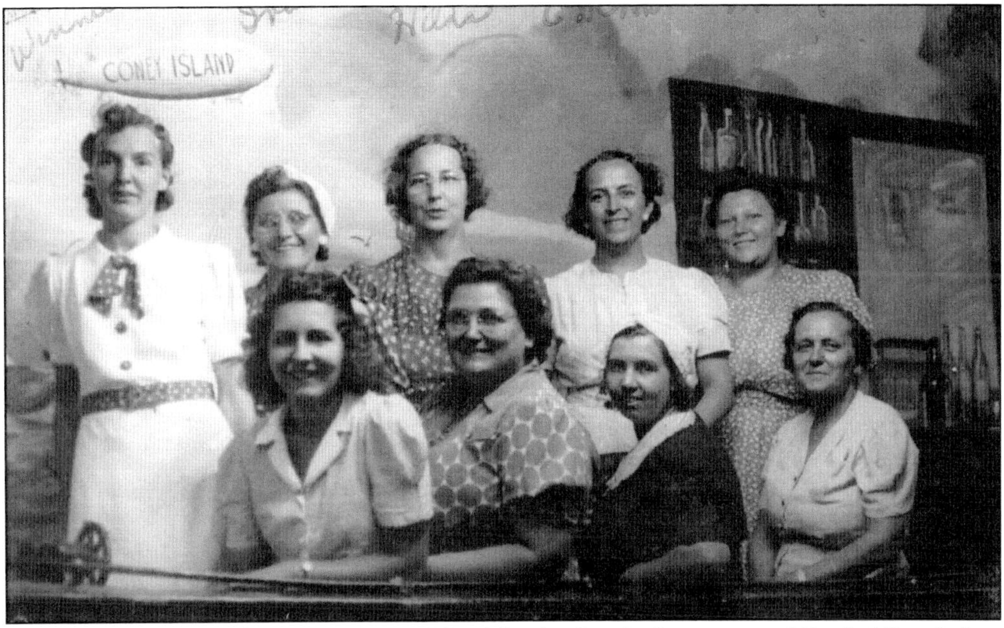

This was just another day trip to Coney Island for the Smith, Swanson, and Rockafellow ladies. They are, from left to right, (first row)) Doris Rockafellow, Anna ?, Ann Rockafellow, and Julia Swanson; (second row) Winifred Smith, Ina Rockafellow, Hilda Smith, Emma Rockafellow, and Mary Popowick (the daughter of Julia Swanson). (Courtesy of Sandra Lewis Terwilliger.)

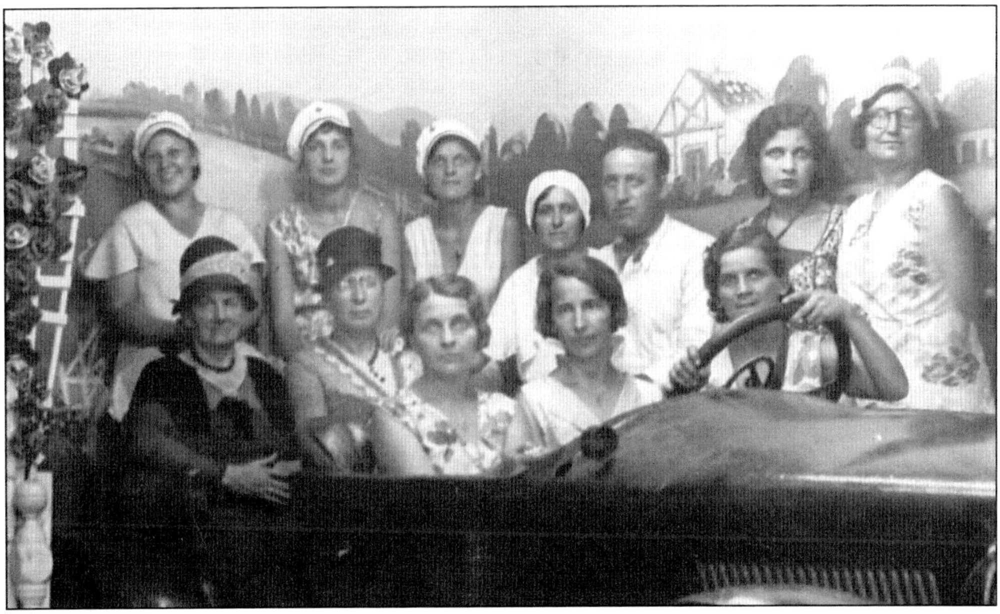

Pictured here on a summer trip are, from left to right, (first row) Hilda Smith, Myra Rumsey, unidentified, Hilda May Smith, and Dorothy Rockafellow; (second row) Mary Popowick Sloboda, Ina Winifred Smith Lewis, Ruth Rockafellow Shenaman, Julia Swanson, two unidentified people, and Anna Rockafellow. Note that the ladies are accompanied by a handsome young man. (Courtesy of Sandra Lewis Terwilliger.)

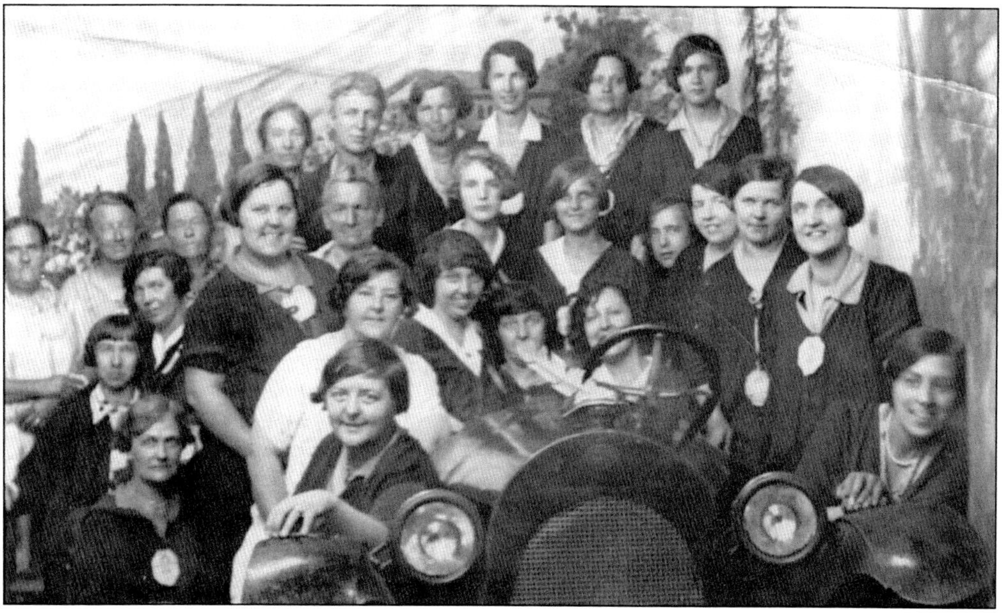

Ladies love to go on trips together. Those pictured here gathered on July 31, 1927, for the 75-mile day trip to Coney Island. Among this group are Hilda Smith, Myra Rumsey, Hilda May Smith, Winifred Smith, Ruth Rockafellow, and Abigail and Geraldine McClure. (Courtesy of Sandra Lewis Terwilliger.)

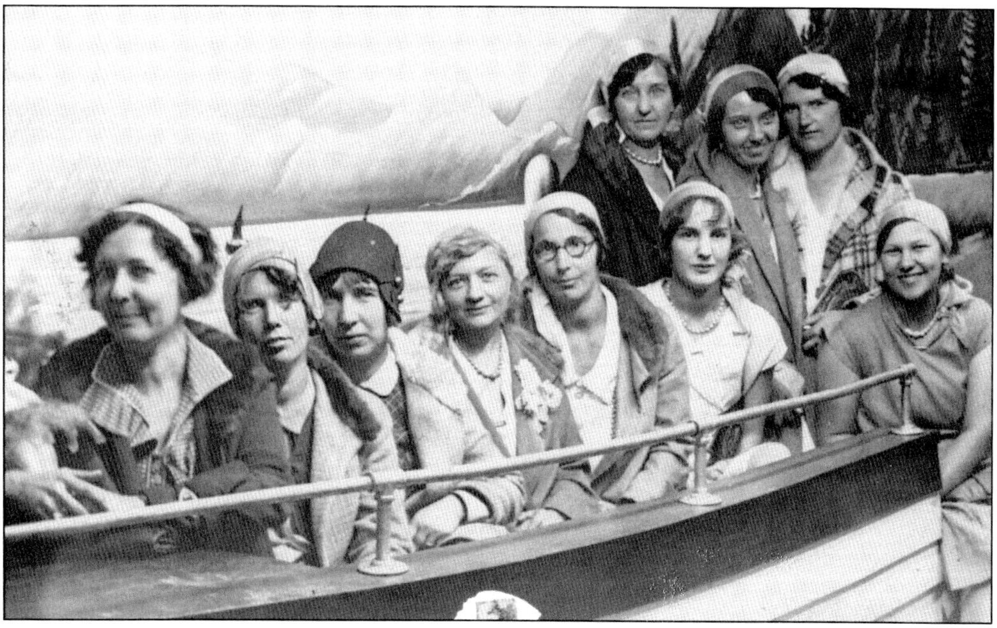

The cold winter of 1928 could not keep the ladies of New Windsor away from Coney Island. They donned their winter coats and hats and headed out for the day. Seated at the far right are Hilda Smith, Winifred Smith, and Mary Popowick. (Courtesy of Sandra Lewis Terwillger.)

Winifred Smith sits on top of Spy Rock on Snake Hill in the late 1930s. In the background, to the left, is Muchattoes Lake, with the smokestack of the Newburgh Bleachery factory visible across the street. The Hudson River can also be seen. (Courtesy of Sandra Lewis Terwilliger.)

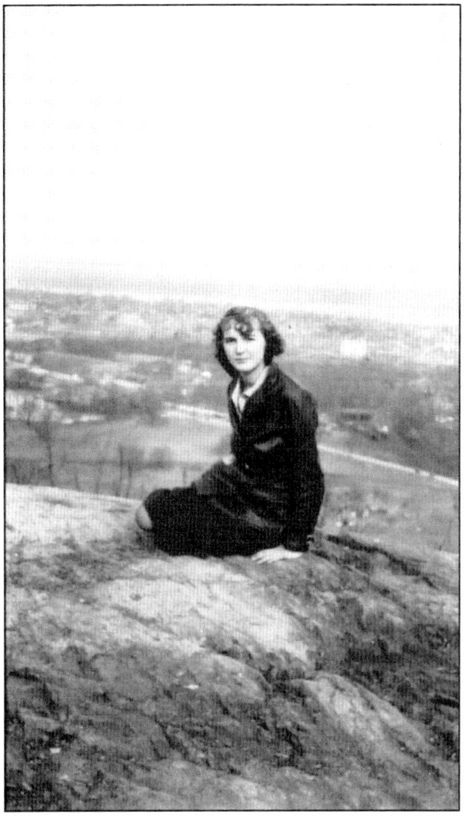

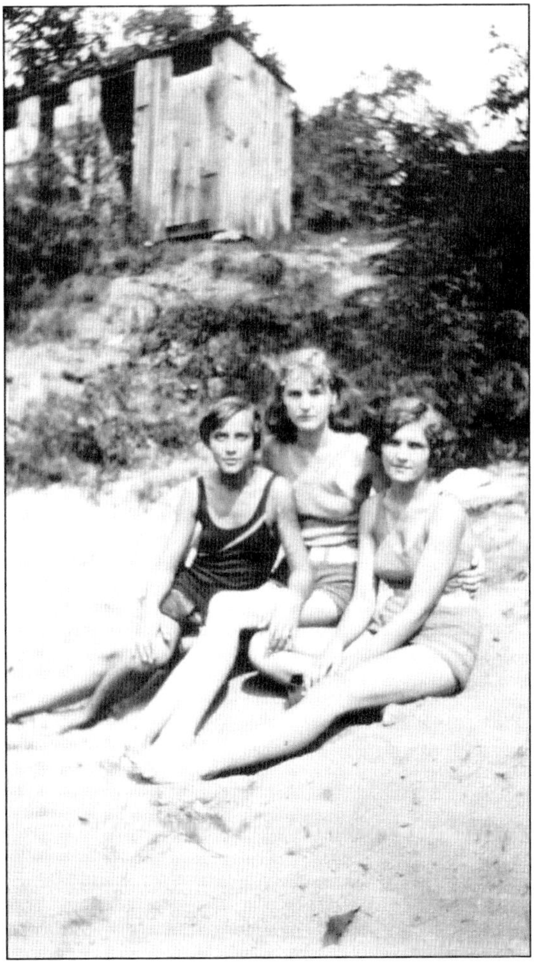

Elizabeth Stavetski (left), Winifred Smith (center), and Ruth Rockafellow sit on the sand, sunbathing on a hot summer afternoon at Seaman's Beach in the late 1930s. Teenagers loved spending time with their best friends at the beach. Note the row of outhouses for beachgoers. (Courtesy of Sandra Lewis Terwilliger.)

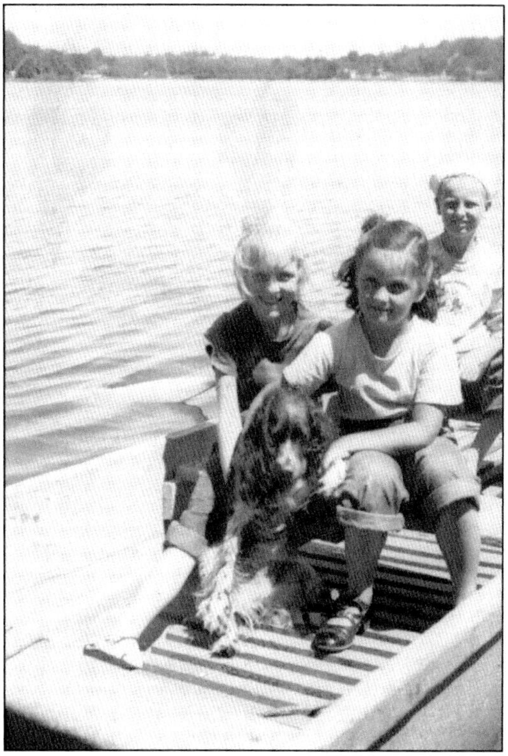

Kathleen Popowick (right) holds on to her dog Puggy, who looks a little frightened. They are waiting to take a boat ride from Seaman's Beach across Beaver Dam Lake. Sandra Lewis and her brother Robert Lewis happily went along for the ride. Puggy finally settled down and enjoyed the trip, too. (Courtesy of Sandra Lewis Terwiilliger.)

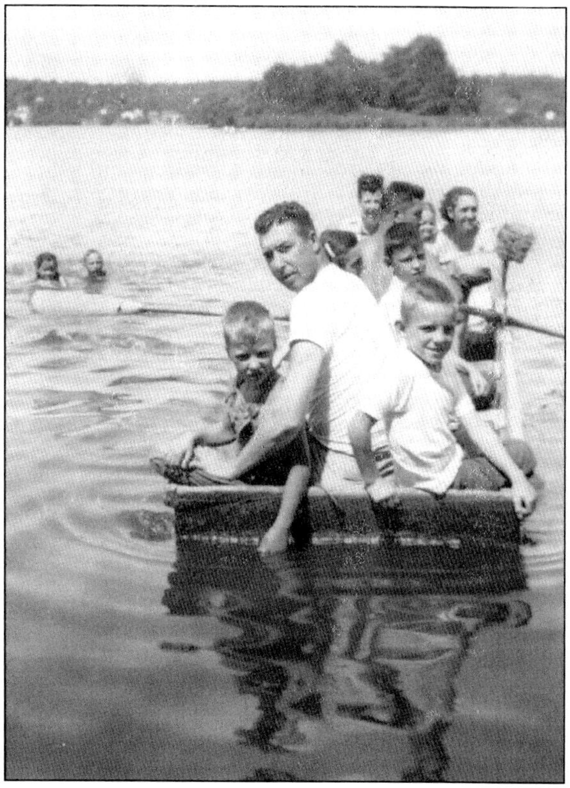

The families of Kenneth and Emily Rumsey and their friends liked to rent boats and spend the day at Seaman's Beach, a popular spot in the 1940s. The Rumseys rented a cottage and boat from Frederick Seaman, owner of the beach property. (Courtesy of Sandra Lewis Terwilliger.)

Standing in the cornfield of the Paul Babcock Sr. Dairy Farm in Little Britain in this 1956 photograph are, from left to right, Arthur Housserman, Frieda Babcock, dog Jerry, and Evelyn Housserman. Frieda, wife of Paul Sr., felt it was her job to measure the corn and keep the weeds to a minimum. (Courtesy of the Robert Babcock family.)

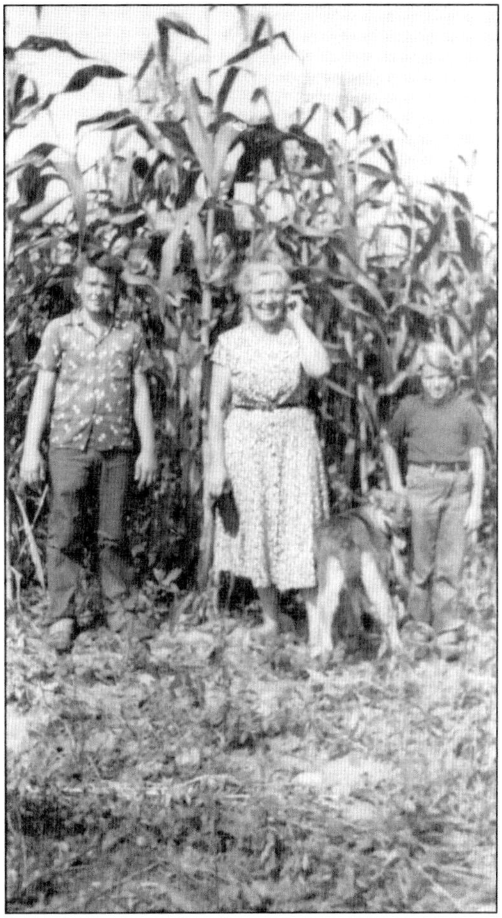

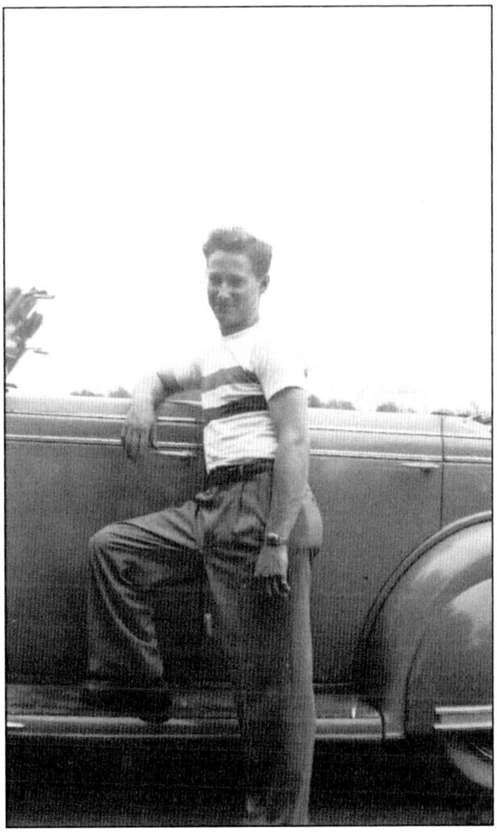

Robert Babcock of Little Britain stands beside his 1936 Dodge Phantom in 1949. Babcock was known in the area as an avid collector and restorer of antique cars. He found this 1936 Dodge in very poor condition but was able to restore it and enjoy driving it for some time. (Courtesy of the Robert Babcock family.)

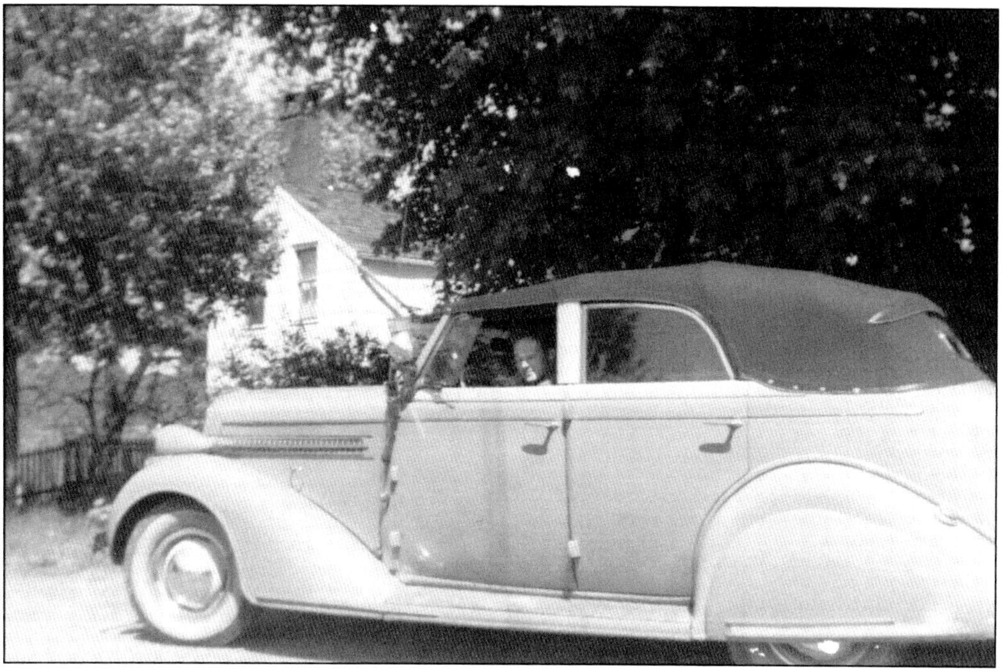

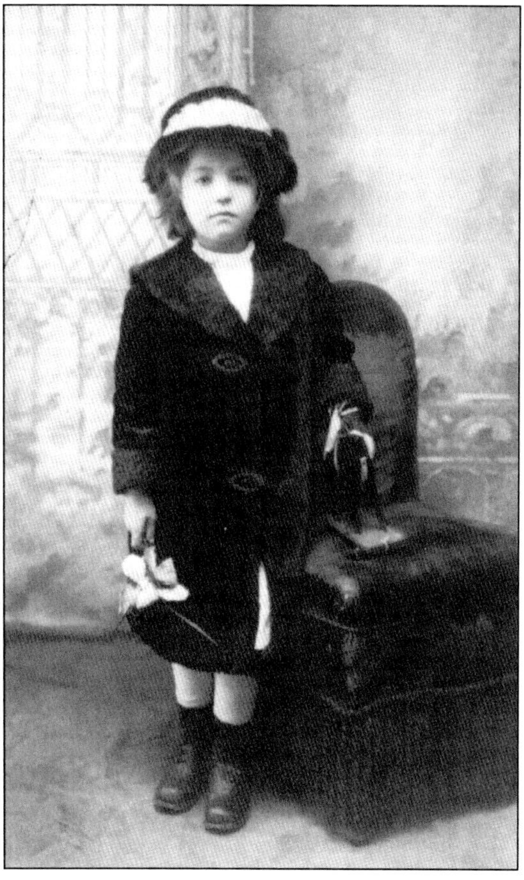

Robert Babcock is seen here in his award-winning 1936 Dodge Phantom. This car won the Grand National First Place Award at Canandaigua, New York, in 1990. Babcock had sold his first restored 1936 Dodge Phandom but had come to regret the decision. By chance, his wife, Catherine, spotted another 1936 Dodge at an antique car show in Hershey, Pennsylvania. He bought it immediately and has kept it to this day. (Courtesy of the Robert Babcock family.)

Sophia was the eldest child of Mary Slovik and George Gastka. She was born on John Street in New Windsor on September 26, 1909. It was rare for even the wealthiest of families to own cameras at that time, so studio pictures were taken by professional photographers. (Courtesy of Irene Pullar.)

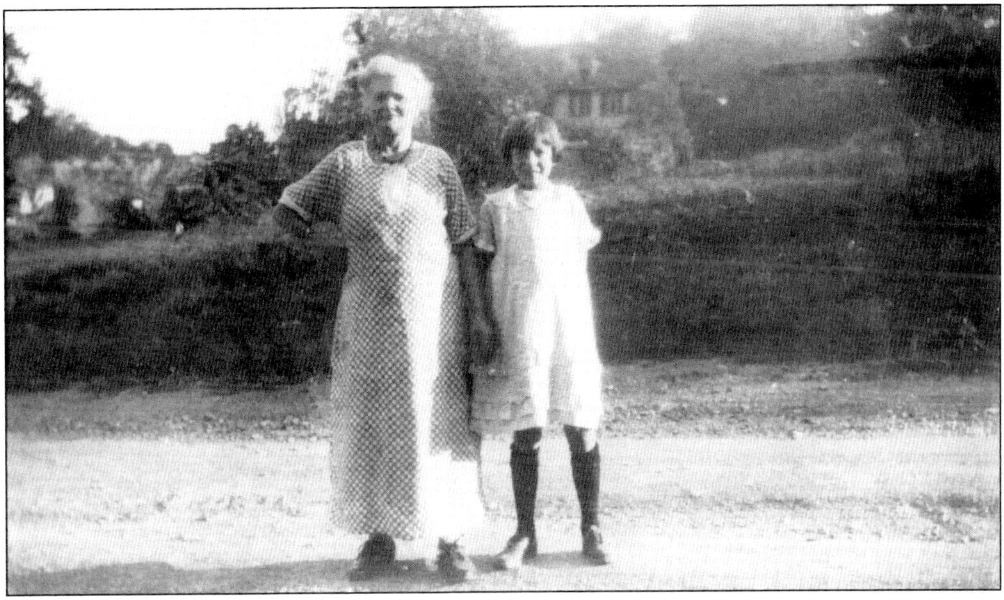

Mary Gastka, grandmother of Irene Pullar, stands next to her daughter Johanna "Jenny" Gastka around the summer of 1925. They are on Ledyard Street, which had not been paved, and are looking up Flynn's Hill toward a dairy and an icehouse. (Courtesy of Irene Pullar.)

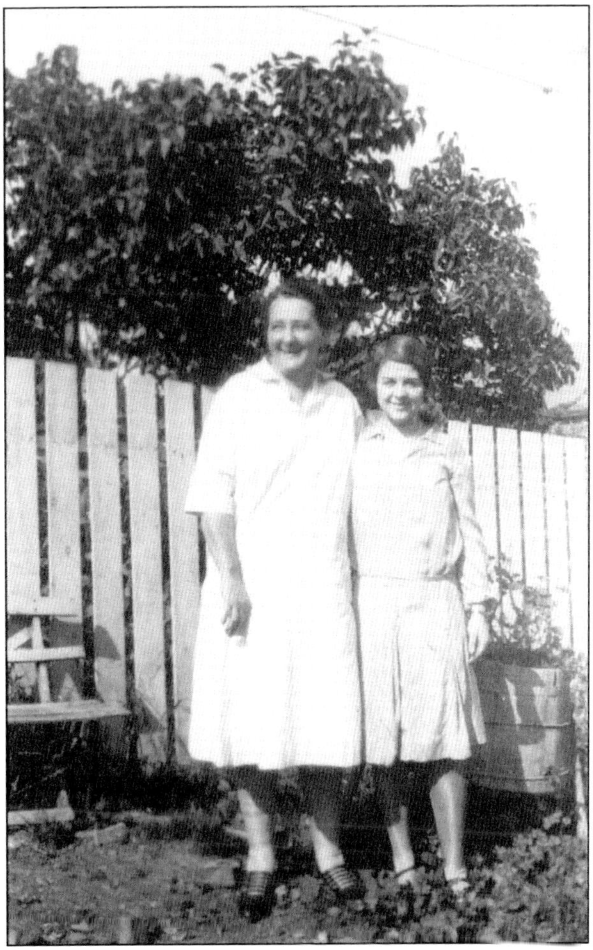

Sunny summer days brought many New Windsor families to their backyards to enjoy picnicking, gardening, and gossiping. Dorothy Sager and her mother are shown in their backyard on Johns Street, around 1925. Dorothy's father was trying out his newly purchased camera. (Courtesy of Irene Pullar.)

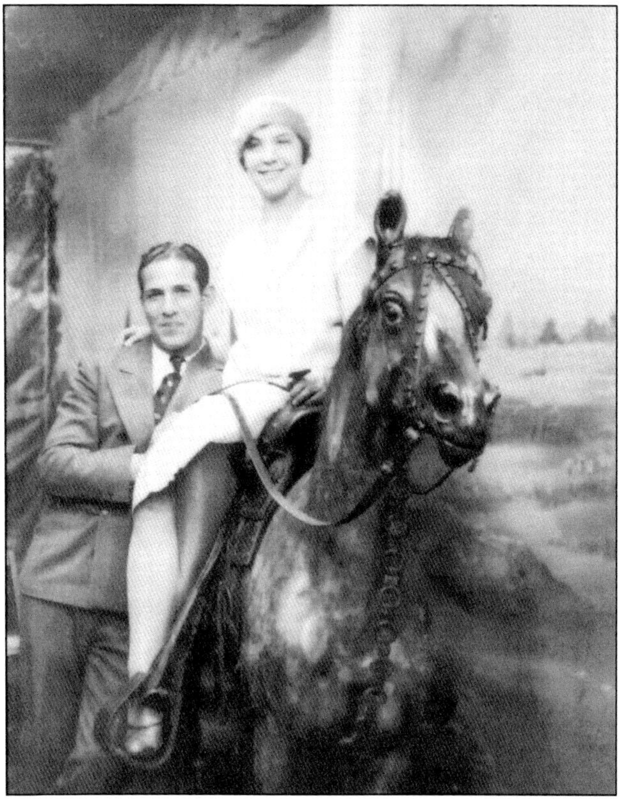

Sophia Gastka DeTurris sits upon a model horse while her husband, John DeTurris, stands by making certain she does not fall off. Coney Island, with its proximity to New Windsor, was an easy destination for a day trip in 1932. There, visitors could pose for photographs with a variety of props. (Courtesy of Irene Pullar.)

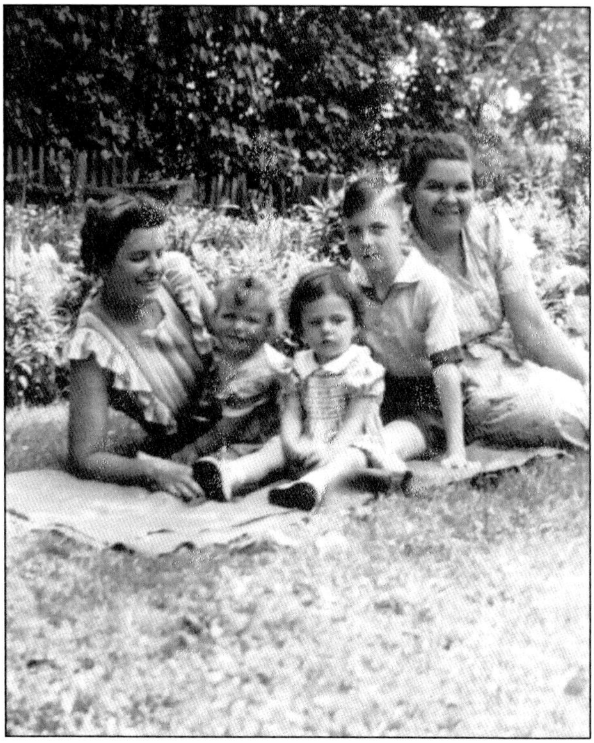

Gardens were popular on Ledyard Street during the 1940s. Enjoying the fresh air in this photograph are, from left to right, Victoria Gastka Zygaldo, Victoria's daughter Hilda, her niece Louise Gastka (the daughter of William and Mary Gastka), Joseph Gastka Jr. (the son of Joseph and Elsie Gastka), and Johanna Gastka Mowsay. (Courtesy of Irene Pullar.)

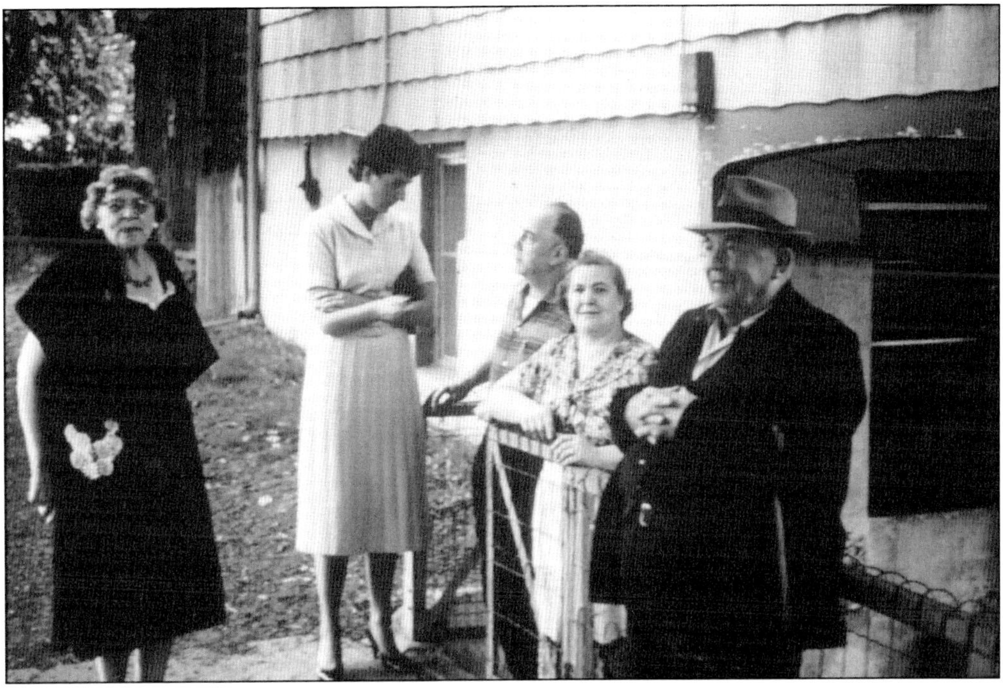

Rosaline Gastka stands to the far left in this 1958 picture, taken by her son John Gastka at 5 Ledyard Street. Also pictured are, from left to right, daughter-in-law Polly Gastka, son-in-law John DeTurris, daughter Sophia, and a delighted George Gaska, who always looked forward to family gatherings. (Courtesy of Irene Pullar.)

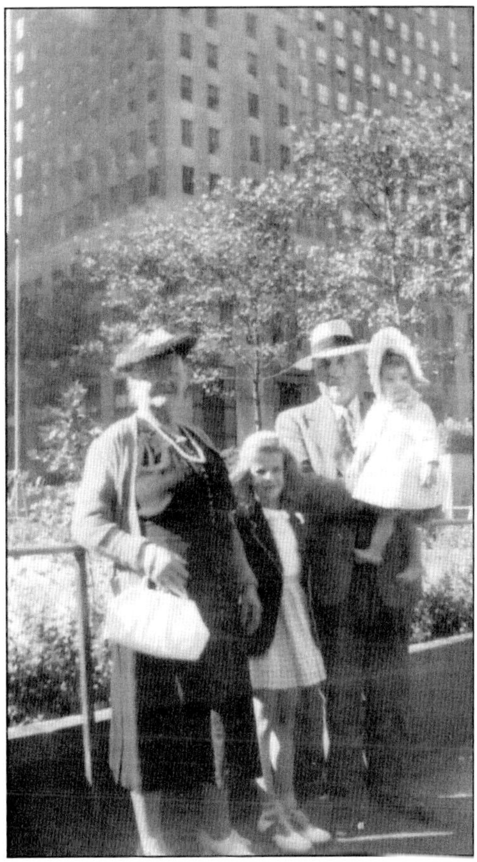

Mary and George Gastka, dressed in their finest, visit New York City's Central Park on Easter Sunday in 1945 with their granddaughters Mary Lou DeTurris Bosacky (age seven) and Irene DeTurris Pullar (age seven months). (Courtesy of Irene Pullar.)

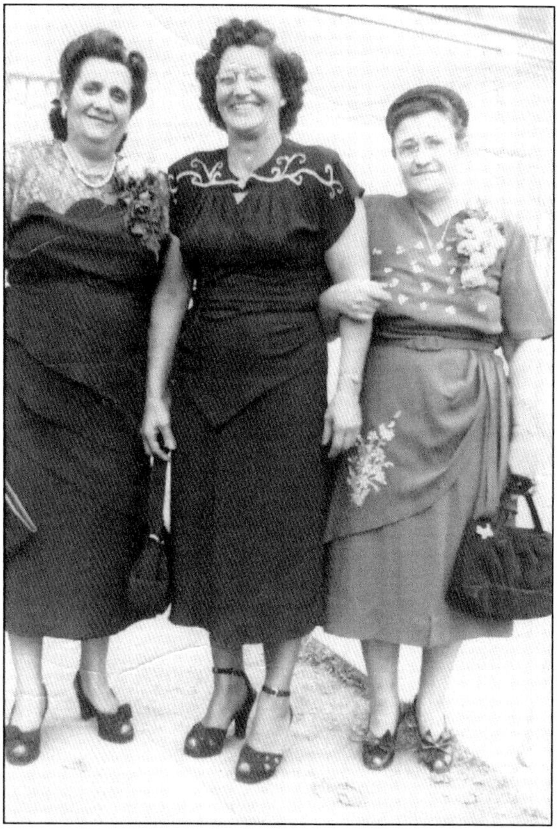

Pictured around 1940 are lifelong friends and Ducktown residents Angelina Spignardo Bucciarelli (left), Elizabeth Petro (center), and Louise Spignardo Crudele. Judging from the Sunday-best outfits and corsages worn by sisters Bucciarelli and Crudele, one can imagine the three are on their way to church, probably on Easter Sunday. (Courtesy of Margaret Spignardo.)

On the right side of this 1974 image, Peter Drennen is seen walking on his hands, supported by neighborhood friend Robert Nixon. To the left, Gregory Palkovic is holding the feet of a young member of the Riley family. All the boys lived in the Park Hill development, where most of the homes had been built by John Petro. Petro and his wife, Martha, still live in the area. (Courtesy of the Drennen family.)

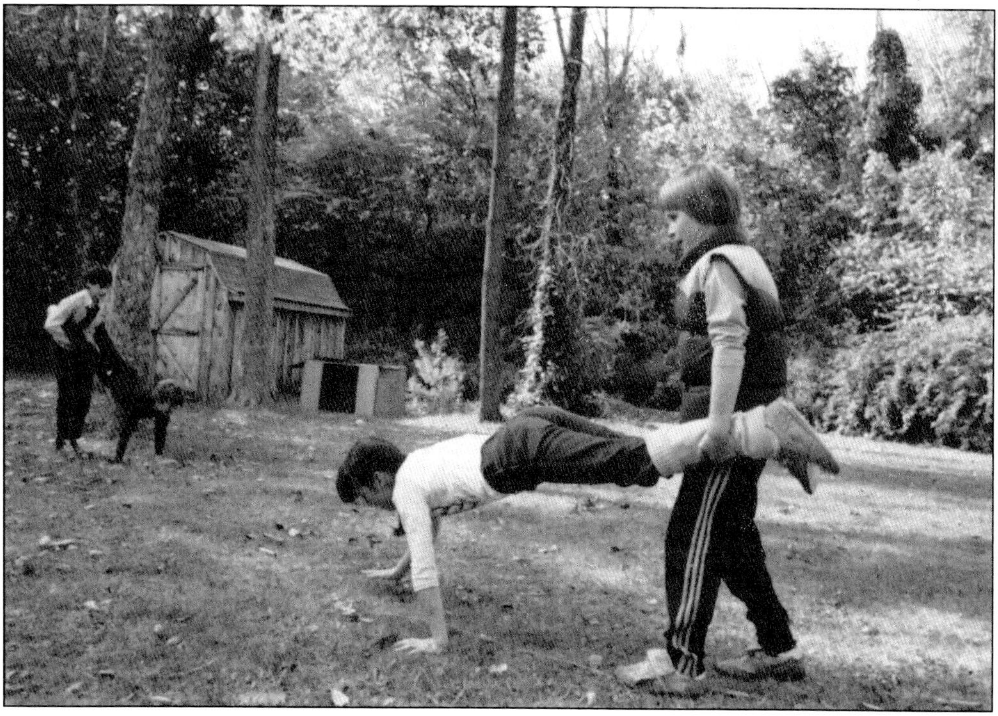

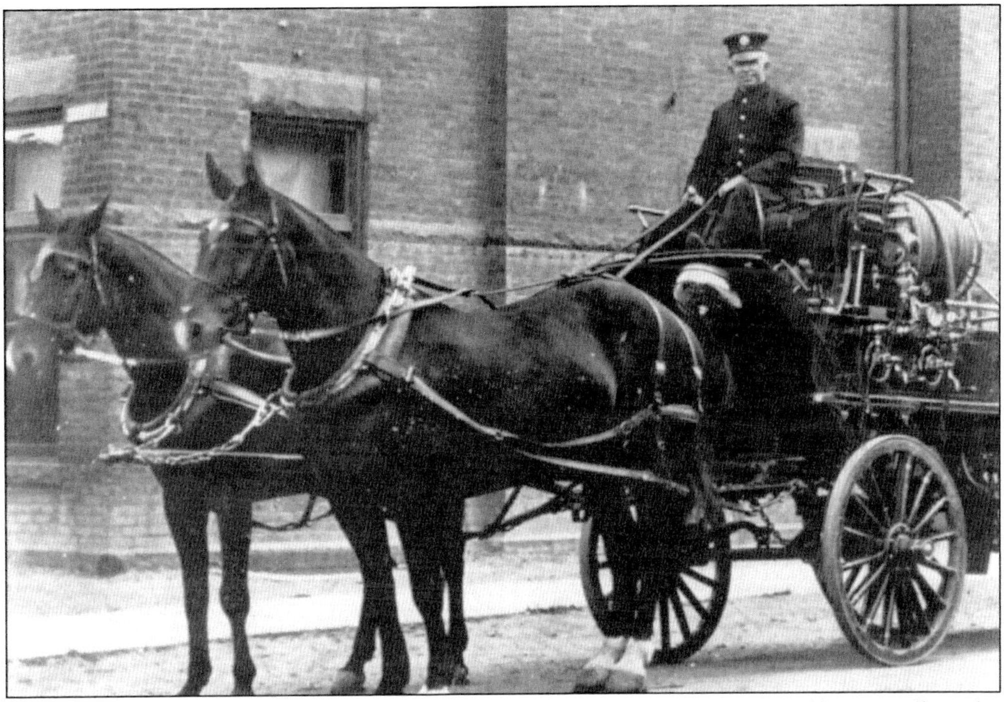

Thomas Balfe, great-grandfather of the Elmer Babcock family, drives a team of horses pulling the firefighting apparatus for the Washington Heights Engine Company of Newburgh. Balfe retired after 25 years of service, just prior to the motorization of the local firefighting equipment around the turn of the century. (Courtesy of the Babcock family.)

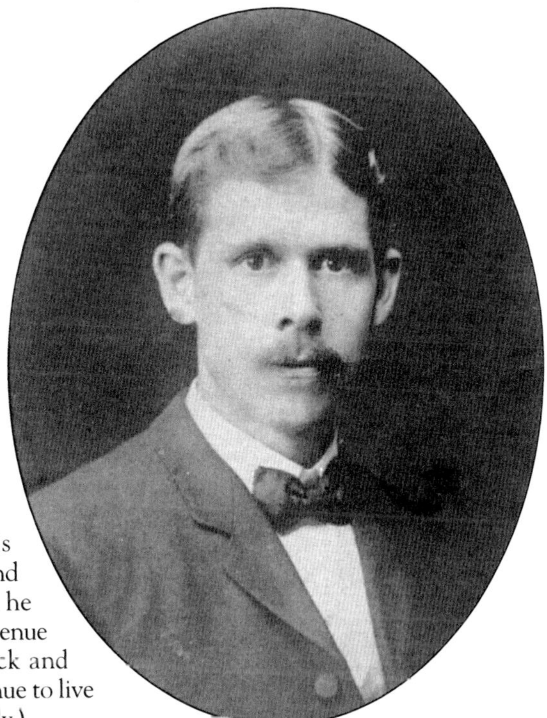

George F. Mills, father of Marion Mills Babcock, was born to William H. Mills and Theresa Cook in the late 1800s. In 1912, he completed construction of the 12 Blanche Avenue house where his grandson John T. Babcock and John's wife, Angela Bugiada Babcock, continue to live to this day. (Courtesy of the Babcock family.)

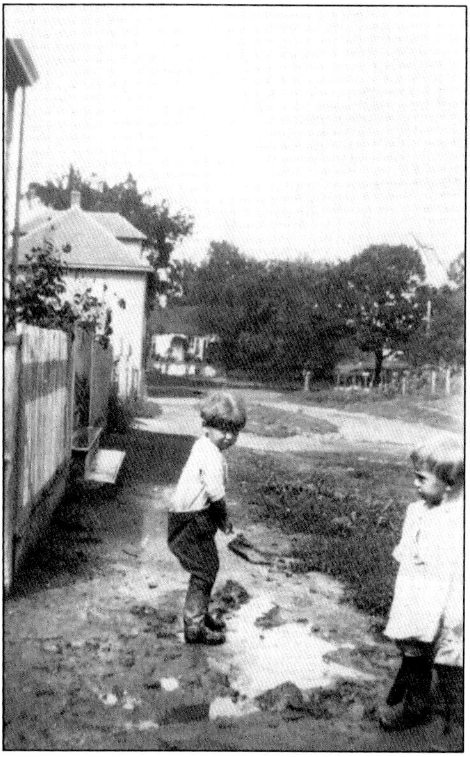

Brothers George (left) and Robert Babcock play at their 12 Blanche Avenue home. Looking down the street toward Walsh's Avenue, note the dirt road. Swanson's house and store is on the left. To get their mail, a family member had to walk toward the corner to a tree that served as a mailbox post. (Courtesy of the Babcock family.)

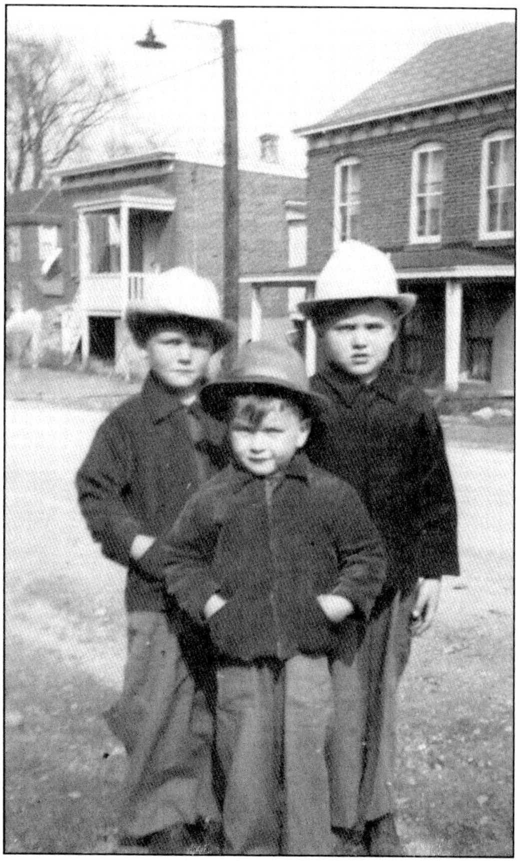

Pictured in 1944 on the dirt road outside their 12 Blanche Avenue home are, from left to right, brothers John, Donald, and Edward Babcock. The boys look so handsome in their hats. In the background are the homes of the Edgars (left) and the Laddicks (right). (Courtesy of the Babcock family.)

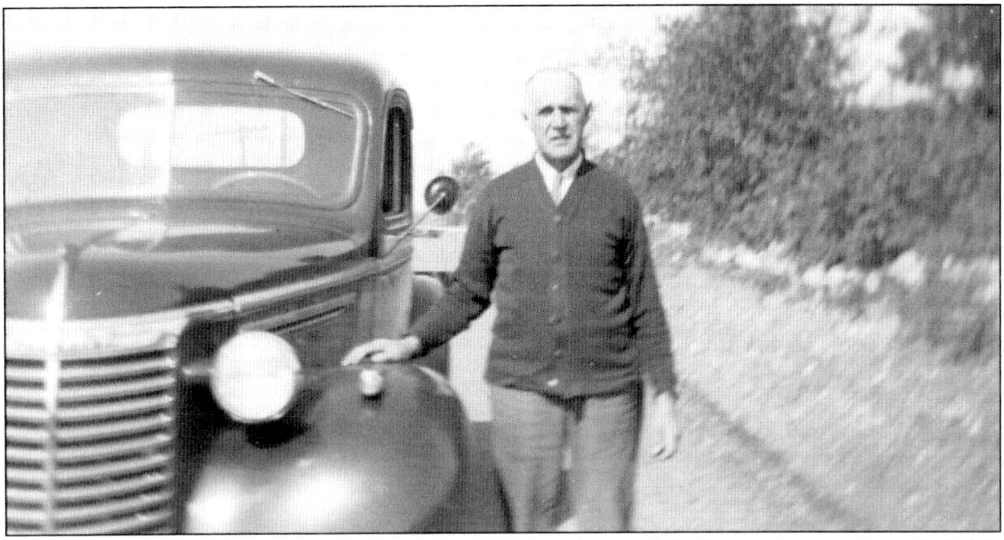

New Windsor highway superintendent John T. Babcock stands by his pickup truck in 1947. He was responsible for maintaining the town roads, many of which were yet to be paved. As the population expanded, so did the highway department and its many responsibilities. (Courtesy of the Babcock family.)

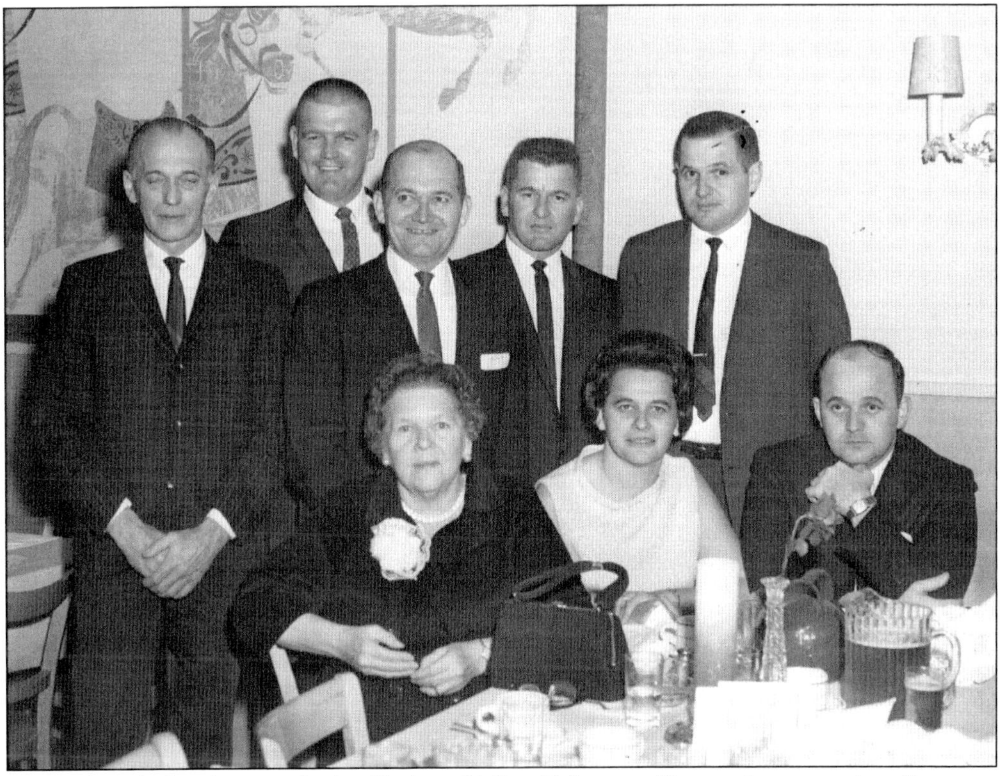

The Babcock family attends the Hudson Valley Volunteer Firemen's convention dinner at Meadowbrook Lodge in 1966. Marion Babcock and her children, Shirley Babcock Early and William Babcock, are seated at the table. Standing behind them are, from left to right, Robert, John, George, Donald, and Edward Babcock. (Courtesy of the Babcock family.)

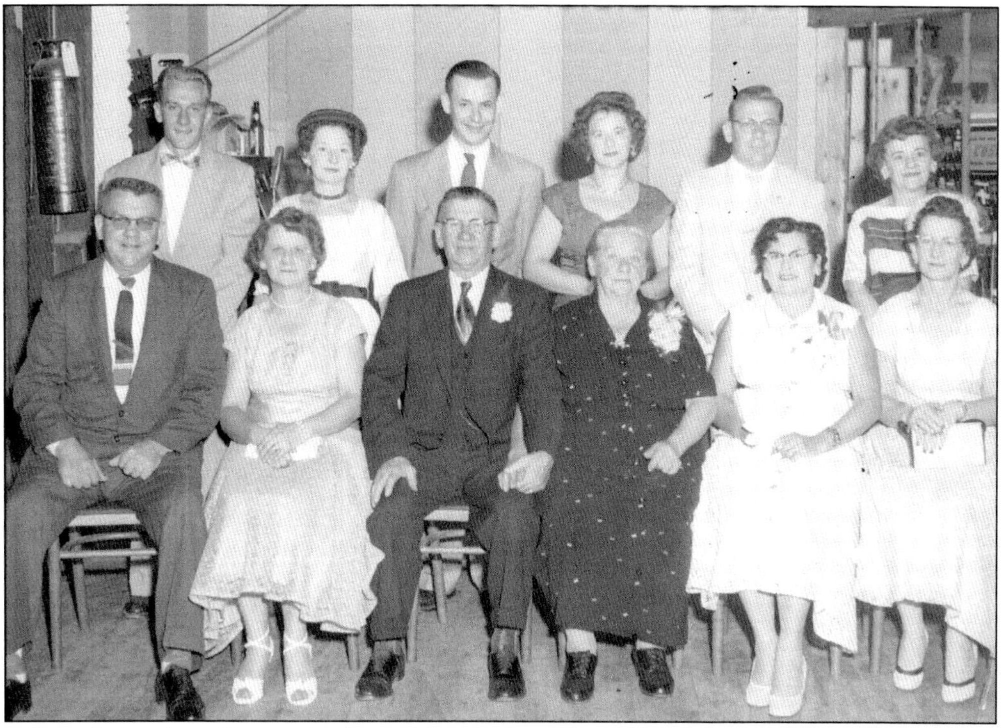

William Dabroski and Frances Doktor celebrate their 50th wedding anniversary with their children in 1956 at the Clamshell Inn on Route 17K. Pictured are, from left to right, (first row) John, Anna, William, Frances, Jay, and Helen; (second row) Edward, Estelle, Joseph, Tillie, Frank, and Loretta. William and Frances Dabroski are representative of the Polish immigrants who arrived in the Clancyville/Ducktown area between 1905 and 1910. (Courtesy of the Dabroski family.)

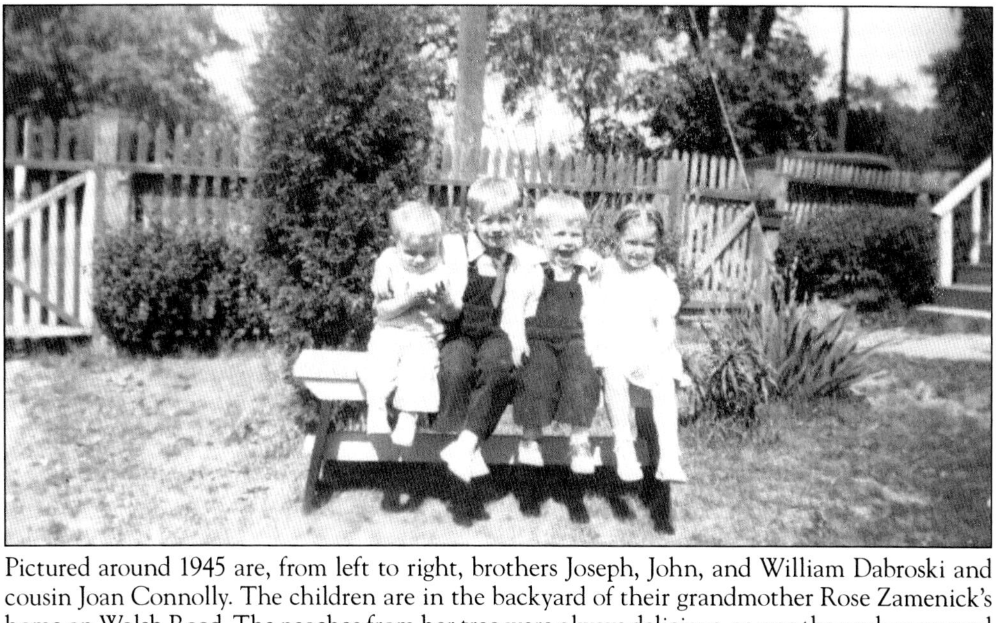

Pictured around 1945 are, from left to right, brothers Joseph, John, and William Dabroski and cousin Joan Connolly. The children are in the backyard of their grandmother Rose Zamenick's home on Walsh Road. The peaches from her tree were always delicious, as was the pork processed in her smokehouse. (Courtesy of the Dabroski family.)

Anne and brother Raymond, children of James and Mary Brennan, are pictured in their yard at 32 Quassaick Avenue around 1923. Their mother, Mary, died when Anne was 13 years old, and Anne was forced to leave New Windsor School to take care of her father and brothers. She felt a sense of loss about having to give up her education. (Courtesy of the Pullar family.)

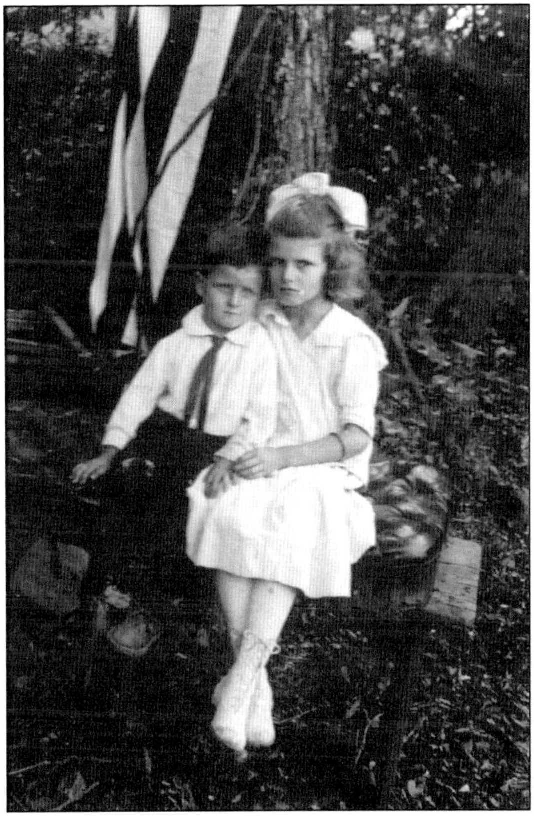

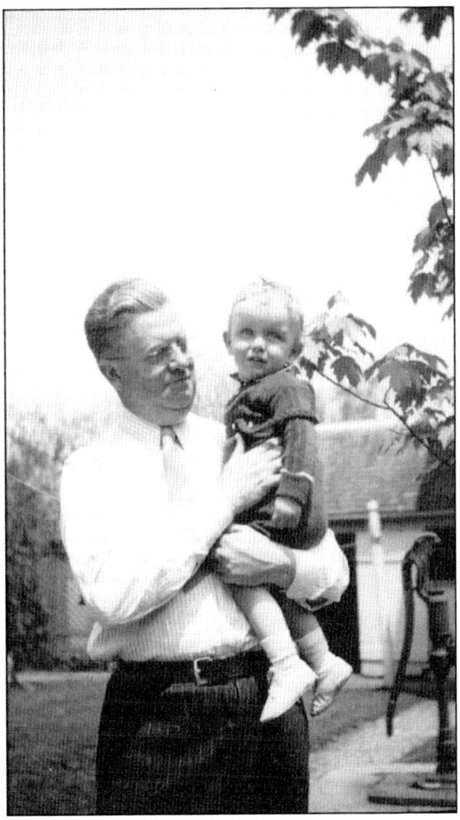

In this May 1940 photograph, John V. Brennan holds nephew James Pullar in the yard of the Brennan home at 32 Quassaick Avenue. Both served New Windsor in political offices—Brennan as justice of the peace for several years during the 1930s, and Pullar as highway superintendent from 1996 to 2000. (Courtesy of the Pullar family.)

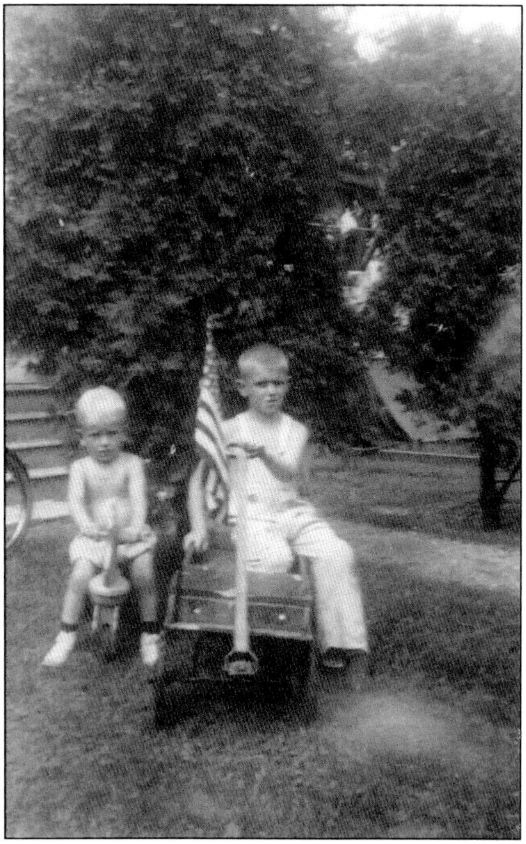

Brothers Jerome (left) and James Pullar play in the backyard at 32 Quassaick Avenue in 1944, patiently waiting for the Memorial Day parade to come down their street. To this day, James displays the American flag at his home. (Courtesy of the Pullar family.)

Jerome (left) and James Pullar are seen with dog Prince in the backyard of their Quassaick Avenue home in 1947. At that time, it was typical to see clothes hanging on the clothesline, a tricycle or bicycle waiting to be ridden, and a dog watching the property. (Courtesy of the Pullar family.)

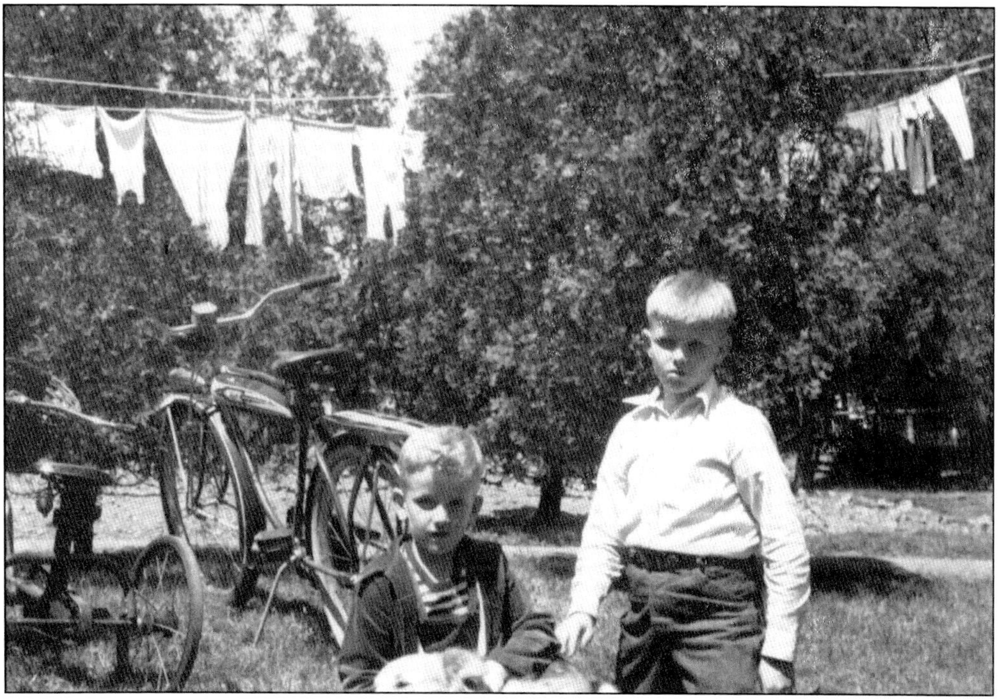

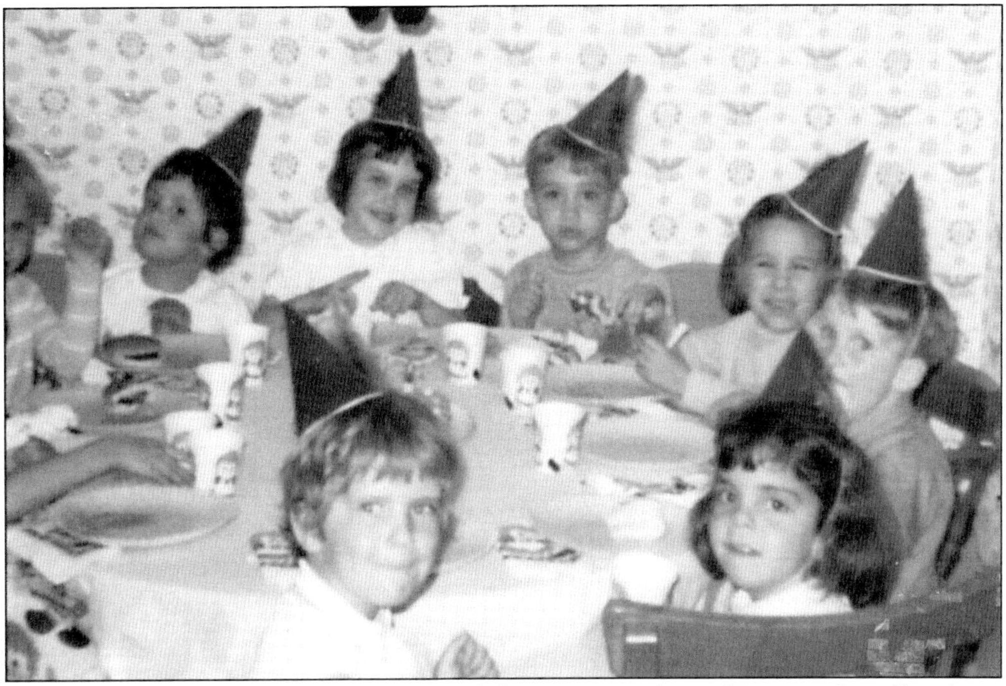

On May 26, 1970, these children attend a birthday party on Valewood Drive in the willow Acres development. In attendance are, clockwise from left, Diane DeWitt (in striped shirt), Cheryl Cummings, Kathleen Smith, Kenneth Parker, Jeri Paffendorf, Brian Smith, Karen DiLorenzo, and Nancy Pullar. (Courtesy of the Pullar family.)

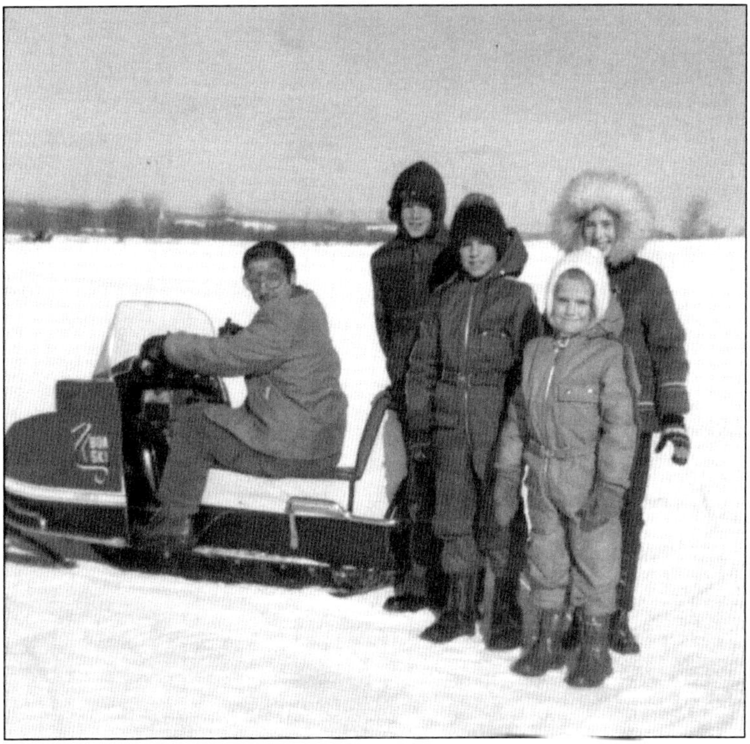

During the 1970s, snowmobiles became very popular; here, Richard Pavlik Sr. is pictured on a rented one in January 1970. Waiting their turn are, from left to right, Richard Pavlik Jr., William Pullar, Nancy Pullar, and Jane Pavlik. (Courtesy of the Pullar family.)

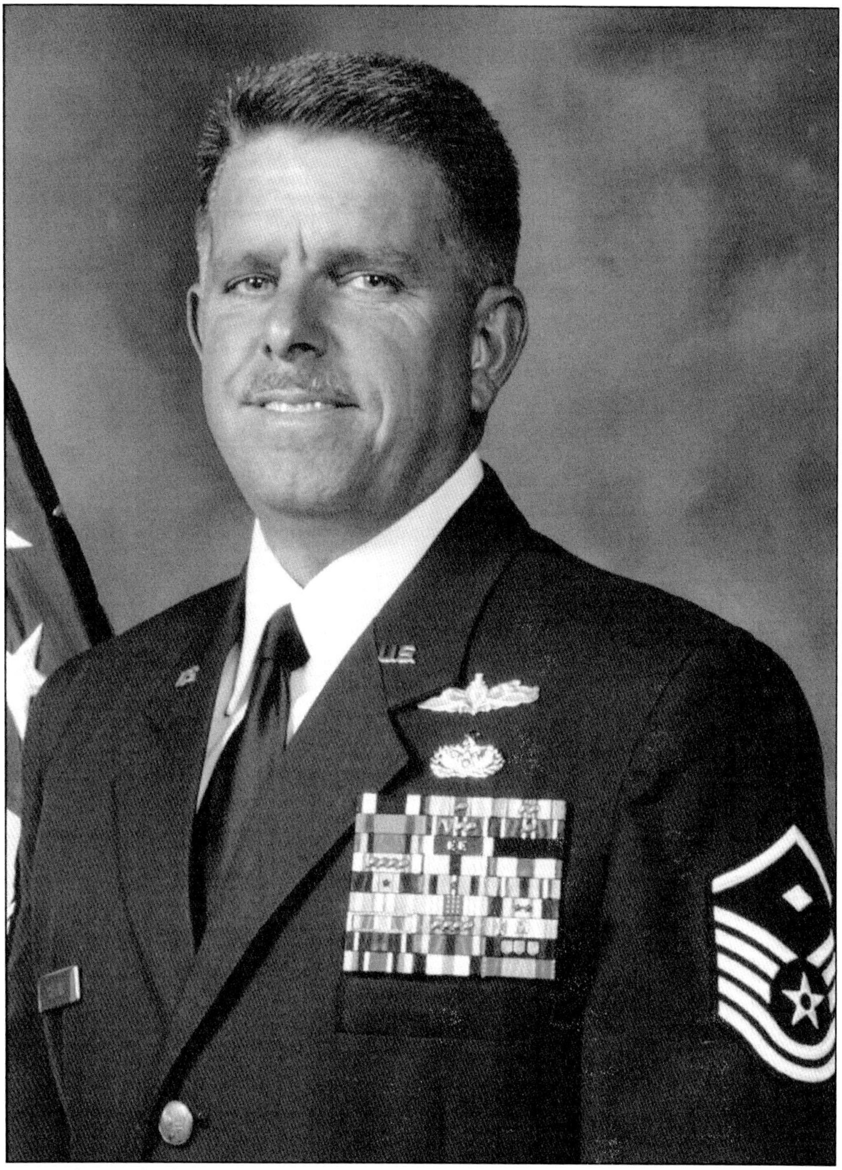

The Lt. Comdr. Nicholas Brooks Memorial Award for exceptional community service was initiated by New Windsor town supervisor George Green in honor of a boyhood friend who was captured and killed in Vietnam. It is the highest honor the Town of New Windsor can bestow. In 1989, William Pullar was the first recipient. Pullar served four years in the US Navy and 26 years in the US Air Force before retiring as a senior master sergeant. He served tours of duty in Iraq, Saudi Arabia, the United Arab Emirates, and Kuwait, and in Operations Desert Storm, Iraqi Freedom, and Enduring Freedom. He is the recipient of the USAF Goddard Medal for his outstanding contribution to military engineering. A recipient of the Quassaick Fire Engine Company Lifetime Achievement Award, he has also served as a New Windsor Little League Board of Directors member, American Legion vice commander, New Windsor Fire Department captain and president, New Windsor Memorial Day Committee chairman, and New Windsor Fire Department 75th Anniversary Committee chairman. He is currently employed by the New York State Department of Transportation as a civil engineer. (Courtesy of the Pullar family.)

Five

Firehouse Volunteers

Firehouses play an important role in communities throughout the United States. Oftentimes, the firehouse is the hub of the community, where people continue to gather to celebrate occasions, share ideas and support, and help each other in times of need. Additionally, the support of firehouse voters can propel politicians to electoral victories.

Vails Gate Fire Company, Inc., did not begin as a firefighting unit, but rather as a 1906 social club. The group, which met in a Vails Gate general store, promoted billiard tournaments and produced one of the area's best baseball teams. In 1907, when aqueduct workers were unable to extinguish a fire that had broken out in a shed, the need for fire protection was recognized. After two smaller buildings became inadequate, a third was built in 1959. In 1980, the company officially became a fire district.

The idea for a New Windsor fire company was first conceived by men of the Quassaick Athletic Club in 1922. Between late 1923 and early 1924, William Donahue, W. Eldridge Sr., and Arthur Smith Sr. met to discuss the need for a fire company and what would be required to bring it to fruition. In May 1927, the first officers were elected. Property at the corner of Walsh Road and Cedar Avenue was purchased from Arthur Smith, and by 1929, the organization was known as the New Windsor Community Club & Fire Engine Company. The first firehouse was built in 1939, and a new, state-of-the-art complex was completed in 2010.

The New Windsor area fire companies continue to grow, as does the quality of their equipment, training, preparedness, and ability to respond and attend to any emergency scene.

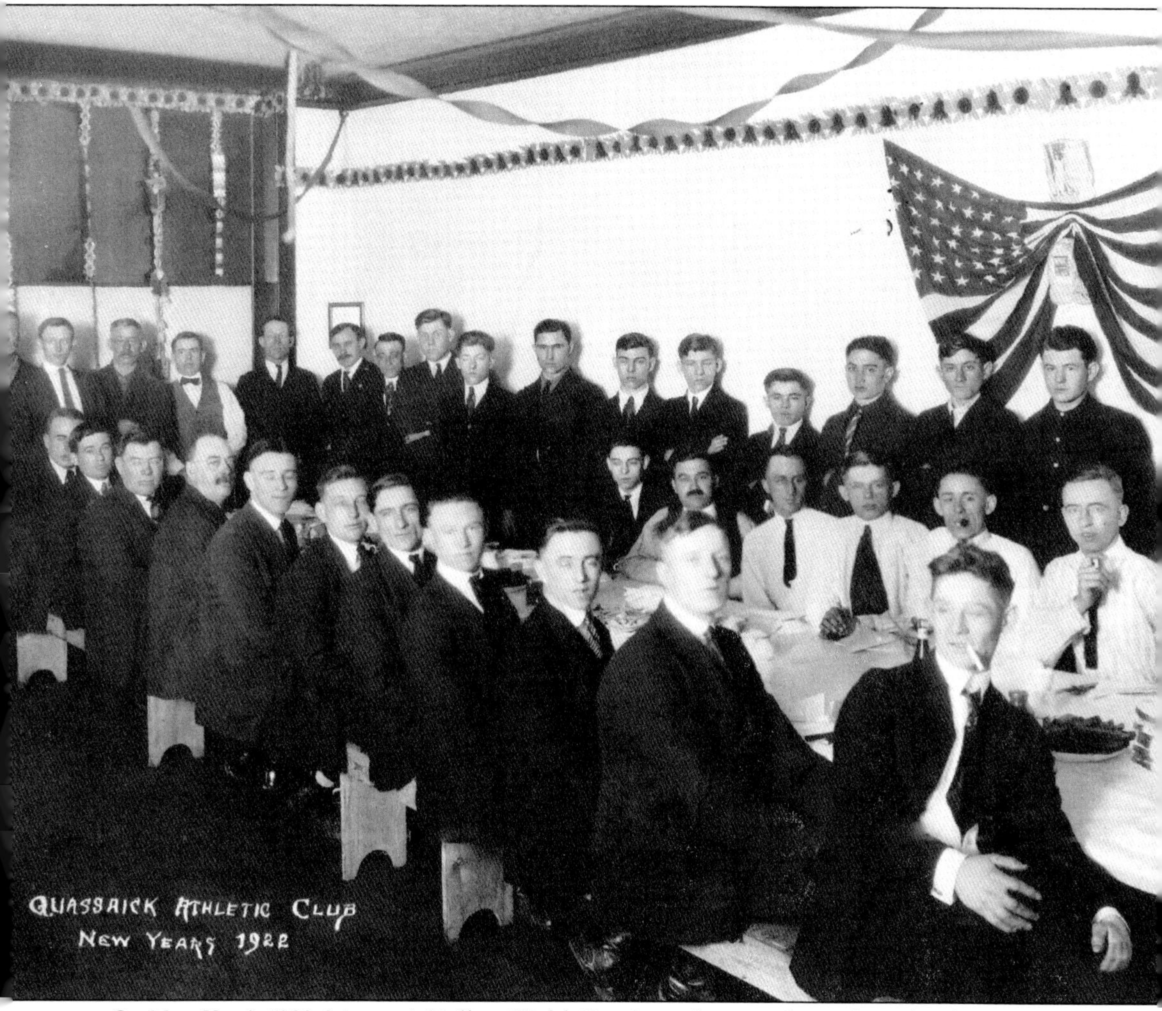

On New Year's 1922, Messina's Hall on Walsh Road was the site of an informal gathering of local community leaders. It was there that the idea for a fire company was discussed. Pictured, from left to right, are (first row, seated) Charles Dusenberry, Warren Sloan, Harrison S. Coutant Sr., Jacob Coutant, Albert Winstanley, Burton Baxter, Anthony Pecka, James Donahue, Patrick Donahue, James Robinson, and Joseph Starr Sr.; (second row, seated) Andrew Hudig, Peter Messina, William Donahue, William Kitsher, John Pecka, and James Quinn; (third row, standing) William Coulter, John Donahue, Walter Haag, James Murray, William Welsh, Fred C. Swanson Sr., Lawrence Youlio, Walter Porter, George Maines, Louis Simek, James Shay, John Perry, Joseph Mangi, Robert Edge, Michael Pecka, John Maderick. The outcome of this discussion was the eventual development of the first volunteer firehouse. (Courtesy of the Quassaick Fire Engine Company.)

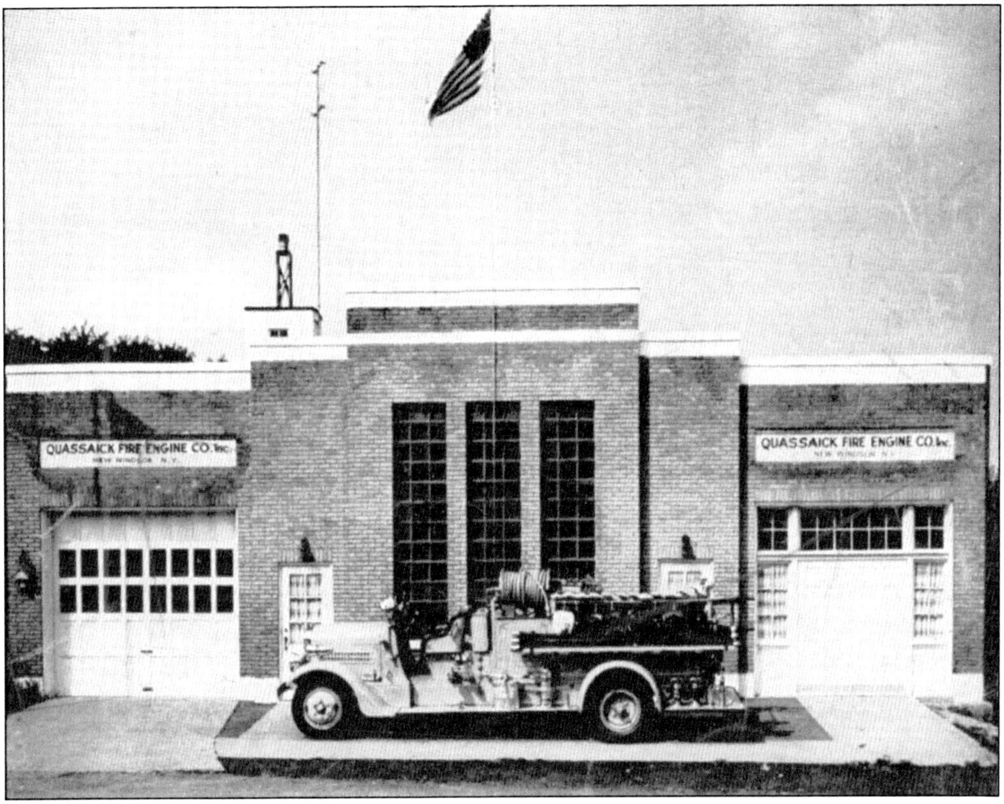

On May 30, 1939, the new facility for Quassaick Fire Engine Company, located on Walsh Road, was dedicated in a ceremony presided over by company president Harry B. Jett. Building committee member Bertram A. Strook turned the building over to Jett. In the building's cornerstone is a metal box of mementos of contemporary history. The company's first fire truck, a 1936 Sanford Fire Apparatus, was manufactured by the Sanford Motor Truck Company in Syracuse, New York. The six-cylinder, 106–brake horsepower apparatus cost $4,700 when delivered. (Both, courtesy of the Quassaick Fire Engine Company.)

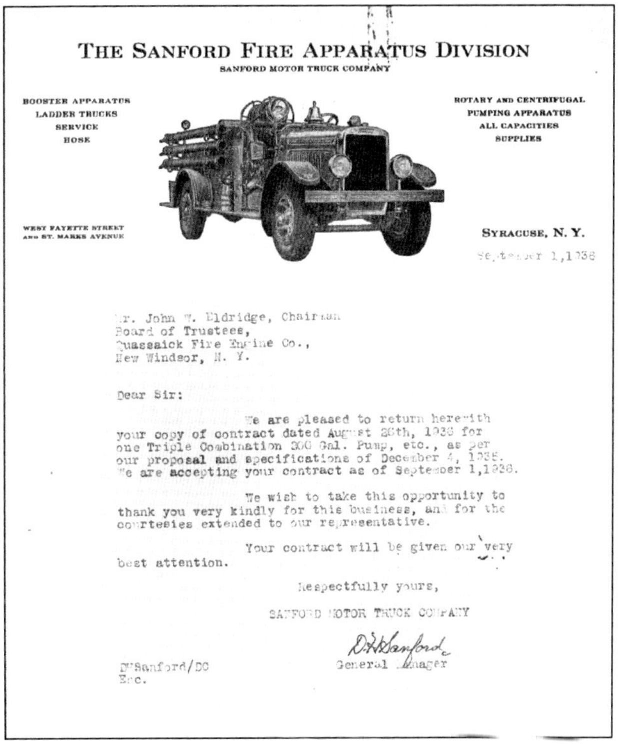

THE SANFORD FIRE APPARATUS DIVISION
SANFORD MOTOR TRUCK COMPANY

BOOSTER APPARATUS
LADDER TRUCKS
SERVICE
HOSE

ROTARY AND CENTRIFUGAL
PUMPING APPARATUS
ALL CAPACITIES
SUPPLIES

WEST FAYETTE STREET
AND ST. MARKS AVENUE

SYRACUSE, N. Y.

September 1,1936

Mr. John W. Eldridge, Chairman
Board of Trustees,
Quassaick Fire Engine Co.,
New Windsor, N. Y.

Dear Sir:

We are pleased to return herewith your copy of contract dated August 26th, 1936 for one Triple Combination 300 Gal. Pump, etc., as per our proposal and specifications of December 4, 1935. We are accepting your contract as of September 1,1936.

We wish to take this opportunity to thank you very kindly for this business, and for the courtesies extended to our representative.

Your contract will be given our very best attention.

Respectfully yours,

SANFORD MOTOR TRUCK COMPANY

D.H. Sanford
General Manager

DHSanford/DC
Enc.

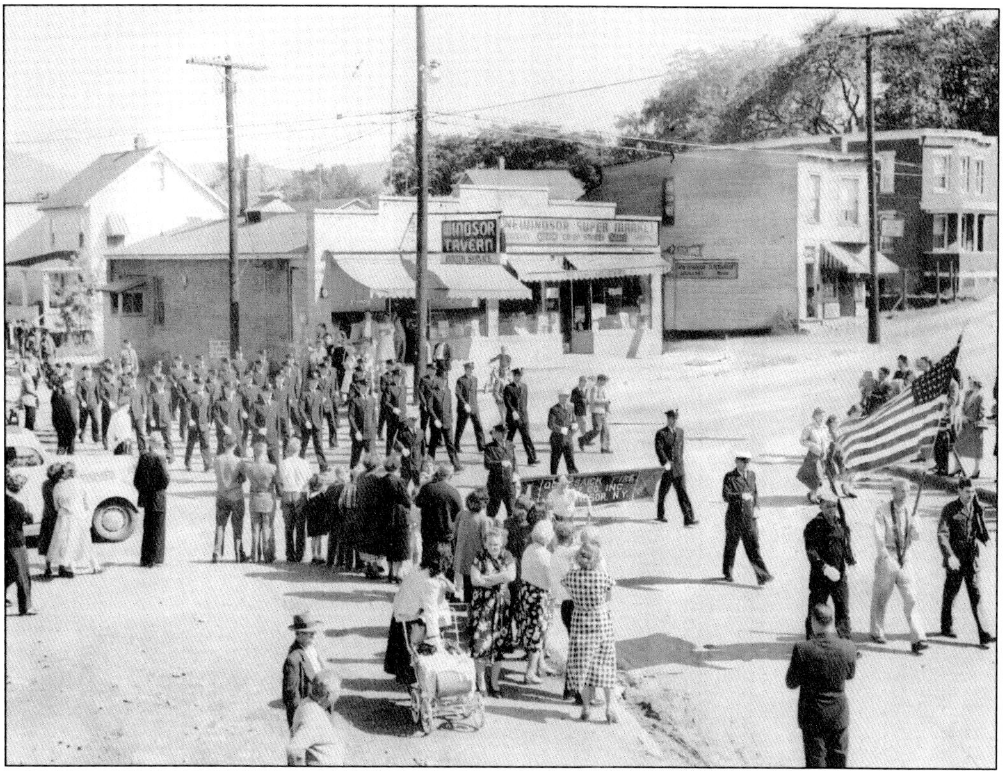

These locals have come out to see the 1950 Victory Parade. Members of the Quassaick Fire Department proudly follow the military color guard as they march on John Street across Quassaick Avenue. There was always a good turnout in support of the fire company's parades. (Courtesy of the Quassaick Fire Engine Company.)

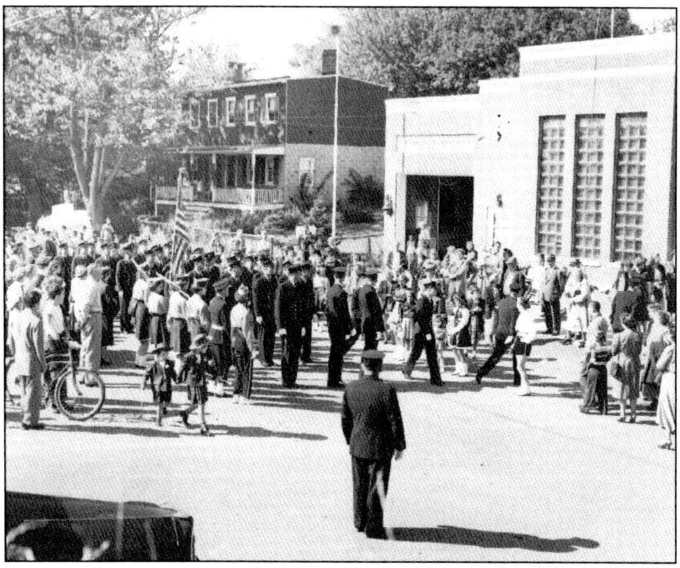

After the parade broke up, participants headed back to the firehouse. The Quassaick Fire Engine Company and the Arthur Smith House provide the backdrop for this photograph. In June 1927, Arthur Smith (grandfather of Sandra Lewis Terwillinger) sold the property for the station to the New Windsor Community Club, whose name was changed in 1929 to the Quassaick Fire Engine Company. (Courtesy of the Quassaick Fire Engine Company.)

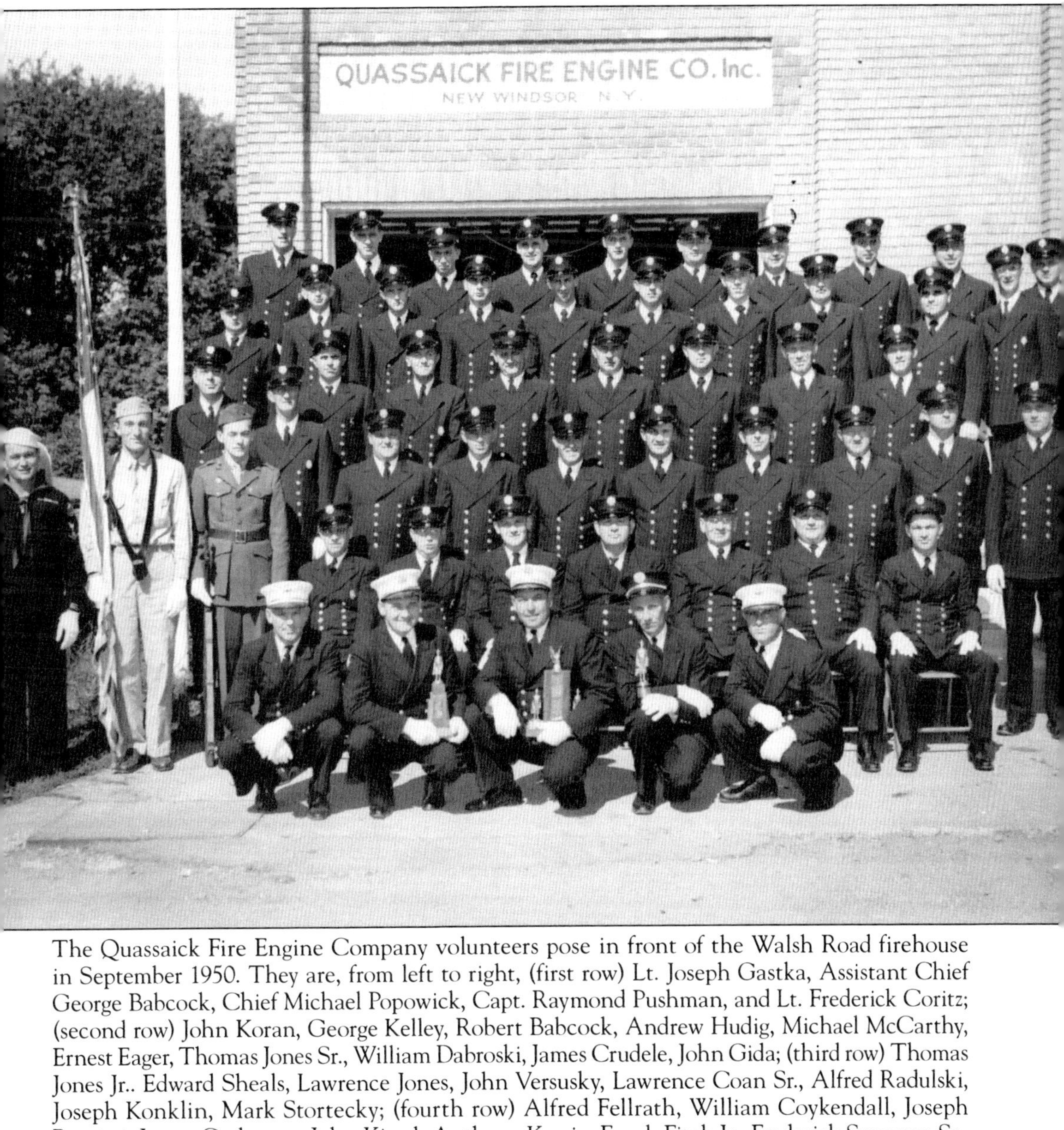

The Quassaick Fire Engine Company volunteers pose in front of the Walsh Road firehouse in September 1950. They are, from left to right, (first row) Lt. Joseph Gastka, Assistant Chief George Babcock, Chief Michael Popowick, Capt. Raymond Pushman, and Lt. Frederick Coritz; (second row) John Koran, George Kelley, Robert Babcock, Andrew Hudig, Michael McCarthy, Ernest Eager, Thomas Jones Sr., William Dabroski, James Crudele, John Gida; (third row) Thomas Jones Jr.. Edward Sheals, Lawrence Jones, John Versusky, Lawrence Coan Sr., Alfred Radulski, Joseph Konklin, Mark Stortecky; (fourth row) Alfred Fellrath, William Coykendall, Joseph Ruscitti, James Carlstrom, John Kissel, Anthony Krazia, Frank Fitak Jr., Frederick Swanson Sr., Frank Giest; (fifth row) Bryan Bauer, Emil Sledzianoski, William Dougherty, Lawrence Coan Jr., Edward Osusky, Lawrence Mowery, Joseph Krazia, Robert Gilfeather, Lloyd Bunting; (sixth row) William Rumsey, George Taylor, Kenneth Downsbrough, Joseph Smith, Joseph Caesar, Flip Weyant, Charles Simanoski, Kenneth Rumsey, Frank Bosacky, and Joseph Tuckosh. (Courtesy of the Quassaick Fire Engine Company.)

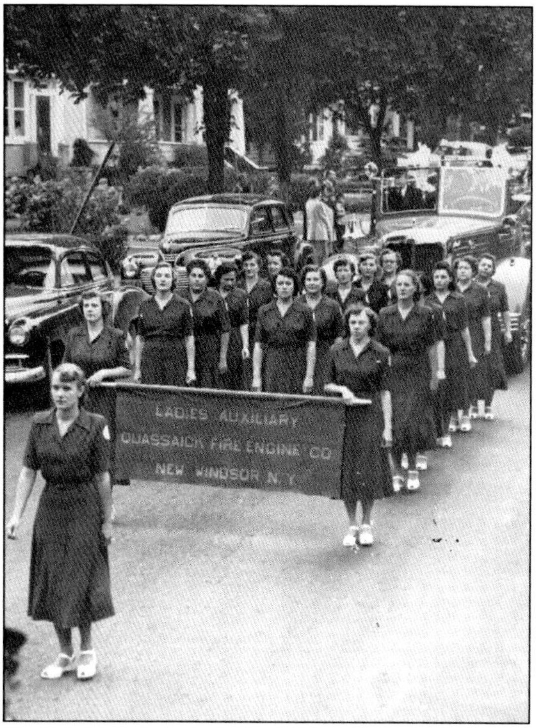

At left, the Quassaick Fire Engine Company's Ladies Auxiliary marches up Fullerton Avenue as part of the Hudson Valley Volunteer Firemen's Convention in 1952. The ladies play an active role in supporting the firehouse and firemen through sponsoring fundraisers, doing kitchen work, and just being there when it counts. Pres. Julia Tuckosh is in front, and Bernice Stortecky (left) and Alvina Krazia follow, holding the banner. Also pictured are, from front to back, (far left column) Winifred Lewis, Sylvia Ruscitti, Helen Mikutis, ? Crudele, unidentified; (center column) Jennie Babcock, ? Kissel, Catherine Jones, ? Hotaling, and Bessie Williams; (far right column) ? Fescoe, Marge Babcock, Elsie Gastka, and Mary Eager. Below, on June 18, 1954, the Quassaick Fire Engine Company's Ladies Auxiliary was awarded first place at the Hudson Valley Convention Parade in Haverstraw, New York. (Both, courtesy of the Quassaick Fire Engine Company.)

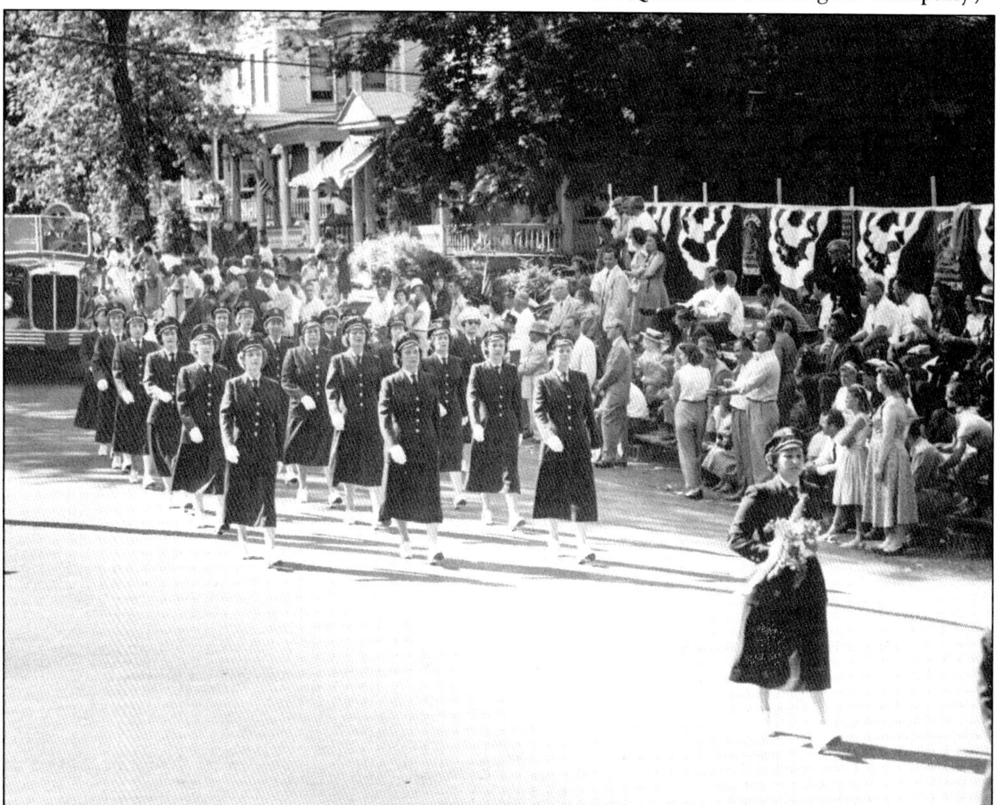

These firemen from the Quassaick Fire Engine Company march in the 1948 Orange County parade in Otisville, New York. Their fire engine follows. Members included Chief Michael Popowick, Capt. George Babcock, 1st Lt. Anthony Mikutis, and 2nd Lt. Joseph Gastka. (Courtesy of the Quassaick Fire Engine Department.)

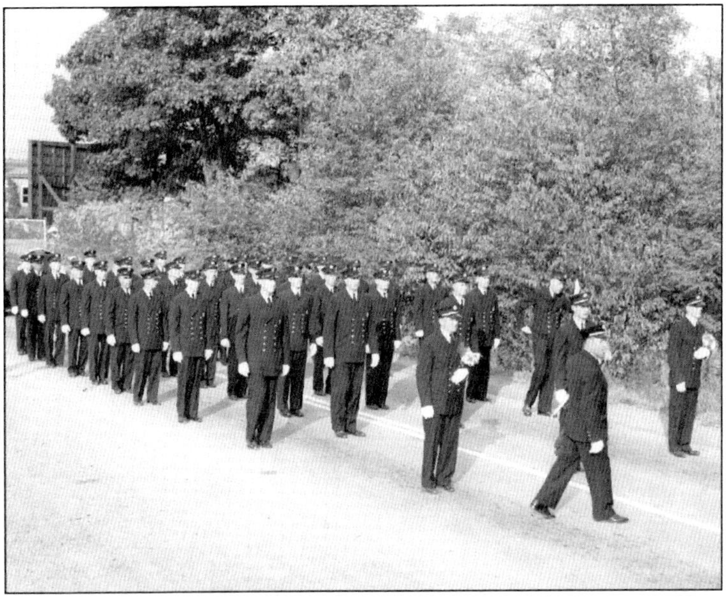

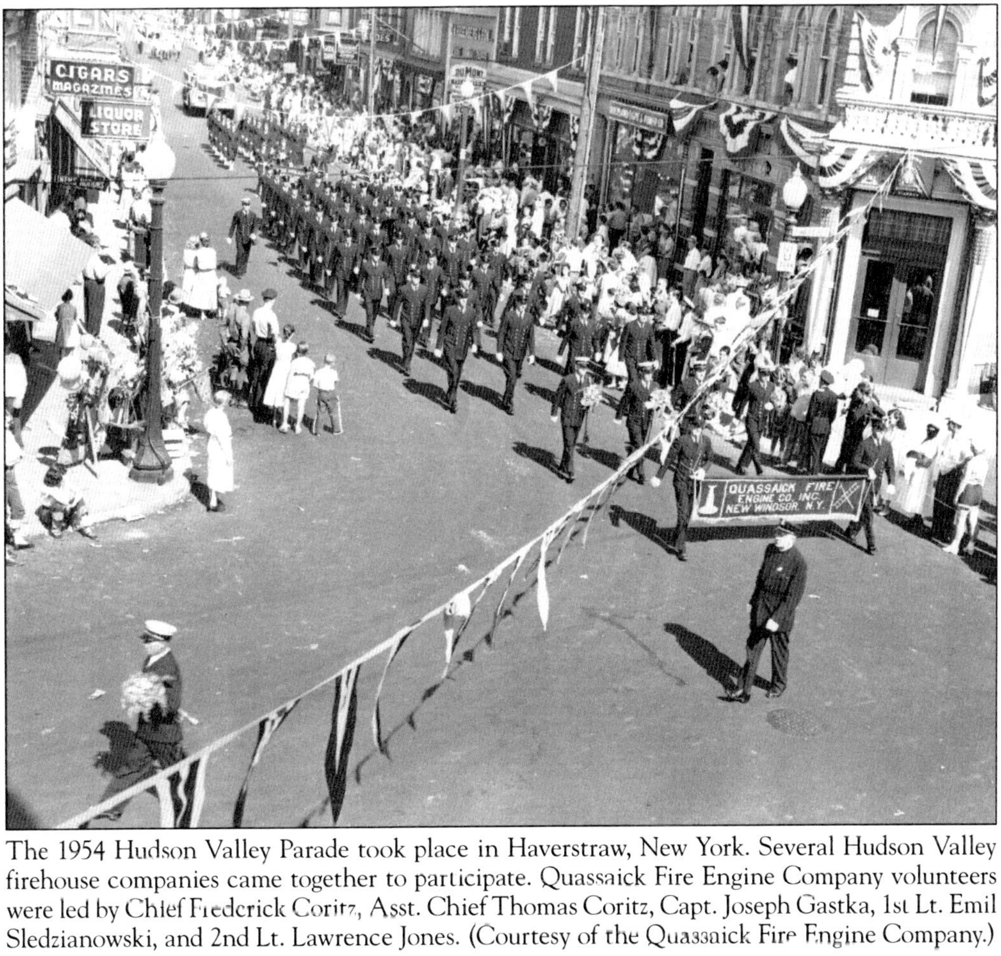

The 1954 Hudson Valley Parade took place in Haverstraw, New York. Several Hudson Valley firehouse companies came together to participate. Quassaick Fire Engine Company volunteers were led by Chief Frederick Coritz, Asst. Chief Thomas Coritz, Capt. Joseph Gastka, 1st Lt. Emil Sledzianowski, and 2nd Lt. Lawrence Jones. (Courtesy of the Quassaick Fire Engine Company.)

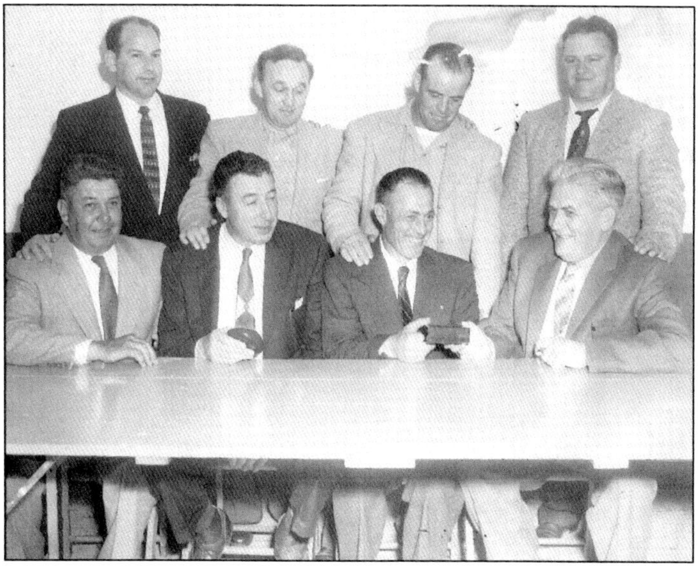

In 1955, the Quassaick Fire Engine Company came together to honor outgoing chief Frederick Coritz. Pictured, from left to right, are (first row) past chief Michael Popowick, past chief Kenneth Rumsey, past chief Frederick Coritz, and master of ceremonies William Doulin; (second row) 2nd Lt. John Crudele, 1st Lt. Charles Babcock, 2nd Lt. Lawrence Jones, and Chief Thomas Jones. (Courtesy of the Quassaick Fire Engine Company.)

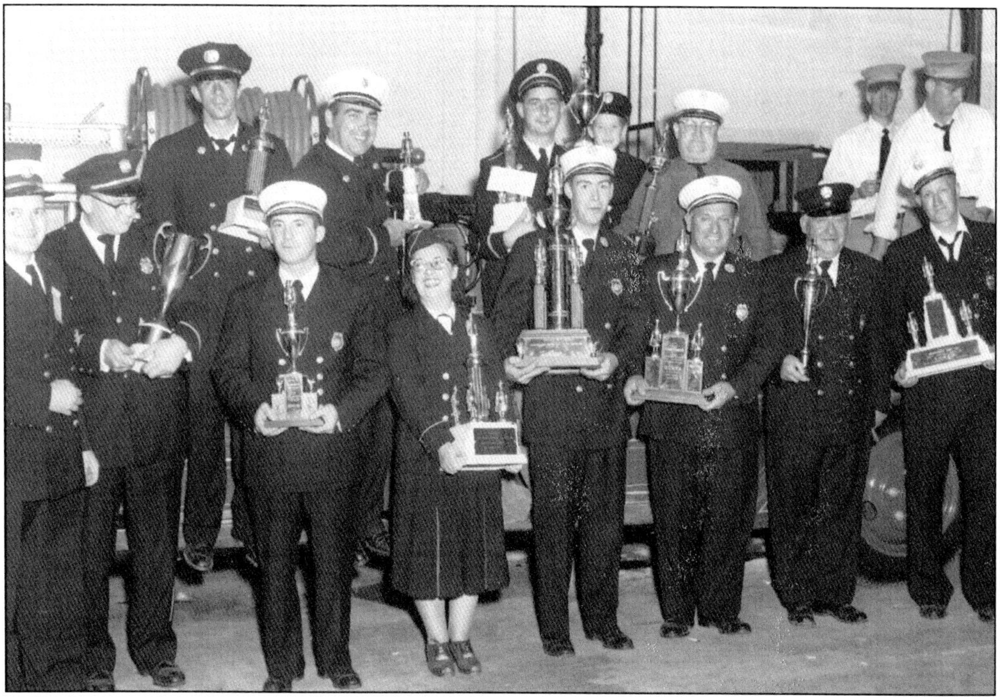

Over the years, participating fire companies competed for coveted awards. The September 17, 1955, Quassaick Fire Engine Company parade at New Windsor resulted in several awards. Quassaick has been a top winner for many years. Identified here are, from left to right, (front row) George Babcock, John Ward, Frederick Coritz, Laura Mazzola, Thomas Wolfrum, Al Diel, and John Fox. People in the back row are all unidentified. (Courtesy of the Quassaick Fire Engine Company.)

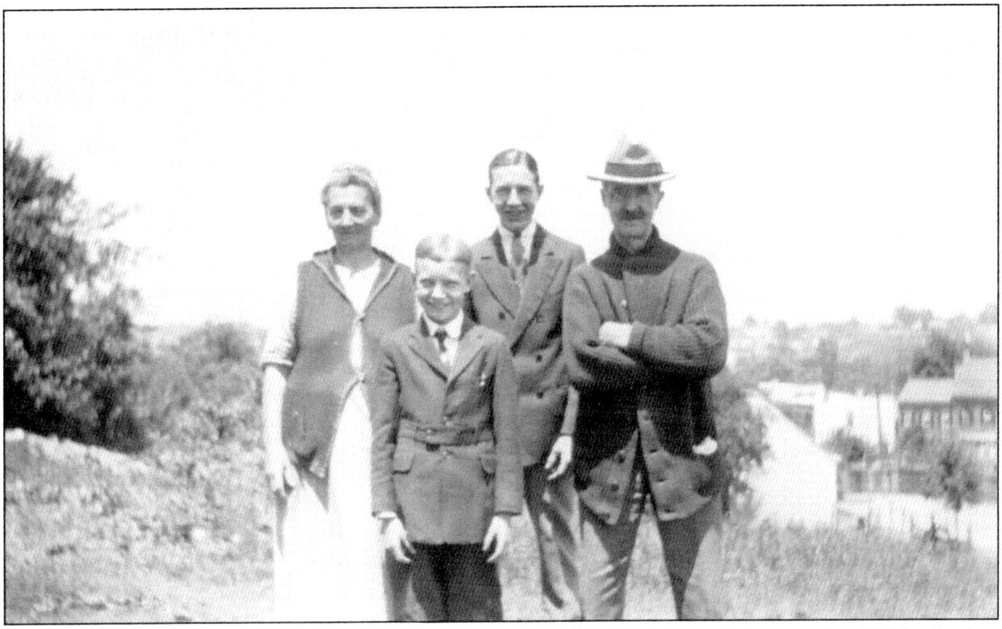

Standing on their Walsh Road property in New Windsor are, from left to right, Hilda, Leslie, Harry, and Arthur Smith. They lived on this site from 1917 until 1959, at which time they sold the property to the New Windsor Fire Department, affording the company room to expand. (Courtesy of Sandra Lewis Terwilliger.)

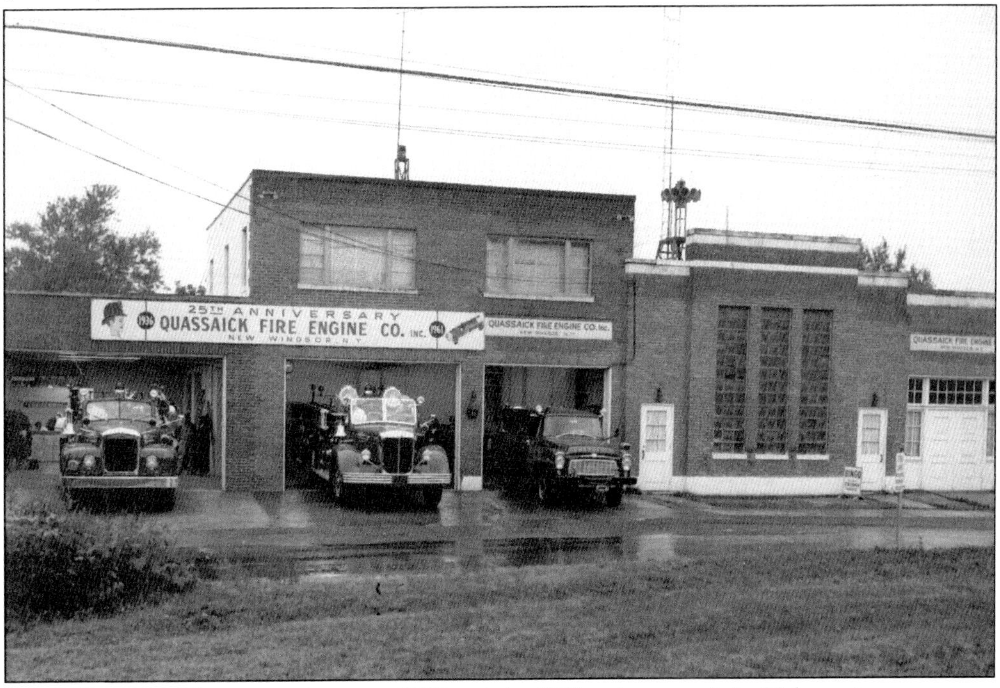

As can be seen in this image, between 1939 and the 1961—the year of the 25th anniversary—two truck bays and a second story were added to the Quassaick Fire Engine Company's original building. The addition of a powerful siren can also be seen on the roof. (Courtesy of the Quassaick Fire Engine Company.)

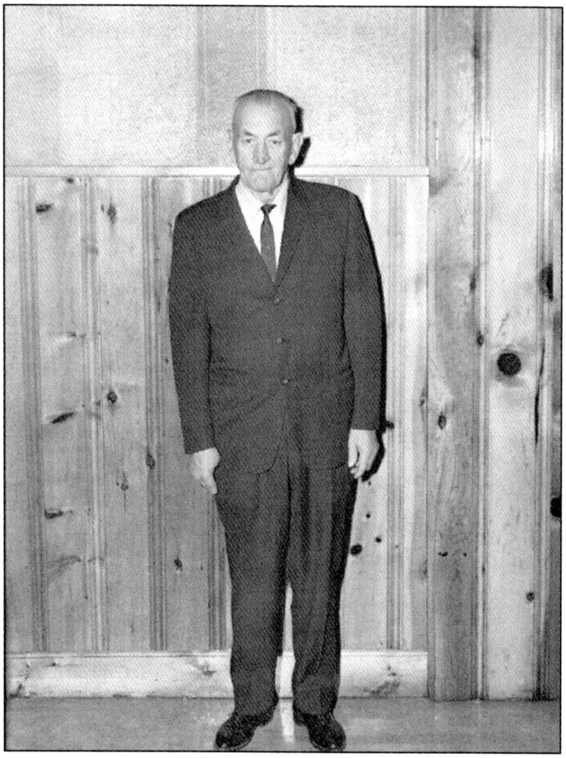

Harry B. Jett attended the 25th anniversary celebration of the Quassaick Fire Engine Company in 1961. Jett had been chosen vice president in the company's first elections, held on November 23, 1936. Also elected that day were John W. Eldridge, president; John S. Evans, secretary; Arthur Smith Sr., treasurer; Elmer F. Babcock, chief; William Gastka, first lieutenant; and Frederick Sloboda, second lieutenant. (Courtesy of the Quassaick Fire Engine Company.)

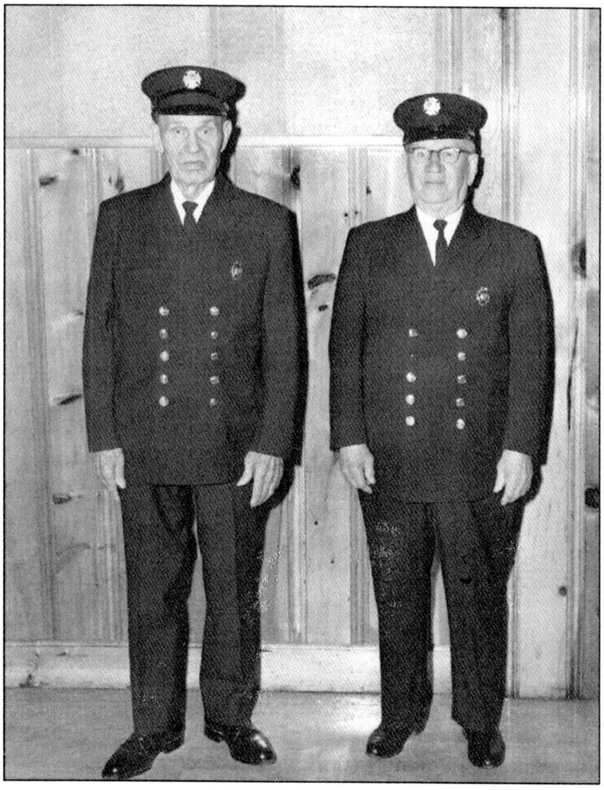

At the Quassaick Fire Engine Company 25th anniversary—a silver jubilee—committee general chairman William Rumsey noted that it was time to honor the members and nonmembers who donated so much of their time and money. It was also time to honor two of the company's oldest living members, Fred Swanson (left) and William Dabroski. (Courtesy of the Quassaick Fire Engine Company.)

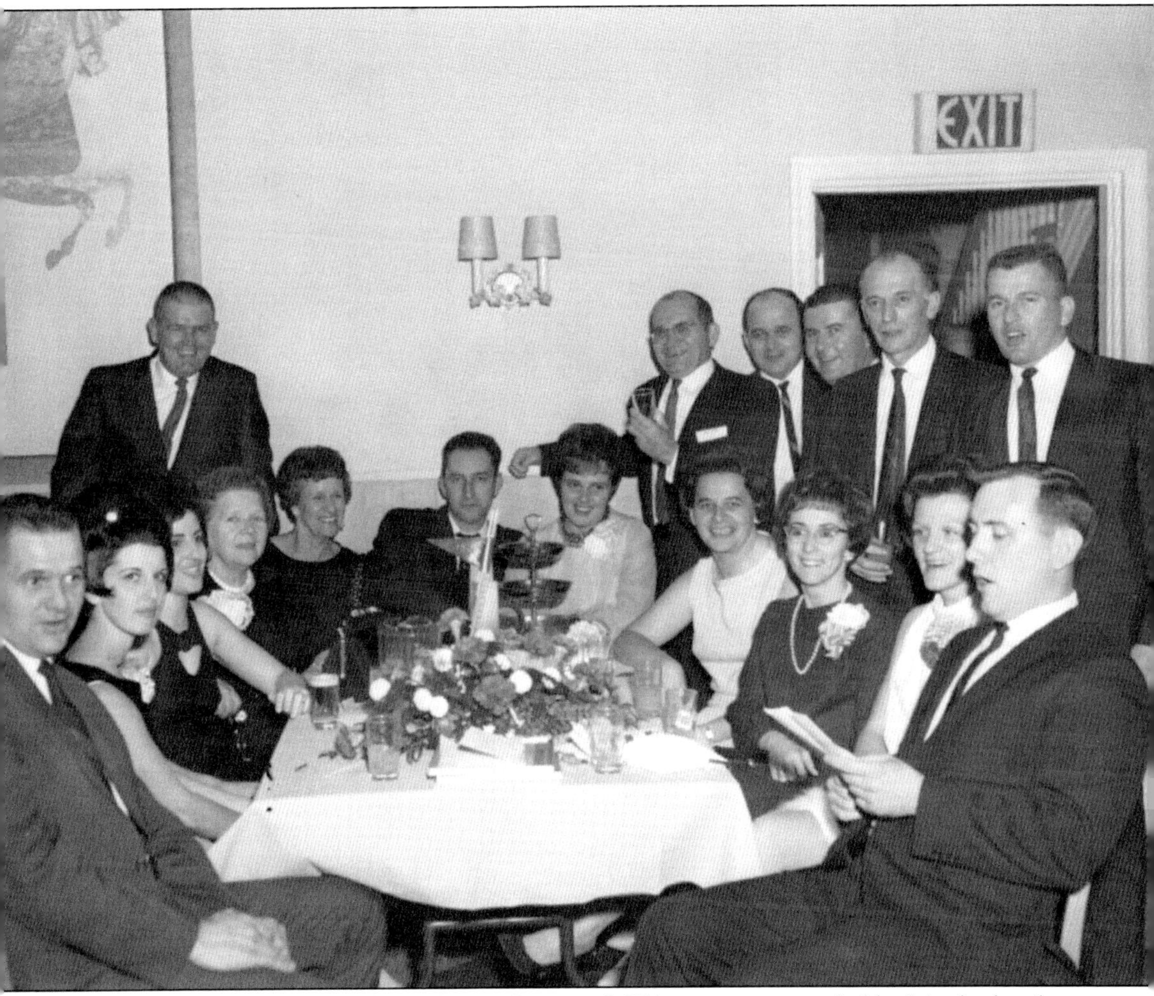

The celebration of the Quassaick Fire Engine Company's 25th anniversary was held at Meadowbrook Lodge. Pictured are, from left to right, (seated) Edward Babcock, Angela Babcock, Phyllis Babcock, Marion Babcock, Jennifer Babcock, Robert Wiggins, Doris Wiggins, Shirley Babcock Early, Gertrude Babcock, Marilyn McDaniel, and John McDaniel; (standing) John Babcock, George Babcock, William Babcock, John Early, Robert Babcock, and Donald Babcock. Elmer F. Babcock became the first chief in 1936, and each of his seven sons belonged to the fire company at the same time, all becoming firematic officers. One went on to become president and chief—a great legacy. (Courtesy of the Quassaick Fire Engine Company.)

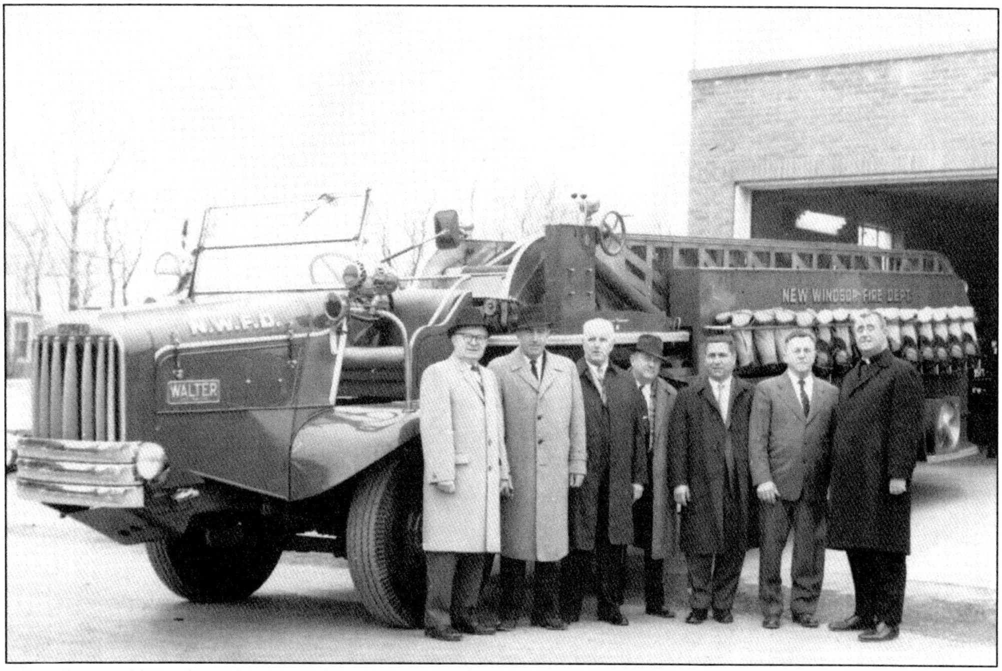

The City of Newburgh turned over its 65-foot, 1937 Walters ladder truck to Quassaick Fire Engine Company for $1 on January 10, 1965. Pictured beside it are, from left to right, Newburgh City Council members William McIntyre and Samuel Cerone, Newburgh Fire Department chief Hubert Dunn, Commissioner Thomas Dowd, New Windsor Fire Department chief Alfred Crudele, Commissioner Zigmunt Orzechowski, and chaplain Gregory Frank. (Courtesy of the Quassaick Fire Engine Company.)

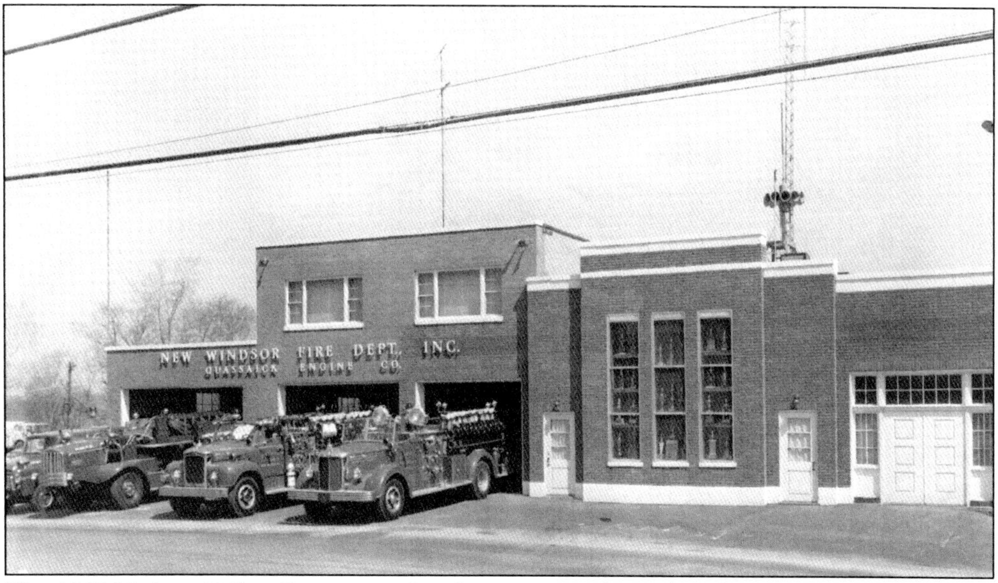

The 1966 Hudson Valley Convention headquarters was housed at the Quassaick Fire Engine Company's Walsh Road location. The proudly displayed fire trucks in this image include, from left to right, the 1961 International Emergency Truck, the 1937 Walters 65-foot ladder truck, the 1957 Mack Pumper, and the 1951 Mack Pumper. (Courtesy of the Quassaick Fire Engine Company.)

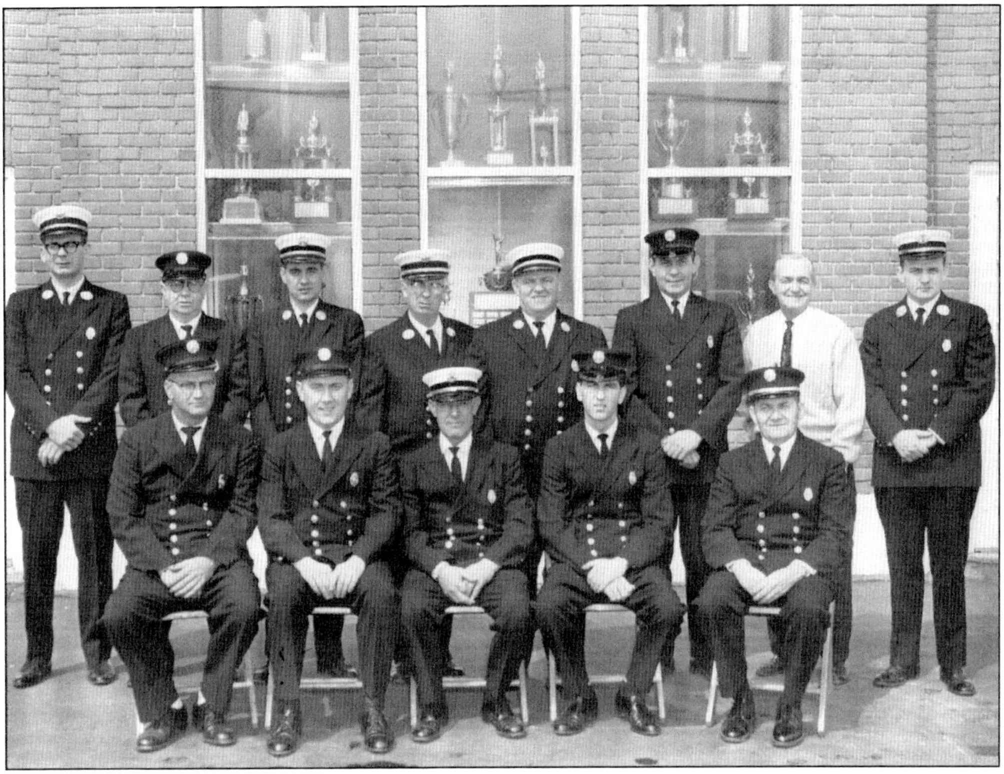

The 1966 Hudson Valley Convention Committee was made up of volunteer firemen. They are, from left to right, (first row) Joseph Smith, Pres. John McDaniels, Frederick Coritz, Donald Smith, George Babcock; (second row) John Kissel, Francis McCarthy Sr., Robert Welsh, Arthur Taylor Sr., Chief Thomas Jones Jr., John Naclario, James Carlstrom, and William Babcock. (Courtesy of the Quassaick Fire Engine Company.)

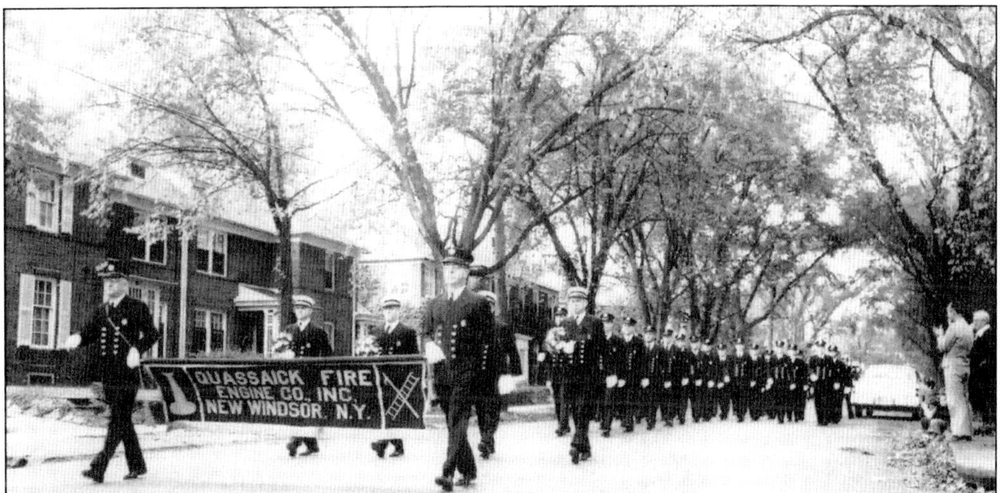

Firemen of the Quassaick Fire Engine Company are seen marching in formation down Fullerton Avenue in Newburgh, proudly carrying their banner. Members of various firehouse companies came together to participate in the much anticipated 1966 Hudson Valley Convention parade. (Courtesy of the Quassaick Fire Engine Company.)

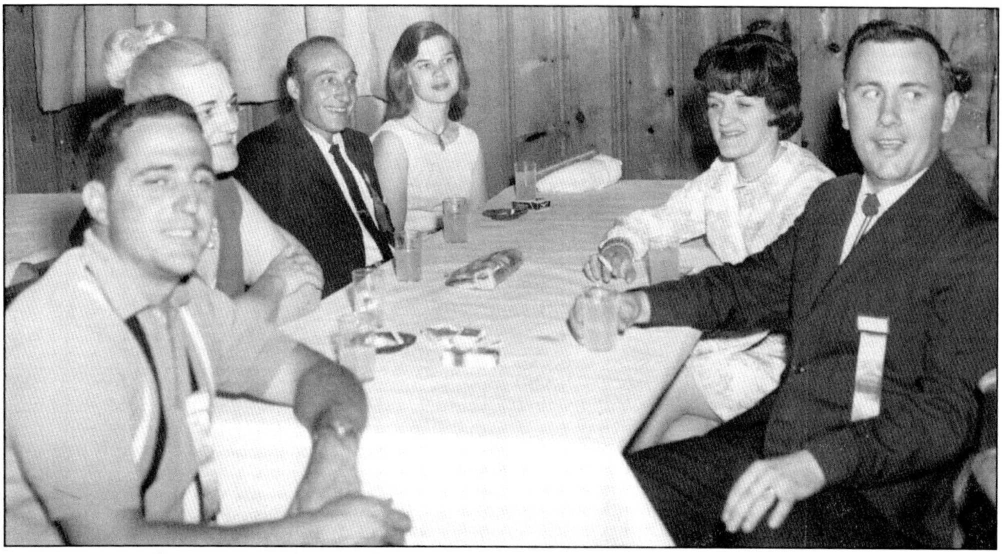

Festivities at the 1966 Hudson Valley Convention took place at the Quassaick Fire Engine Company. In attendance are, from left to right, John Marullo, Elizabeth Marullo, Al Huck, ? Huck, Marilyn McDaniel, and John McDaniel. Fire companies belonging to the state association from as far south as White Plains and as far north as Lake George came to the New Windsor parade. (Courtesy of the Quassaick Fire Engine Company.)

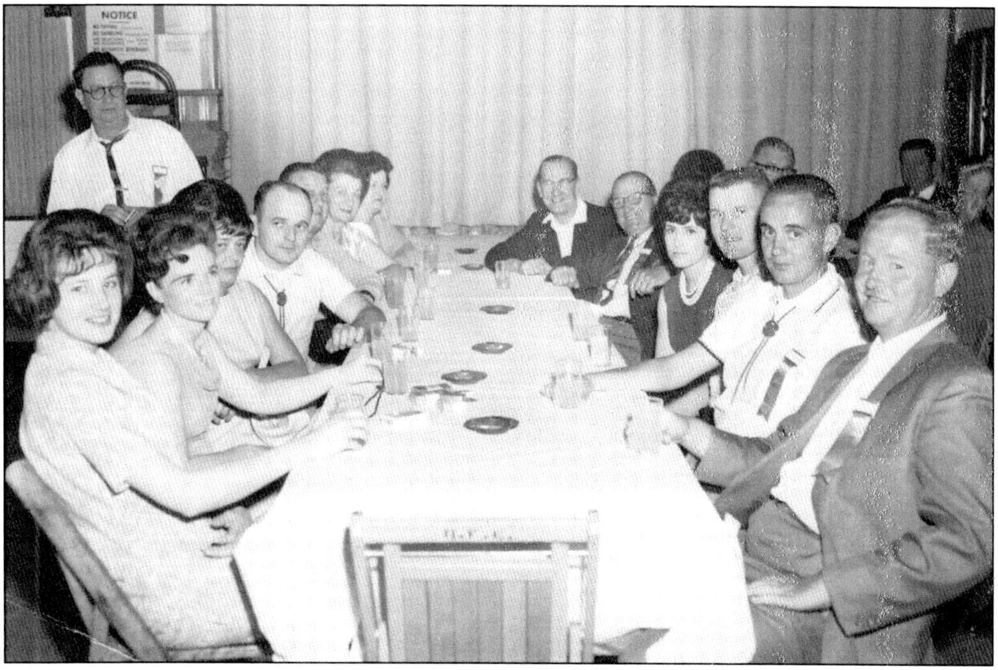

Also attending the same 1966 Hudson Valley Convention celebration are Michael McCarthy (standing), and, seated from left to right, three unidentified women, William Babcock, James Crudele, ? Crudele, unidentified, John Versusky, George Manuche, Phyllis Babcock, Donald Babcock, Robert Welsh, and Red Jones. The convention and inspection parade is held at a different location each year, with potential hosts submitting bids. (Courtesy of the Quassaick Fire Engine Company.)

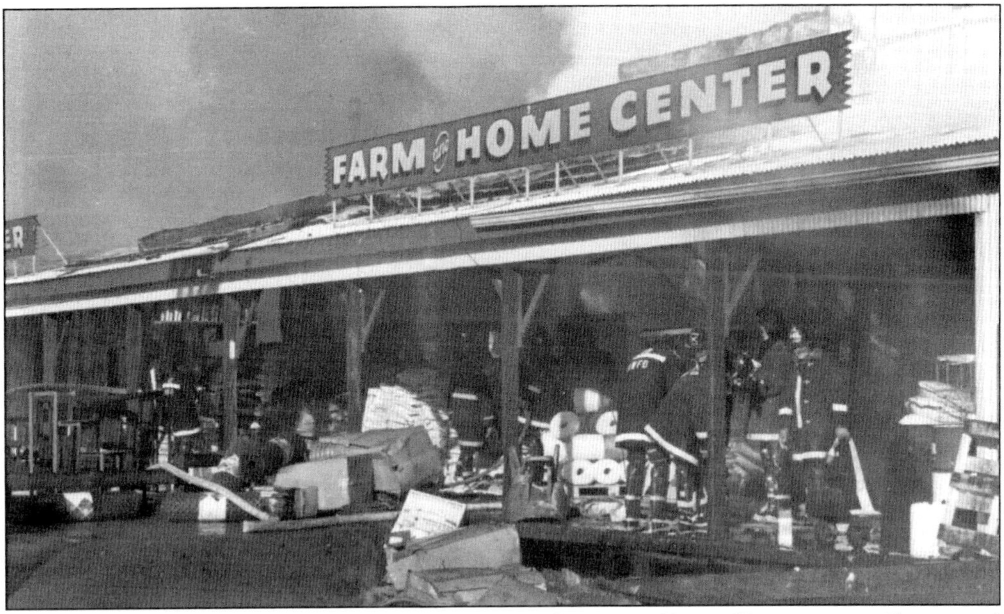

On January 10, 1980, John Devitt's Farm & Home Center on Route 32 went up in flames and smoke, though responders from several firehouses fought valiantly to save it. For years, Devitt's Farm & Home had provided high-quality products, advice, and services to the community. (Courtesy of the Quassaick Fire Engine Company.)

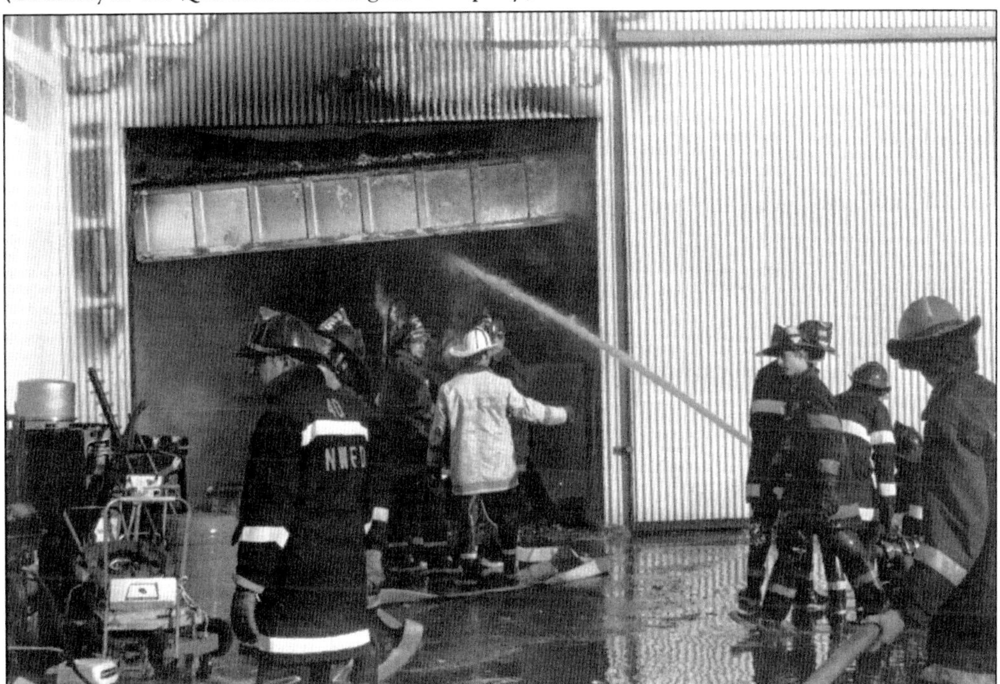

Before its destruction, Devitt's was known for its Christmas on the Farm display, which included animals, an electric train, and, most important of all, Eggbert the Talking Egg. Over the years, Egbert drew thousands, somehow always remembering each child's name. (Courtesy of the Quassaick Fire Engine Company.)

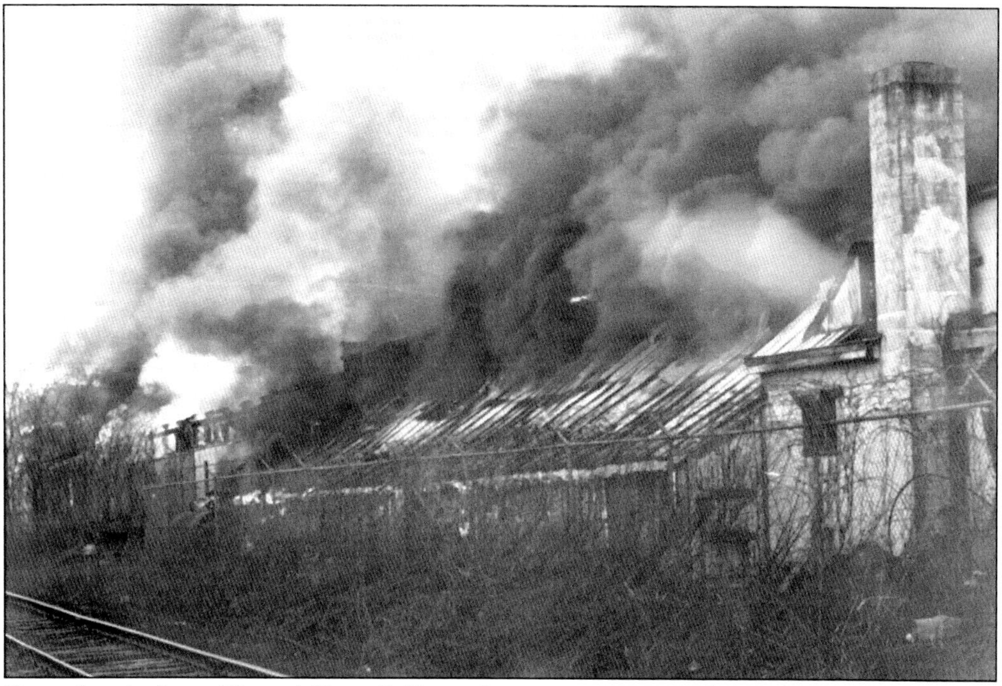

Years after the loss of Devitt's Farm & Home Center, new owners Christopher Fitch and Joseph Gizzarelli renewed the tradition of providing quality services and products and, to everyone's delight, revived the traditional Christmas display. (Courtesy of Quassaick Fire Engine Company.)

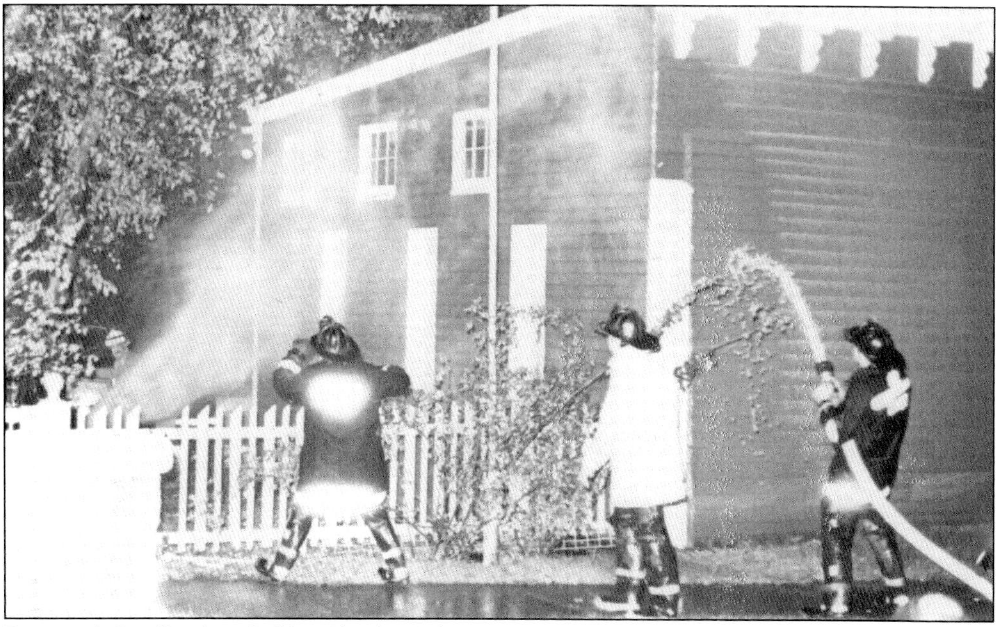

Diamond Candle, founded by Charles Schisano in 1919, specialized in pure beeswax products that were used by the Vatican, Roman Catholic churches, and in private homes. In 1980, firemen from various firehouse companies fought a blaze at the business, with volunteer firemen shown here protecting the neighboring Paffendorf's Upholstery Shop from flames. (Courtesy of the Quassaick Fire Engine Company.)

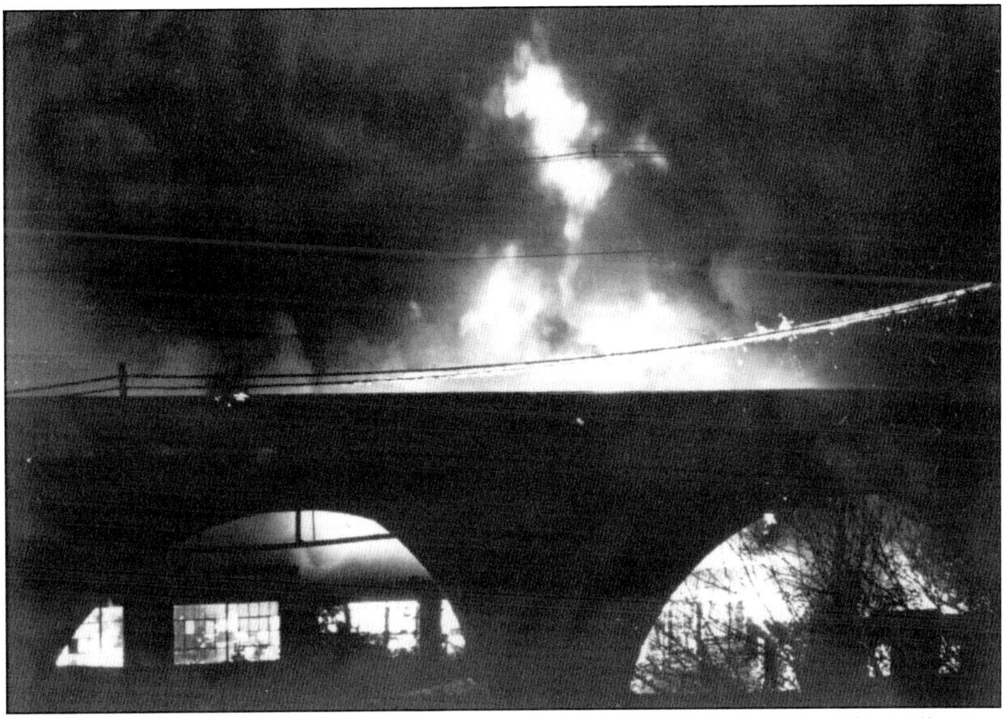

A half dozen buildings beneath the Quassaick viaduct had been occupied by woolen mills since the 1890s when Diamond Candle purchased the defunct Hudson River Woolen Mills plant in February 1942. In this image, flames from the 1980 fire can be seen erupting on the bridge and into the night sky. Despite the valiant efforts of several firemen, little could be done to save the structure. (Courtesy of the Quassaick Fire Engine Company.)

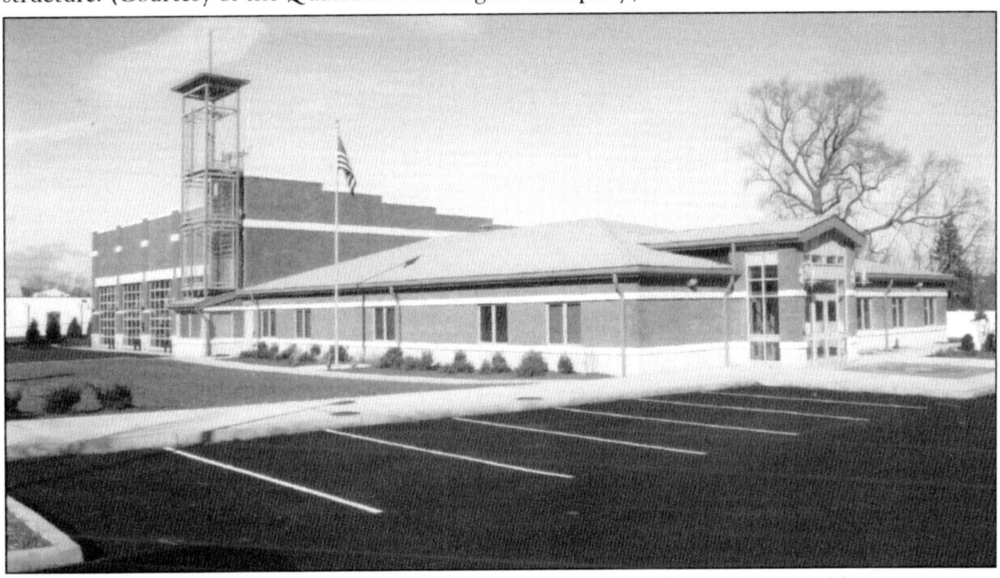

The Board of Fire Commissioners and chairman John T. Babcock launched a publicity campaign to raise awareness about the need for a new fire station. The bond vote was set for July 31, 2007, and residents came out in full force, voting 3-1 in support of the bond. The new Quassaick Firehouse was completed in 2009. (Courtesy of the Quassaick Fire Engine Company.)

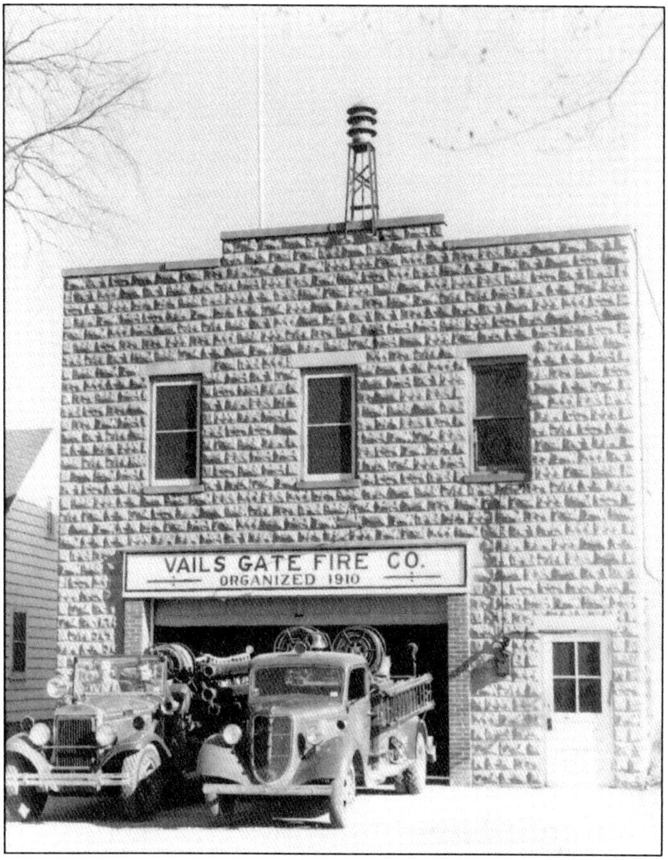

In 1925, this two-story building was erected to accommodate the Vails Gate Fire Company. Nicholas Marshall had donated the land the previous year. Seen on the left is a Franklin-Wright fire engine, and on the right is a Ford fire engine. (Courtesy of Mary Jane Miller.)

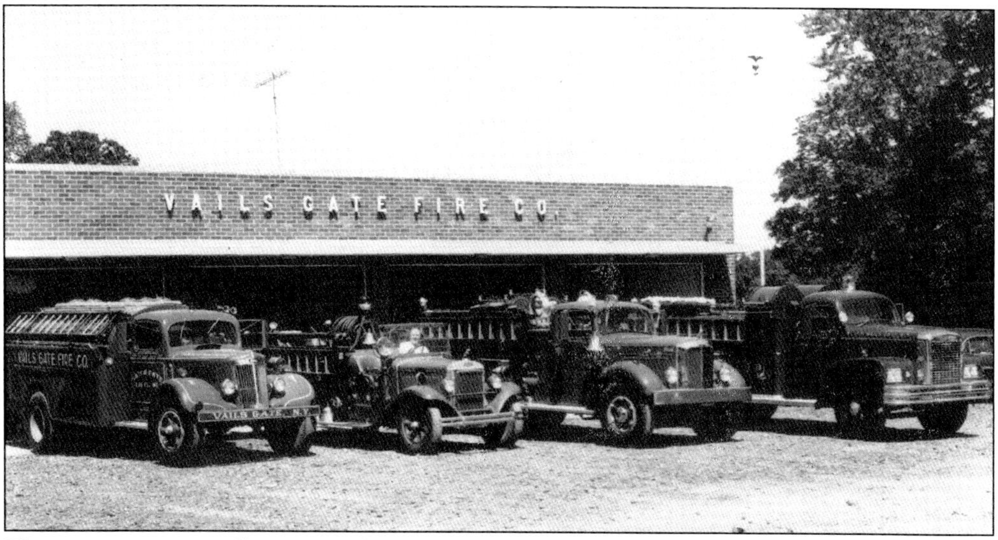

The company eventually outgrew the old building, which was too small to house the additional apparatus that had to be added as area development mushroomed. Property was obtained from the Forge Hill Farm, and construction commenced in the fall of 1958. The new structure was completed in 1959, with a new seven-horn siren that could be heard for 10 miles. (Courtesy of the Vails Gate Fire Company.)

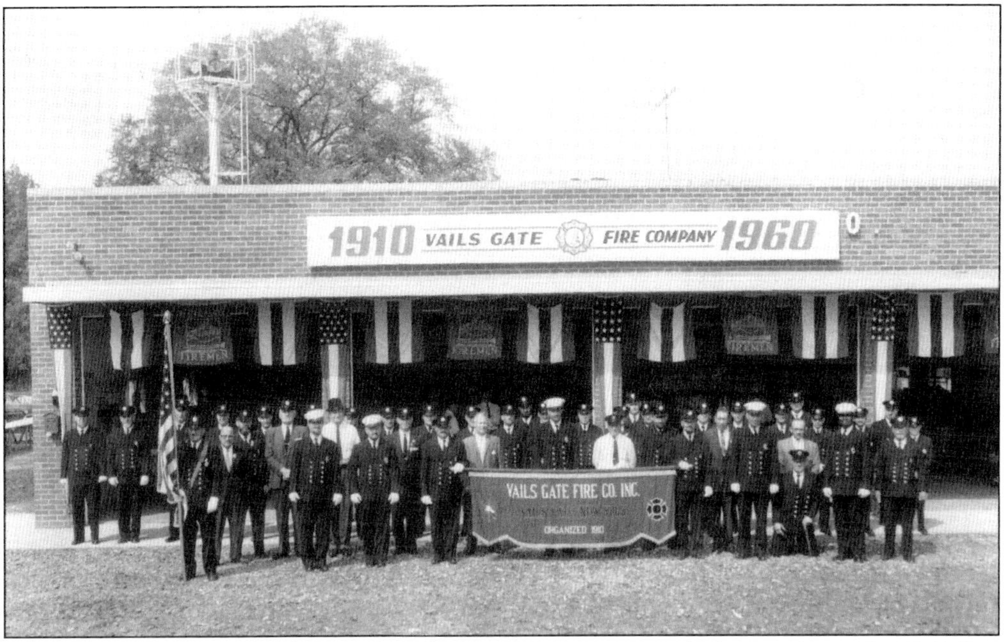

The year 1960 marked half a century of strong organization with the purchase of a 1960 Reo chassis that had a John Beam high-pressure fog and a 750-gallon volume pump with a 500-gallon booster tank fire truck. In 1963, the social hall was expanded to twice its original size. (Courtesy of the Vails Gate Fire Company.)

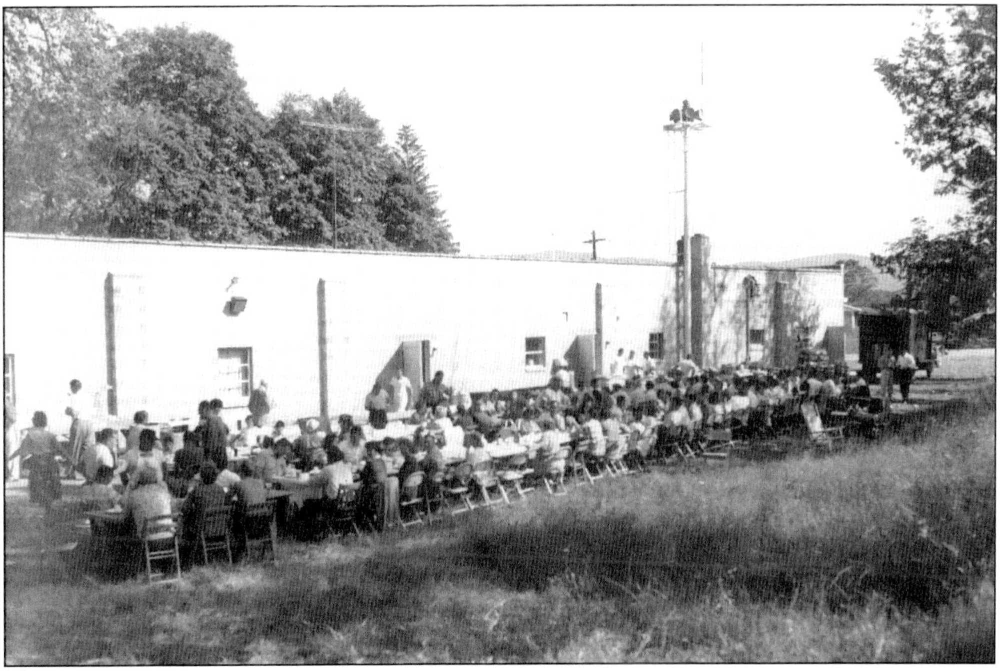

In the mid-1960s, the Vails Gate Firemen began a tradition of a softball game that pitted old-timers against younger competition. A picnic for firemen and their families always followed, and all could attend and enjoy the food, no matter who won the game. (Courtesy of the Vails Gate Fire Company.)

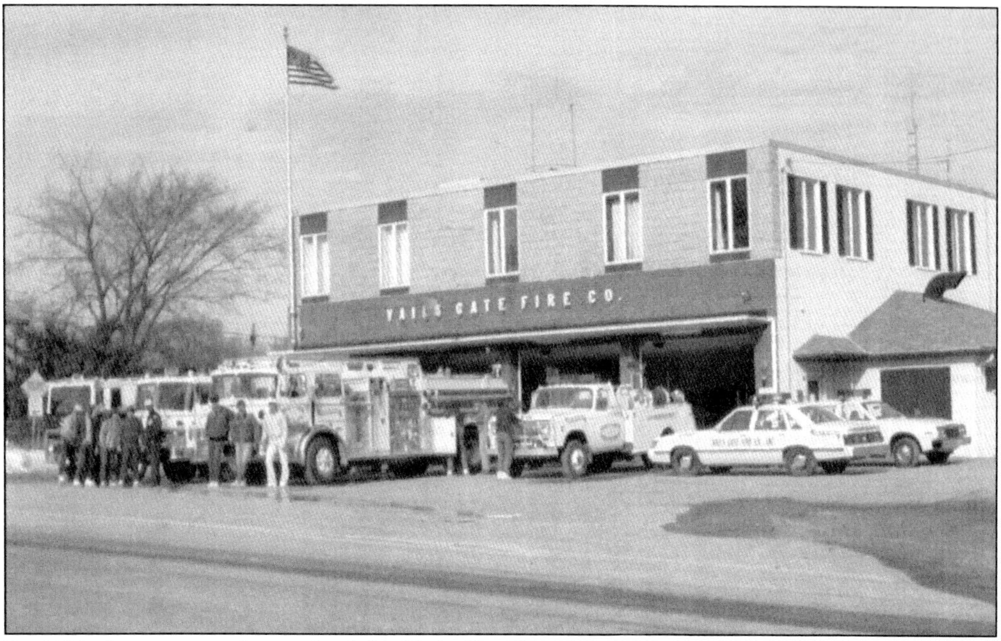

By 1971, the continued growth of the Vails Gate Fire Company necessitated more room, and a lounge, conference room, and chief's office were added to the second floor of Station No. 1. The year 1978 saw the company updating and modernizing its vehicle fleet with the addition of a 1978 Duplex 1,250-gallon-per-minute pumper. (Courtesy of the Vails Gate Fire Company.)

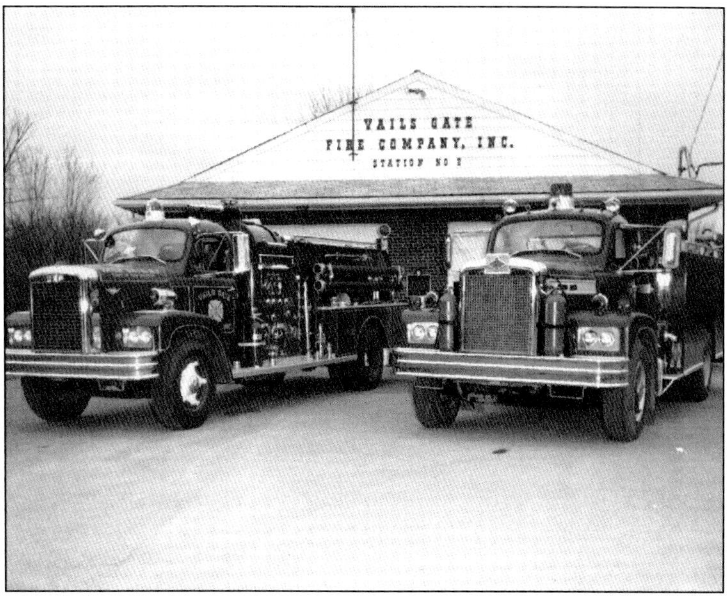

In 1965, a new firehouse, designated Station No. 2, was built on Weather Oak Hill Road to better serve the western end of the district. Between 1967 and 1970, the need for additional fire protection need became apparent. The company purchased a Diamond Reo 1,600-gallon tanker and placed it in service at Station No. 2. (Courtesy of the Vails Gate Fire Company.)

This Vails Gate Fire Department aerial ladder is primarily used to allow firefighters and other rescue personnel access to high or hard-to-reach places. It is outfitted with a platform, or bucket, on the end to give firefighters and rescue personnel a stable place to stand. Demonstrating the equipment's capabilities in 1985 are Leonard McDonald, Dominick Lucera, and Christopher Barrett. (Courtesy of the Vails Gate Fire Company.)

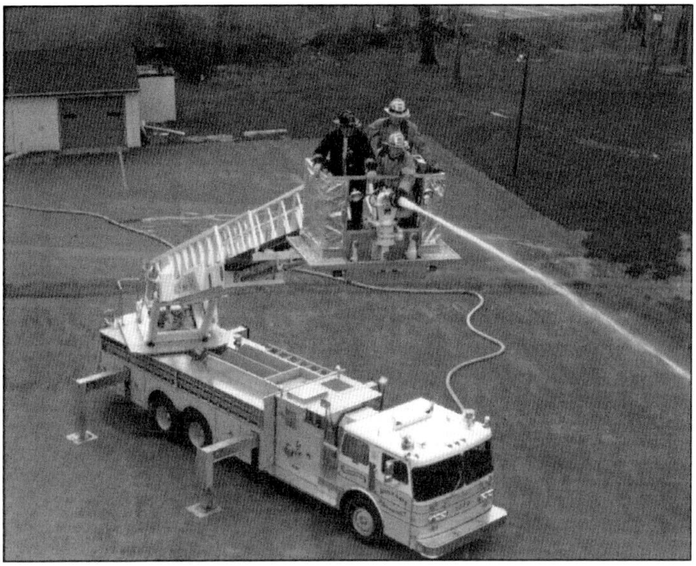

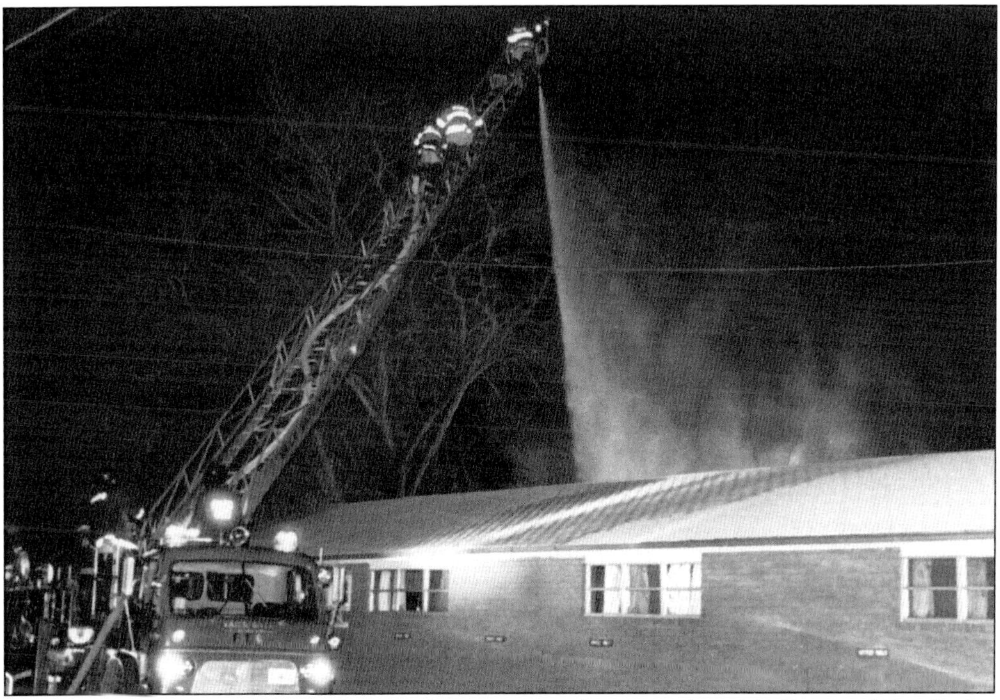

The Vails Gate aerial ladder truck is seen here covering the November 1980 Diamond Candle fire on John Street. Firemen from Vails Gate, Quassaick, and Newburgh joined in battling the fire at the candle-making firm, which once employed up to 100 people. (Courtesy of John T. Babcock.)

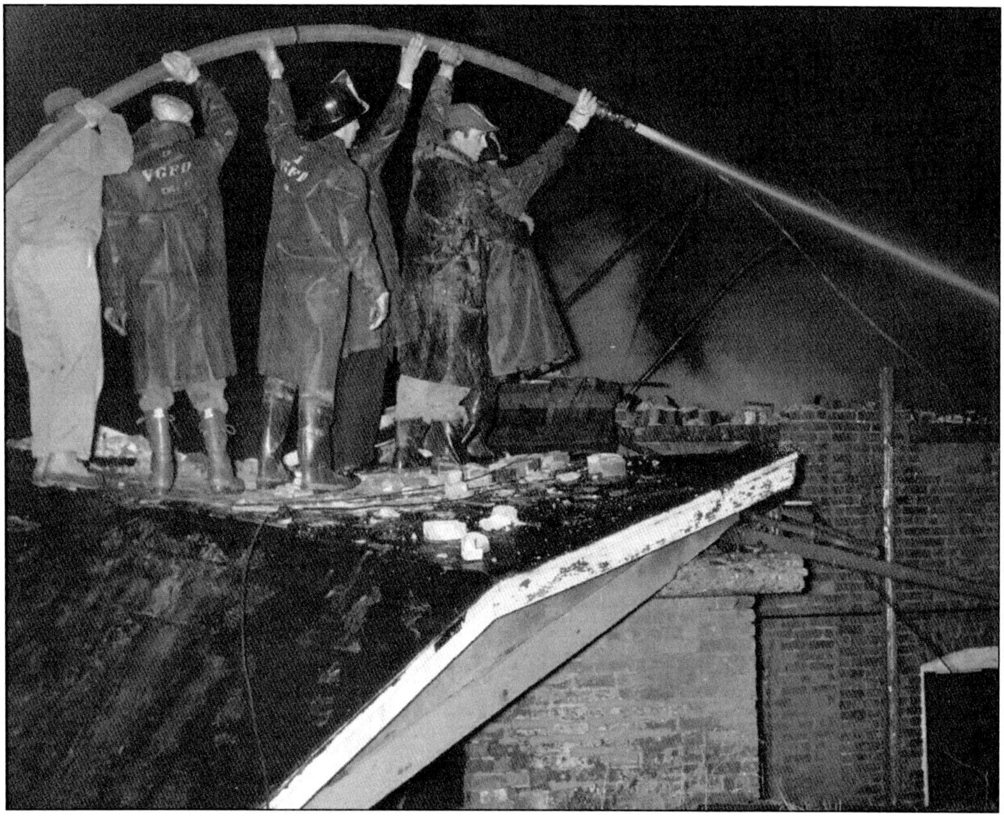

The Little Falls Paper Mill was destroyed on March 30, 1960, by a fire that raged on for more than five hours. The blaze was discovered at about 9:00 p.m. and lasted into the early morning hours. Firemen from five different companies came together to fight the flames. Fortunately, there were no injuries. (Courtesy of the Vails Gate Fire Company.)

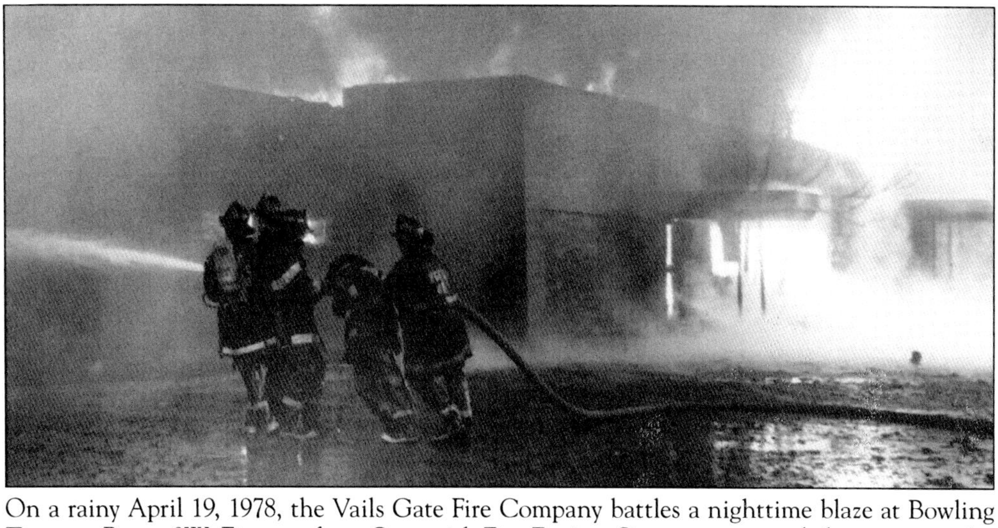

On a rainy April 19, 1978, the Vails Gate Fire Company battles a nighttime blaze at Bowling Time on Route 9W. Firemen from Quassaick Fire Engine Company responded to assist in the effort. The structure was rebuilt and remains a popular bowling spot to this day. (Courtesy of the Vails Gate Fire Company.)

Six

Business Evolves

As the population of early New Windsor grew, so did the number of businesses. The Hudson River, with all its promises and proximity to what is now New York City, drew people from all over the world.

In the 18th century, wheat was the area's leading agricultural product. Roads leading from the interior stretched to piers built on the Hudson River. There, homegrown products were either shipped out or exchanged for manufactured or imported goods. The *New Windsor Gazette* was established in 1797 by Jacob Schultz; other early entrepreneurs and their businesses included Samuel Brewster, sawmill; Capt. Jonathan Lawrence, store; Abraham Van Deusen, house of entertainment; William Scudder, land office; Jonas Williams, flour mill; Benjamin S. Hoyt, medical practice; Matthew C. Lyons, medical practice; and Richard Edgetton, dry goods/groceries. In 1753, the same area saw the first glass factory in this country, producing simple tableware and window glass.

At the turn of the century, the *New Windsor Ferry* sailed to Fishkill. The steamboat *Barge Experiment*, built in New Windsor in 1828, supported the Cornwall trades and sailed from New Windsor. This freighting method continued until the Erie Railroad came on the scene, around 1850. The commercial brick industry was at its peak during the 1800s.

As decades passed and laws changed, the number and variety of businesses grew. Today, businesses like Argenio Brothers, Coach Diner, and Ann's Gift Shop dot the landscape.

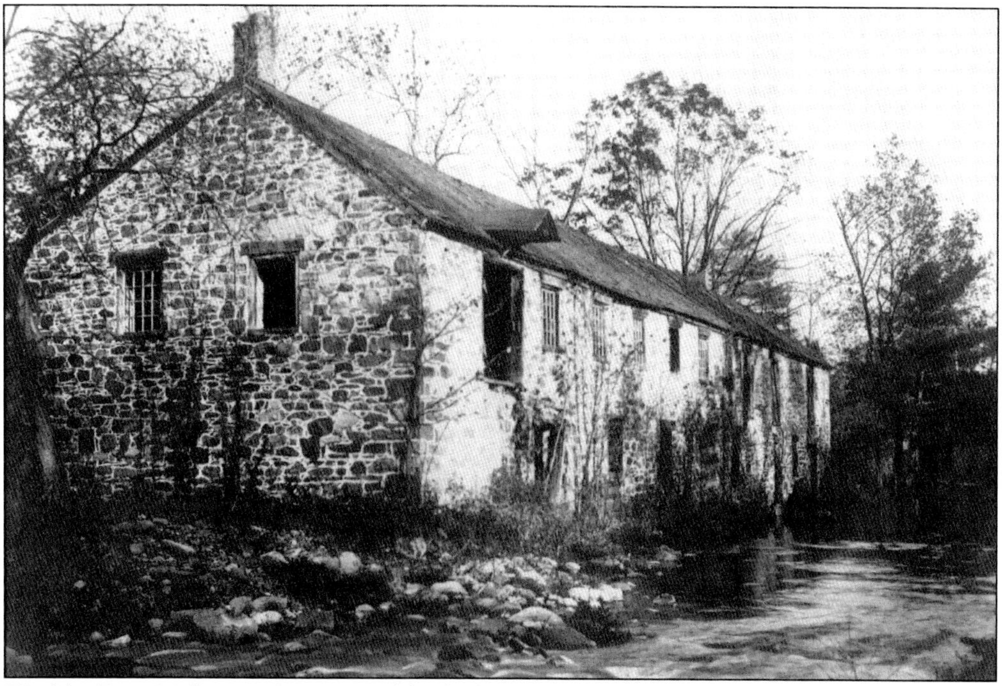

Wealthy Rose Miller was known worldwide for her fine-cut "Rose-leaf Snuff and Tobacco" in the late 1700s. To ensure an adequate supply of rose leaves, she planted four acres of land with a variety known as the Philadelphia rose. The tobacco business continued for many years under the management of her son-in-law Andrew H. Mickle, onetime New York City mayor. (Courtesy of the Historical Society of Newburgh Bay and the Highlands.)

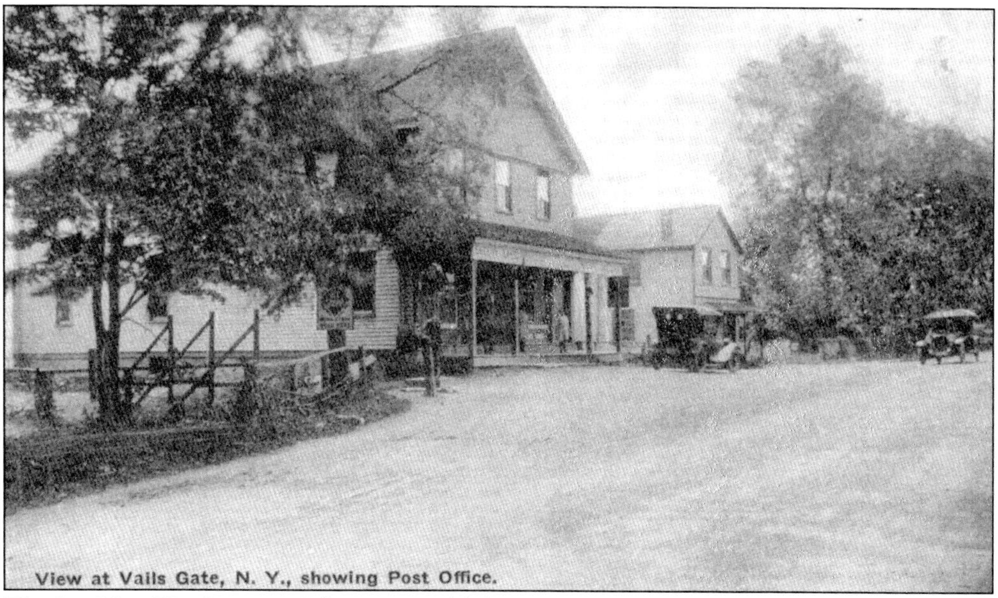

The first New Windsor Post Office was established in Little Britain on May 29, 1824; the second was established in New Windsor on February 19, 1829. Cushing's Hall in Mortonville—now known as Vails Gate—was a general store and the location of the third post office, established on April 10, 1850, with John D. Vail as postmaster. (Courtesy of the Whitehill Collection.)

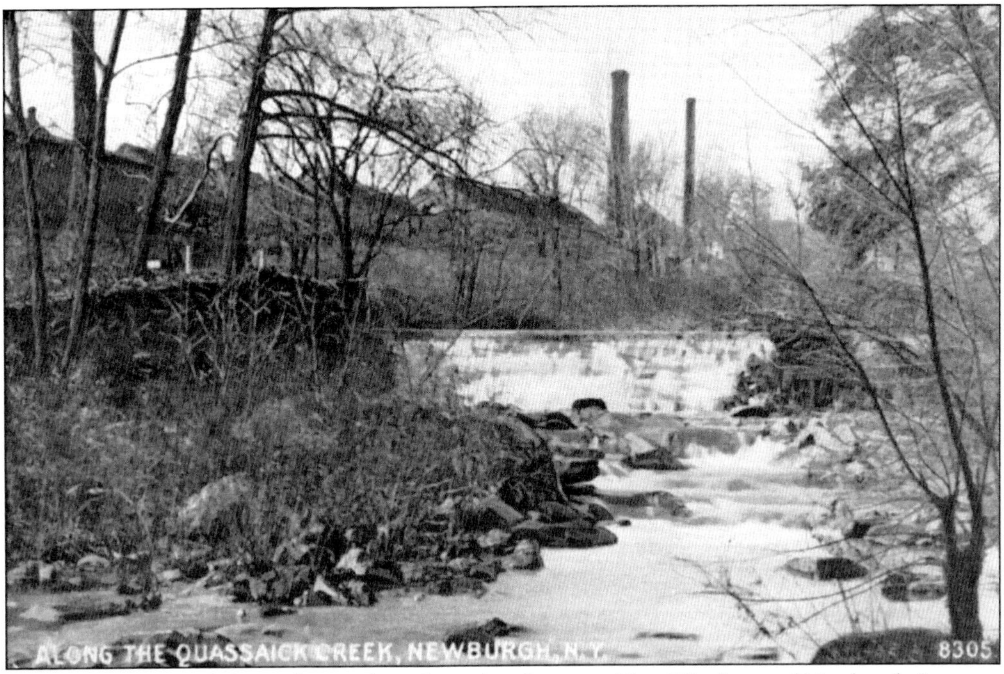

The Quassaick Creek forms the northern boundary between New Windsor and Newburgh. It enters New Windsor from Muchattas Lake and empties into the Hudson River. Early settlers built mills along this waterway, and its creek banks provided convenient sites from which their products could be taken to ships on the Hudson River to be transported. (Courtesy of Mary Jane Miller.)

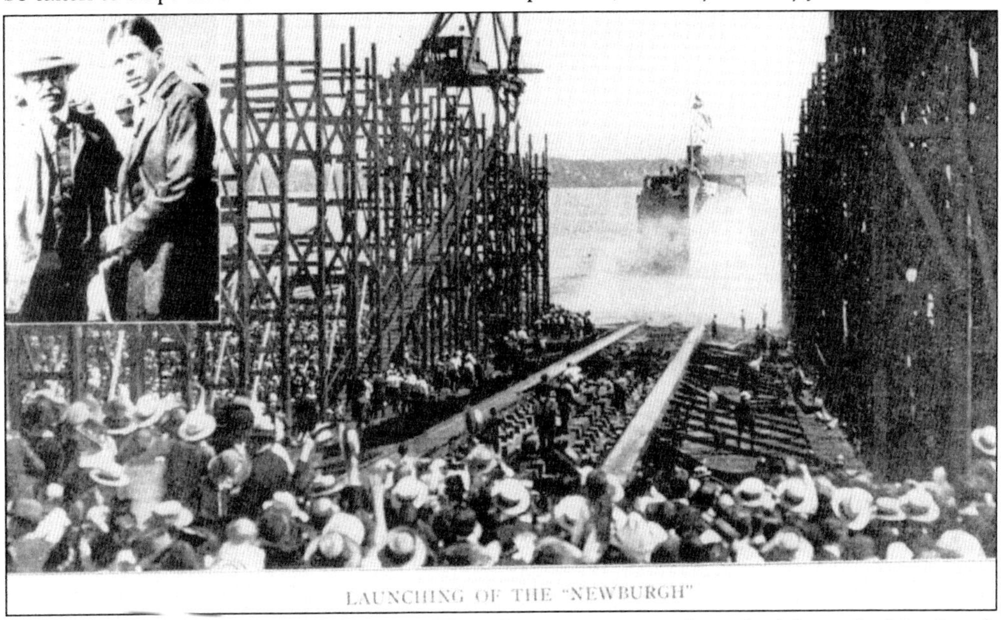

The *Newburgh*, built for the Emergency Fleet Corporation, was launched from the Newburgh Shipyard on October 19, 1918. Its sister ship, the *New Windsor*, had been launched first, on September 2, 1918. Alcoa Steamship Corporation bought the *New Windsor* in 1940, renaming it the *Alcoa Mariner*. In 1942, it was struck by three torpedoes 100 miles south of Trinidad and sunk with no losses. (Courtesy of the Dabroski family.)

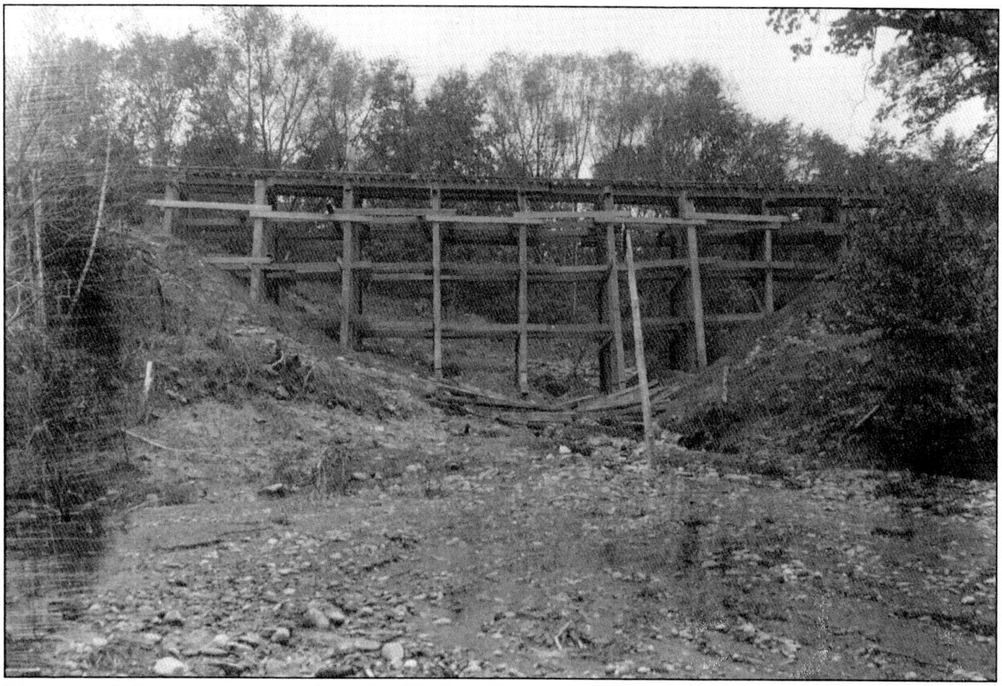

Many goods being transported on the Hudson River took to the rails. This c. 1905 photograph shows a light-construction trestle that was erected to transport fill dirt along the Ontario & Western rail line as it was being built from Cornwall through New Windsor to Middletown. (Photograph by Ludwig Diemer, courtesy of the Historical Society of Newburgh Bay and the Highlands.)

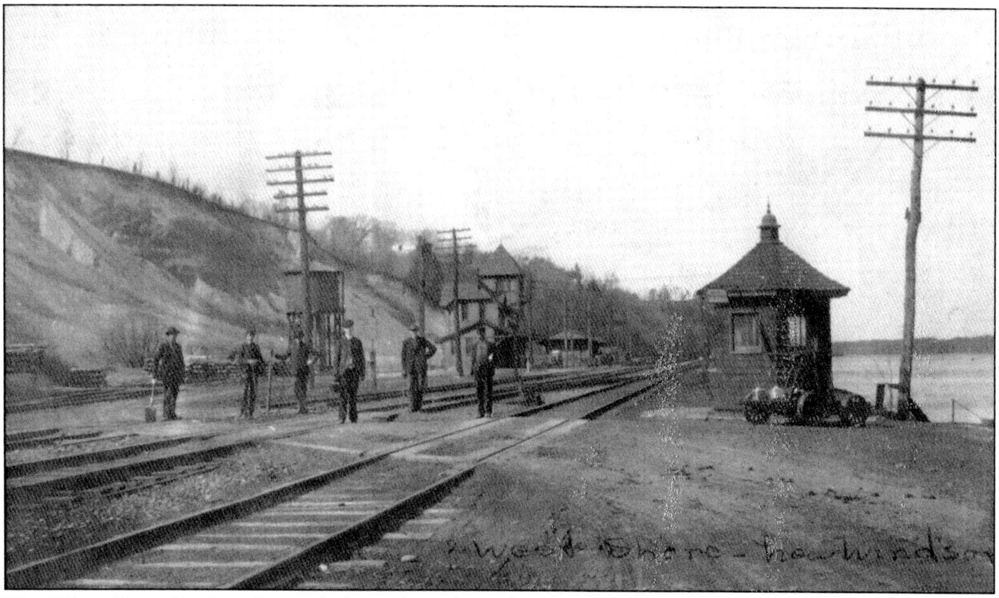

The West Shore Railroad traveled north and south along the banks of the Hudson River through New Windsor. The area prospered with the advent of the railroad, and people, products, and goods were moved on a daily basis during the late 1800s. The railroad provided hard work for local men who were only too happy to have the job. (Photograph by Jerry Huddleston, courtesy of the Historical Society of Newburgh Bay and the Highlands.)

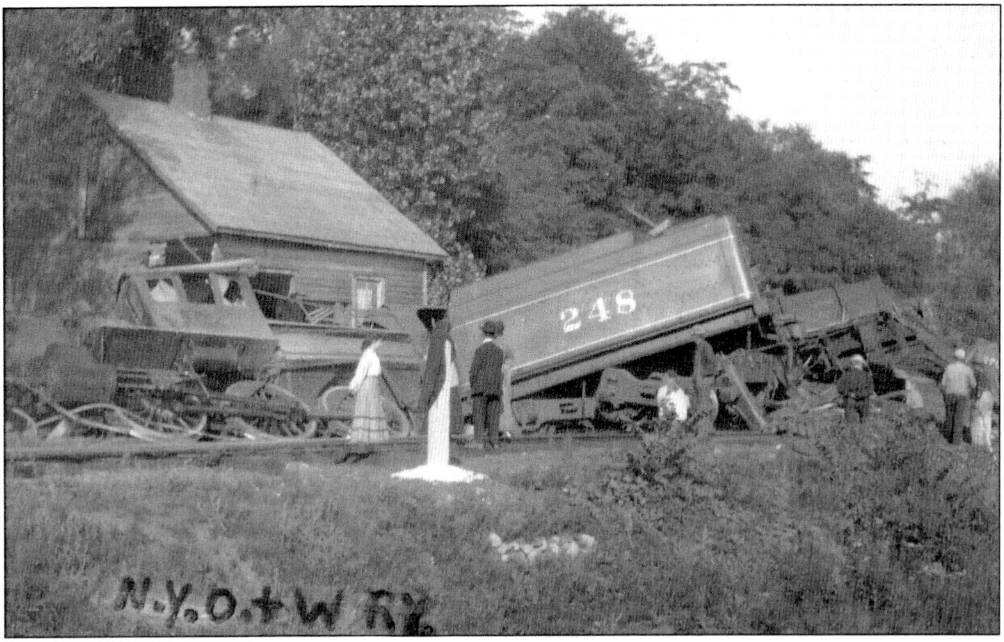

Nearby Cornwall was the site of a 1908 Ontario & Western train wreck. Local people gathered to see the derailed engine and cars strewn all over the tracks. Reportedly, no one was hurt. It was no easy matter to determine the cause of the derailment and to clear the tracks in preparation for the next train. (Courtesy of the Whitehill Collection.)

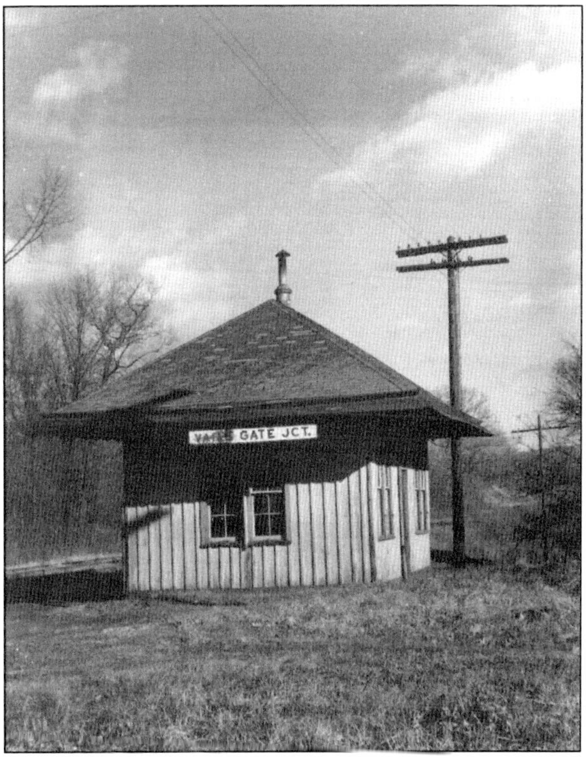

The Erie Railroad operated in six states, including New York, from 1832 to 1960. In 1845, an amended charter sought to build a Newburgh branch running north from Harriman through Vails Gate Junction. Splitting at Vails Gate, the Newburgh Short Cut line went to Central Valley; the branch proper went under the viaduct through Salisbury Mills. (Photograph by Dr. William Small, courtesy of the Historical Society of Newburgh Bay and the Highlands.)

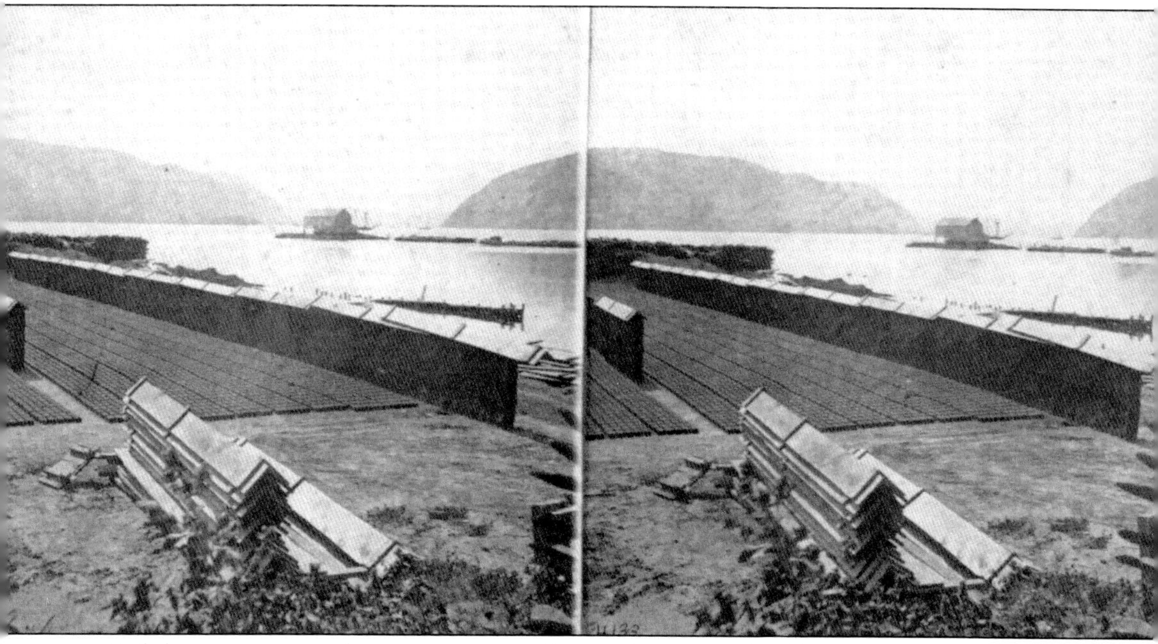

Early businessmen saw there was only a small strip of somewhat level land along the riverbank with a steep bluff rising in the back. It was composed of surface sand and gravel along with a substratum of clay, which could be used for making an excellent-quality brick. This image is an example of a stereoscope, invented in 1838 by Charles Wheatstone. The stereoscope required two separate pictures to be positioned two and one-half inches apart. When viewed through the prismatic lenses by the viewer, the two images are blended by the eyes into one, which is perceived by the brain—as with normal vision—in three dimensions. (Courtesy of the Whitehill Collection.)

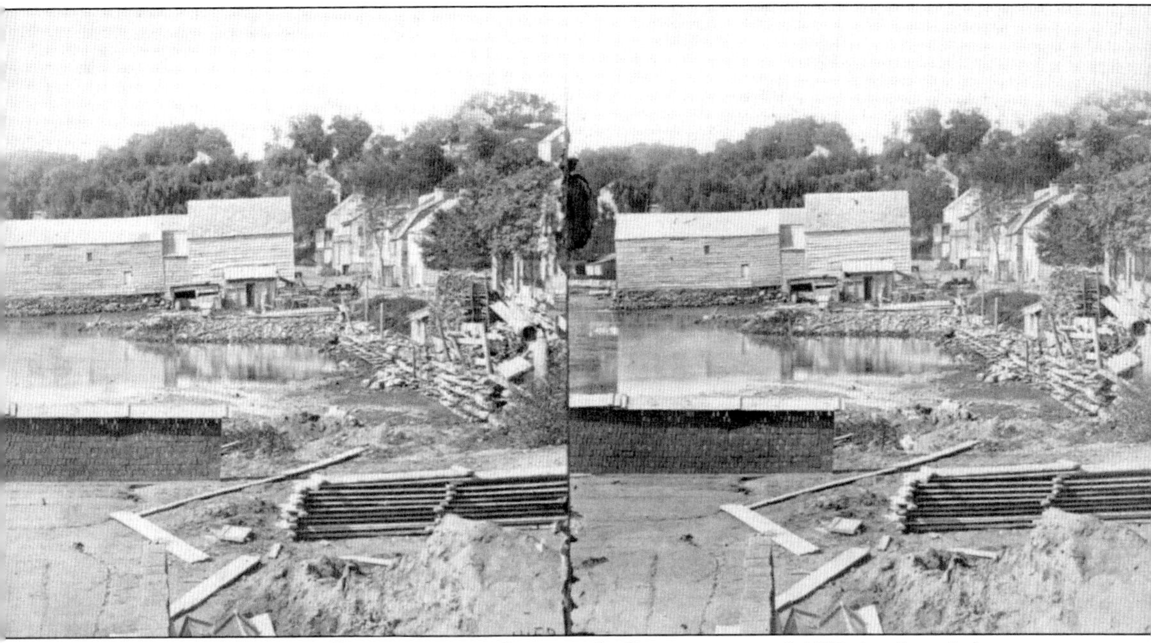

This is another example of a stereoscope photograph. Starting around 1850, brickyards became one of New Windsor's dominant industries as six establishments sprang up around the same time. The industry remained the principal commercial business of the area thanks to the combination of available natural elements and access to Hudson River docks and ramps for shipment. The Lahey Yards, owned by leading manufacturer William Lahey, covered 40 acres and produced 165,000 brick per day. Loaded on four Lahey barges, the popular, high-quality bricks headed down the Hudson River toward New York City. Hugh Davidson and a Mr. Walsh were also prominent brickyard owners. By the beginning of the 20th century, with 130 manufacturers, the brick-making industry dominated the Hudson River. By 2002, after three and a half centuries, the once powerful industry vanished along these shores. (Courtesy of the Whitehill Collection.)

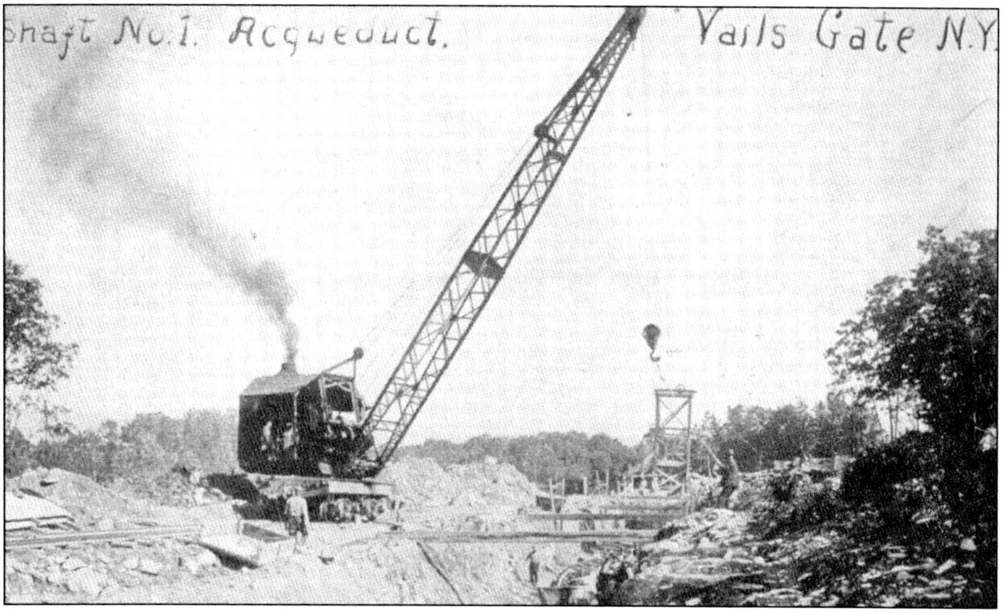

Construction on the Catskill Aqueduct began in 1907 and was completed in 1916. The entire system, including three dams and 67 shafts, was completed in 1924 at a cost of $177 million. It brings water from the Ashokan Reservoir through Vails Gate to New York City and remains the town of New Windsor's sole water source. (Courtesy of Mary Jane Miller.)

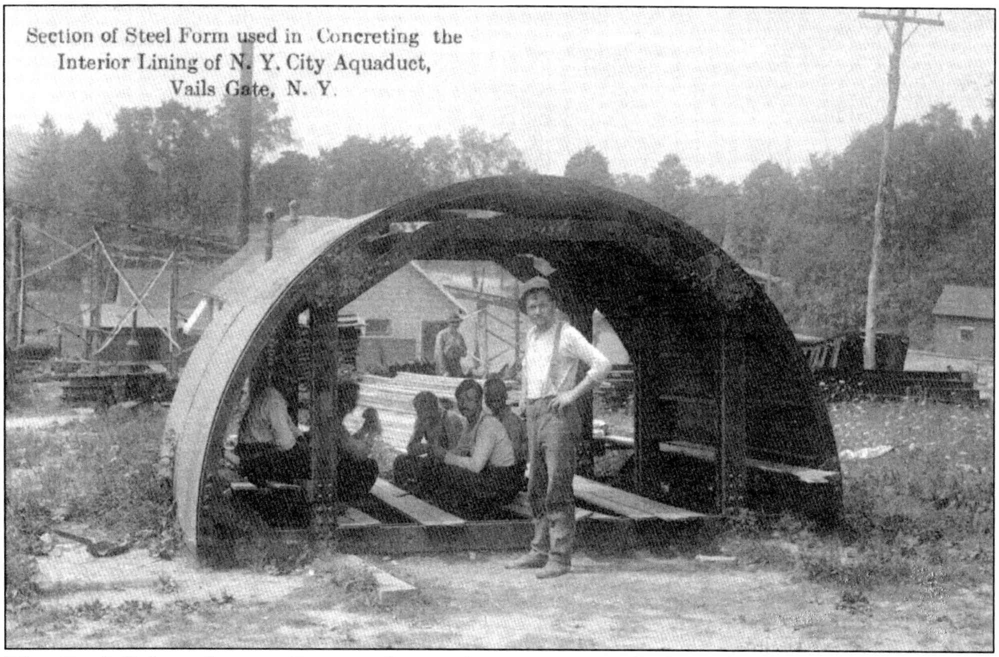

The Catskill Aqueduct, with water flowing by gravity, travels from the Catskill Mountains to Yonkers, where it connects to other parts of the tunnel on its way to New York City. As seen in this c. 1920 photograph of workers on a break, steel forms were used in concreting the interior lining. (Courtesy of the Whitehill Collection.)

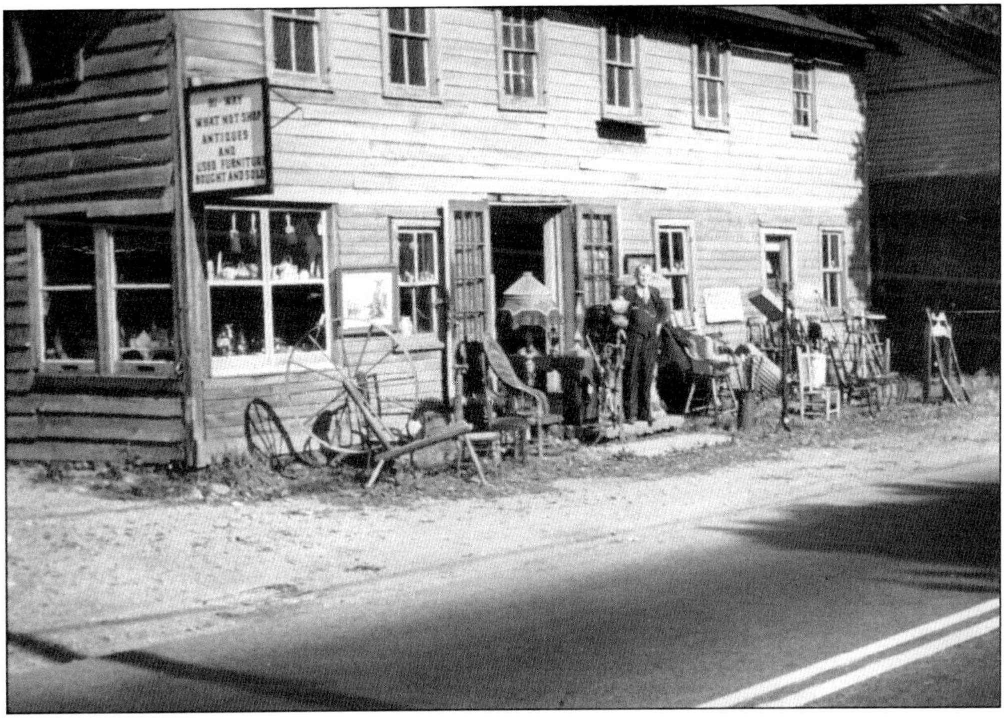

The Hi-Way What Not Shop on Route 32, pictured around 1930, was a popular stopping-off place for early travelers who liked to browse. Antique and used furniture was bought and sold, and it was not unusual to hear patrons bargaining over prices. (Courtesy of the Historical Society of Newburgh Bay and the Highlands.)

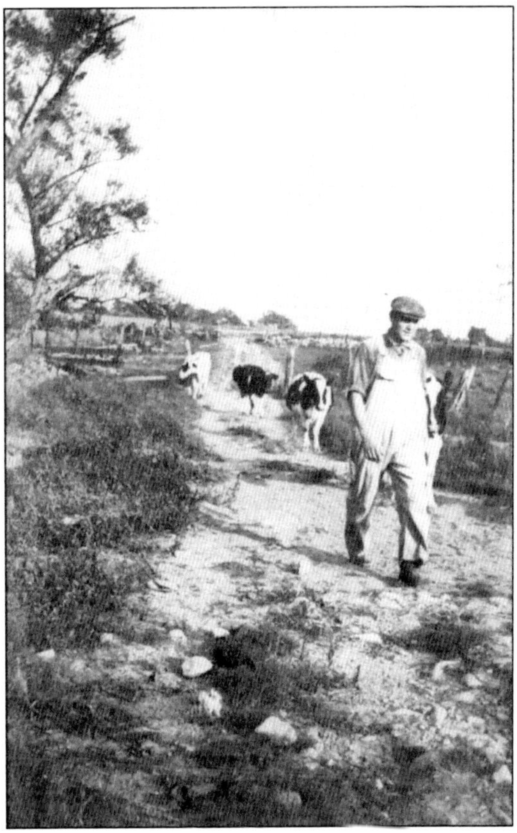

Paul Babcock Sr., owner of the Paul Babcock Sr. Dairy Farm in Little Britain, is shown bringing in the cows to be milked in 1939. Babcock came to the United States from Germany when he was 20 years old with the equivalent of $2 in his pocket. After working on a farm in Craigsville for two years, he bought his own farm, which still bears his name. (Courtesy of the Robert Babcock family.)

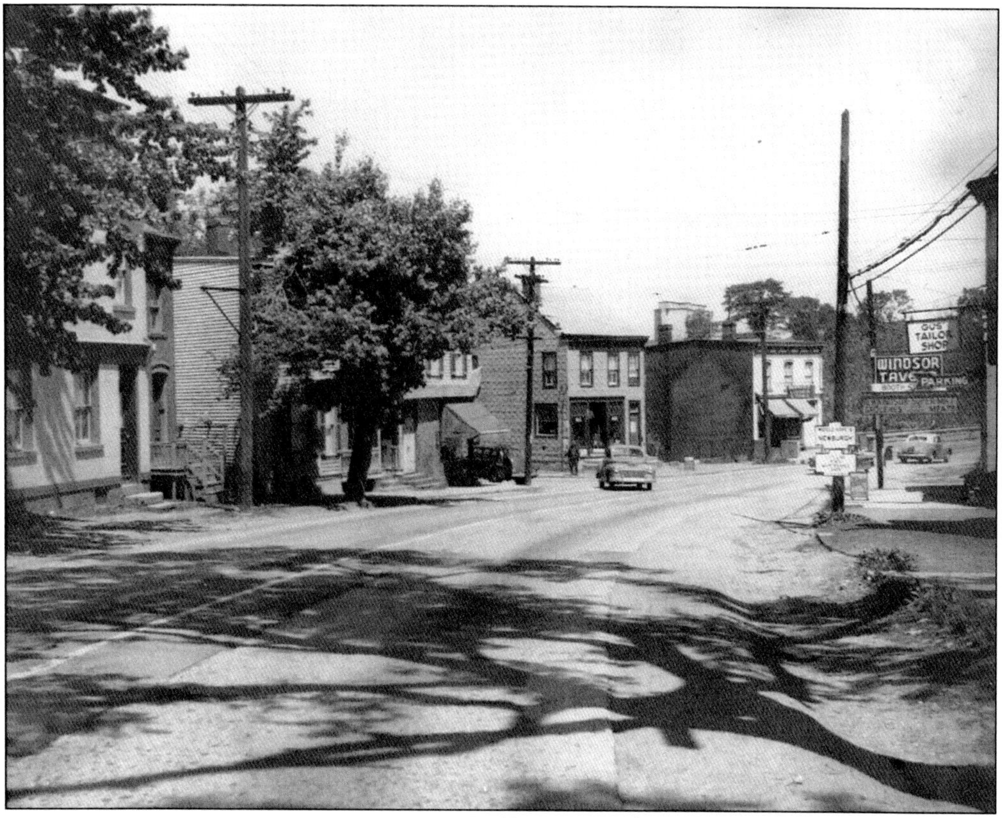

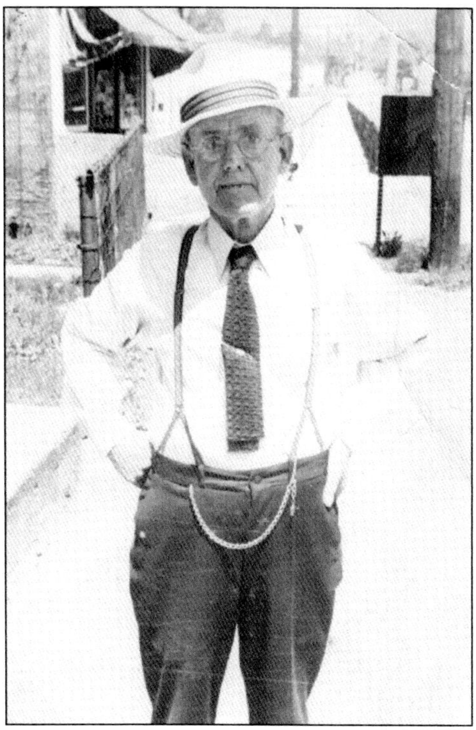

Businesses along Quassaick Avenue, like those pictured here around 1940, catered to locals as the road approached the bridge toward Newburgh. On the right are Gus's Tailor Shop, New Windsor Super-Market, and Windsor Tavern. Around the corner on John Street is Hudig's Tavern, with Andrew Hudig's living quarters upstairs. On the left are two unidentified residences, Gus's Tavern, Nellie Murray's Ice Cream Shop, and Bianco's Liquor Store. (Courtesy of Margaret Spignardo.)

? Murray stands in front of Nellie Murray's Ice Cream Shop, located to the left of the old New Windsor Bridge and near the original Gus's Tavern. Winter or summer, cold or hot, all the local children looked forward to Nellie Murray's ice cream cones. (Courtesy of Sandra Lewis Terwilliger.)

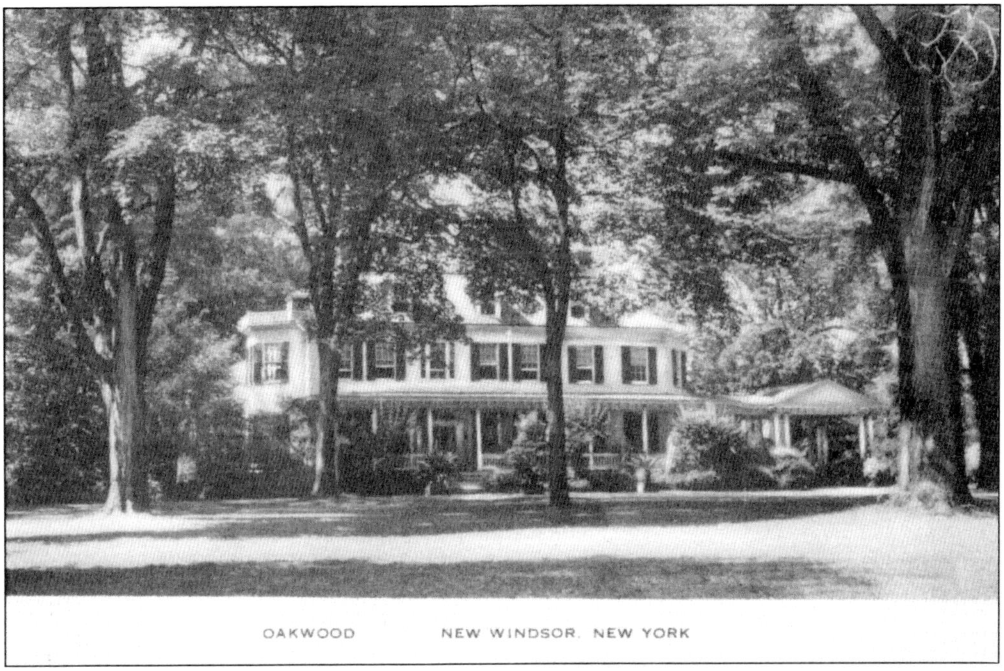

In the 1930s and 1940s, this large Colonial estate, known as Oakwood, was used as a private resort. Located on Blooming Grove Turnpike, it was only 60 miles from New York City. Among other things, its advertising boasted the use of a private lake. (Courtesy of Mary Jane Miller.)

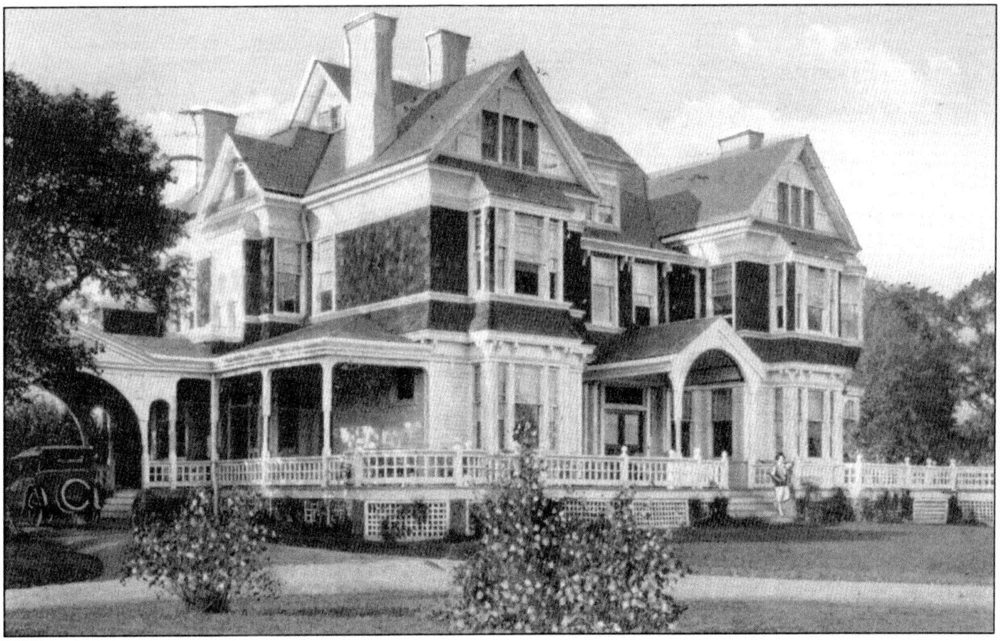

The Aspetong (a Mohegan word for "hilltop") Farm began along Route 94, beside an Indian burial ground. In 1899, Charles S. Bryan bought 34 acres for his summer home. The model 185-acre dairy farm had its own electricity, steam plants, and waterworks. The processes that Bryan developed ensured the quality and purity of milk being shipped to Newburgh. (Courtesy of the Whitehill Collection.)

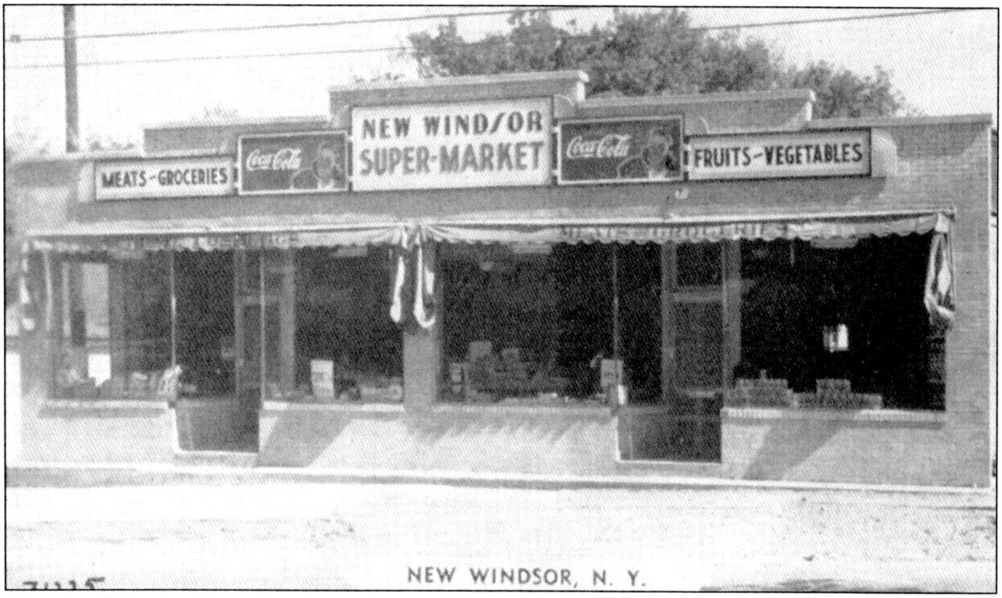

The New Windsor Super-Market, a favorite of local shoppers that offering a wider variety of foods and products, was located on Quassaick Avenue near the old New Windsor Bridge. Supermarkets like this one had begun to replace the small, family-run grocery stores. The building still stands but has changed owners numerous times. (Courtesy of Mary Jane Miller.)

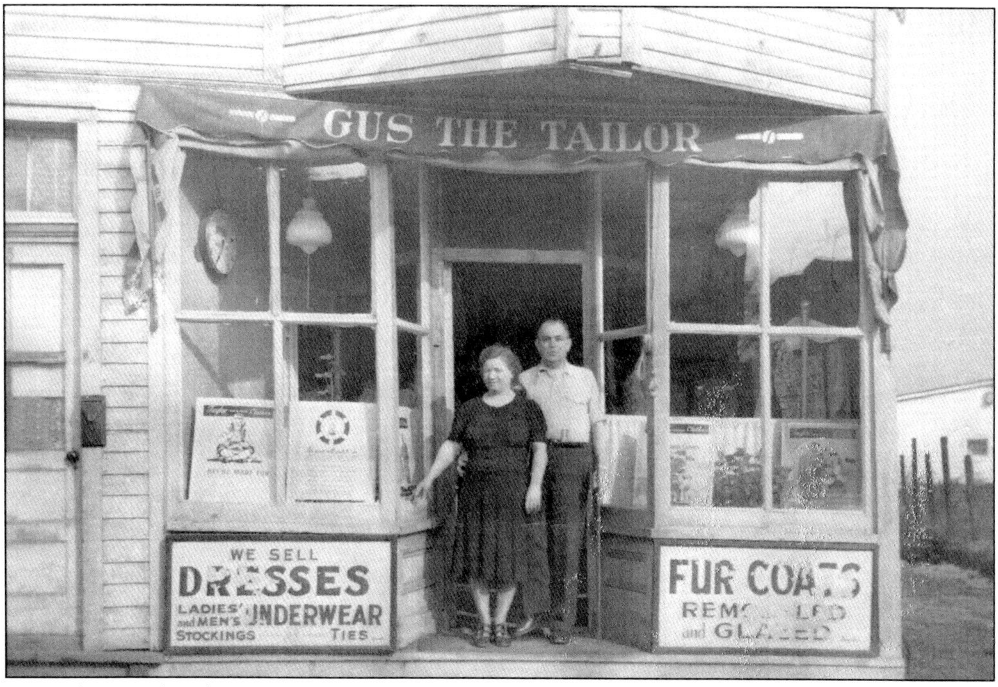

Gus Zilavy and wife, Margaret, are pictured around 1940 in front of their first tailor shop on Quassaick Avenue, where they sold clothes for men and women. Area residents brought clothes to be mended, tailored, or altered. The shop was later relocated to 38 Quassaick Avenue. Gus, a former tailor at the US Military Academy, had previously made uniforms for West Point cadets. (Courtesy of Margaret Spignardo.)

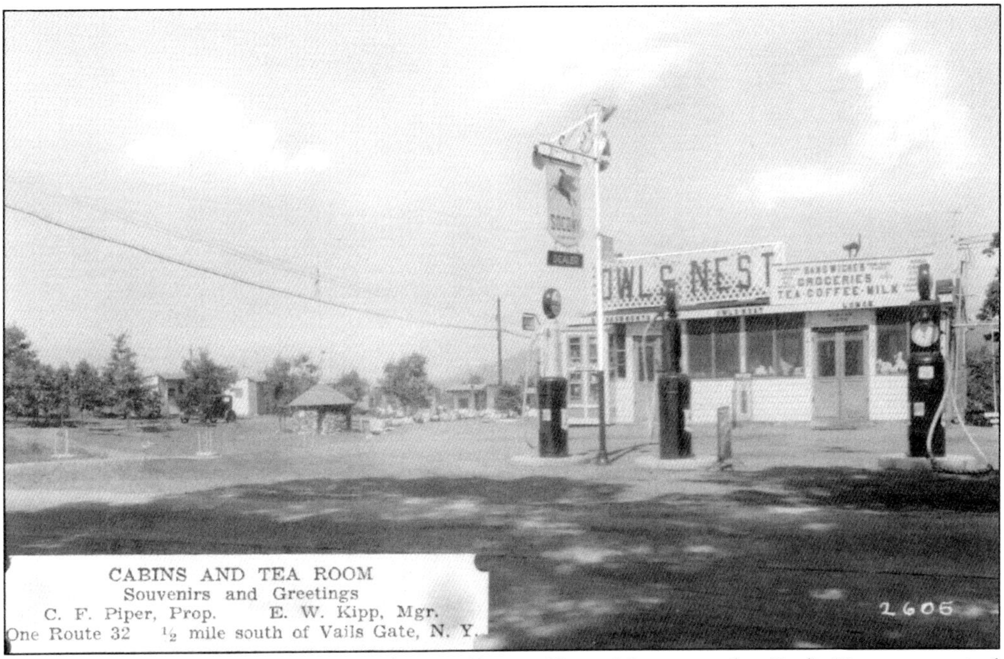

Around the mid-19th century, travelers on Route 32 could stop at the Owl's Nest—a typical gas station of the times—located one half mile south of Vails Gate. Socony, the brand of gas advertised in the photograph, was founded in 1911 and eventually became Mobil. The telephone booths to the left of the building allowed travelers to make calls, and cabins afforded a place to rest. (Courtesy of the Whitehill Collection.)

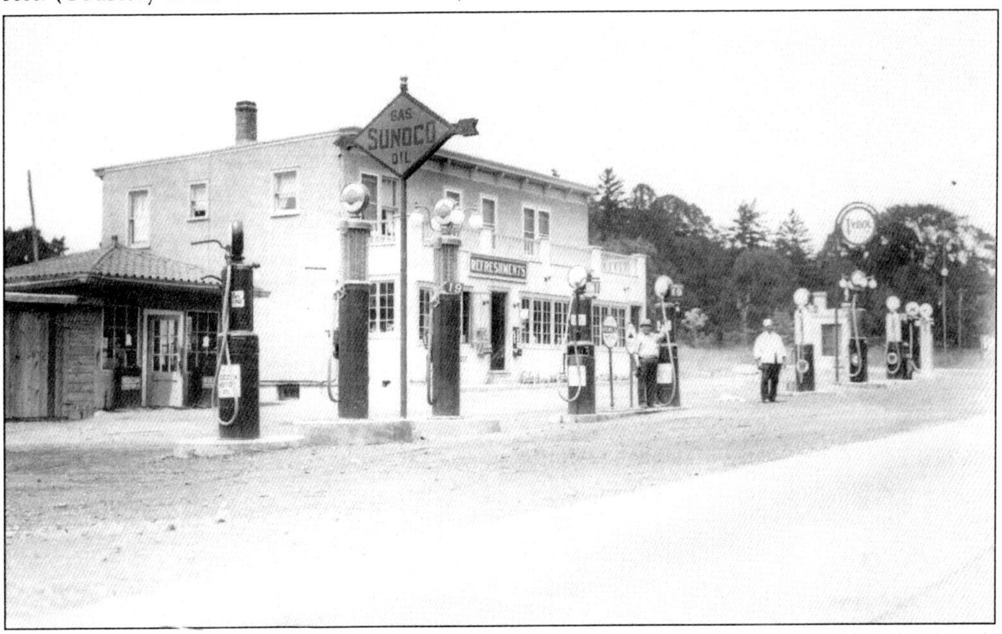

The Blue Bird restaurant and gas station was a rest stop along Route 9W. Original builder Joseph Favino and his family lived above the restaurant. A miniature golf range was behind the Tydol gas station. The Sunoco station at the corner of Union Avenue and Route 94 was south of the original gas station. (Courtesy of Catherine Molloy Nugent.)

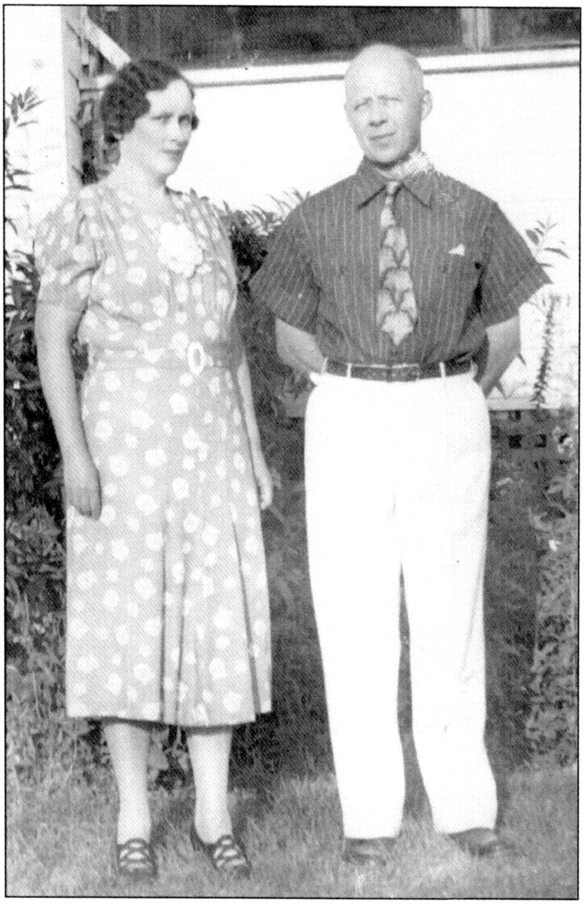

Herbert and Lucille Paffendorf were married around 1920. His father, Christian Paffendorf, began a furniture business in the late 1800s at 57–59 Colden Street in Newburgh. Herbert joined the business as a young man and, along with Lucille, continued building an outstanding reputation as a fair and honest businessman and friend. His sense of humor and generous nature drew people to his shop to visit every day. (Courtesy of Jeri Paffendorf.)

This 1941 Dodge panel truck was used to pick up and deliver the furniture that Herbert Paffendorf repaired or sold. Furniture stores in the Newburgh area would often send furniture that had been damaged in shipping to be repaired. At the time, panel trucks like this one were very popular and were also used for a variety of purposes by the military. (Courtesy of Jeri Paffendorf.)

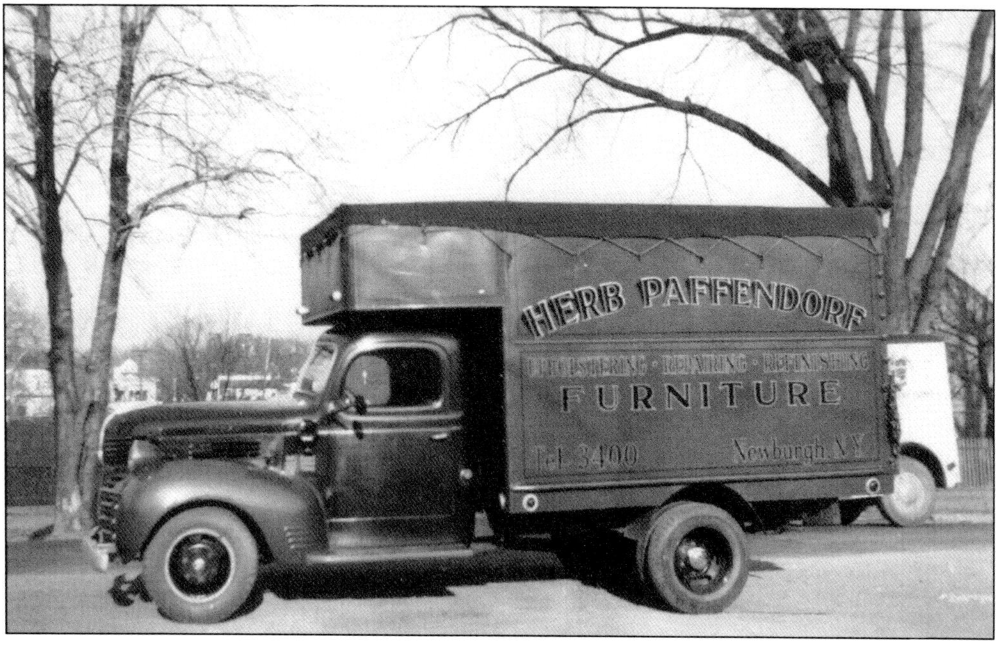

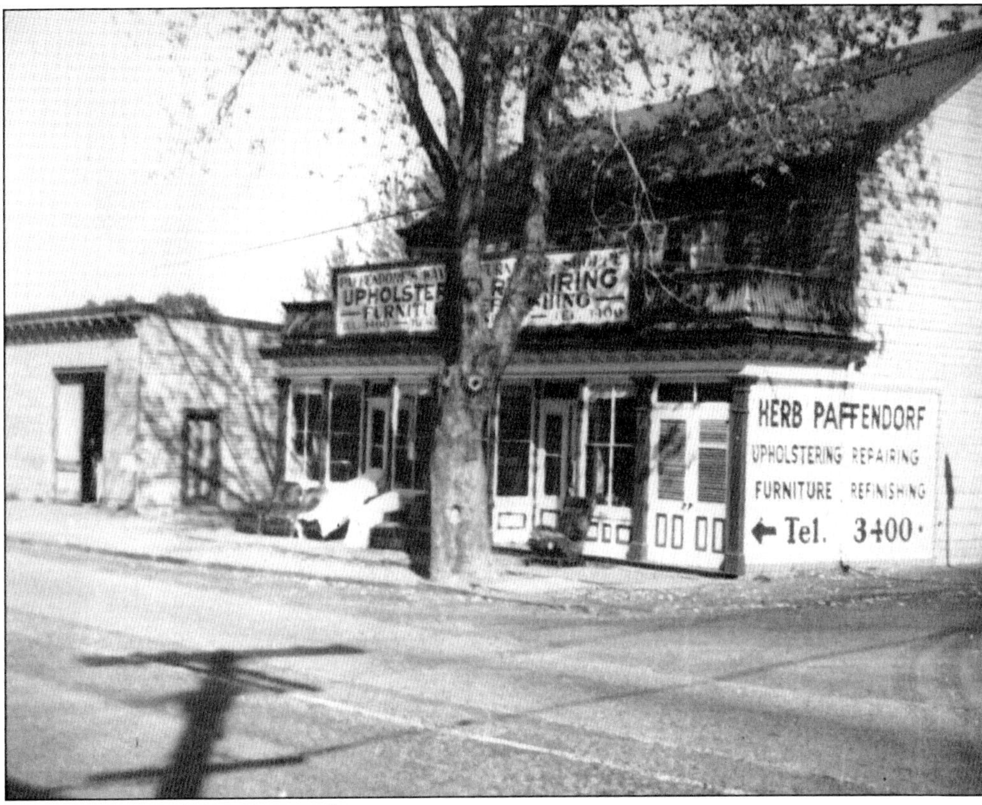

Prior to 1947, and the closing of the Colden Street location, the Paffendorf Wayside Furniture Shoppe, pictured here, was opened in the family-owned building on Quassaick Avenue. At that time, Herbert Paffendorf employed as many as six men to work with him selling new furniture and reupholstering, repairing, and refinishing older pieces. He specialized in refurbishing antique furniture. The building stayed in the family until it was sold in 2012. (Courtesy of Jeri Paffendorf.)

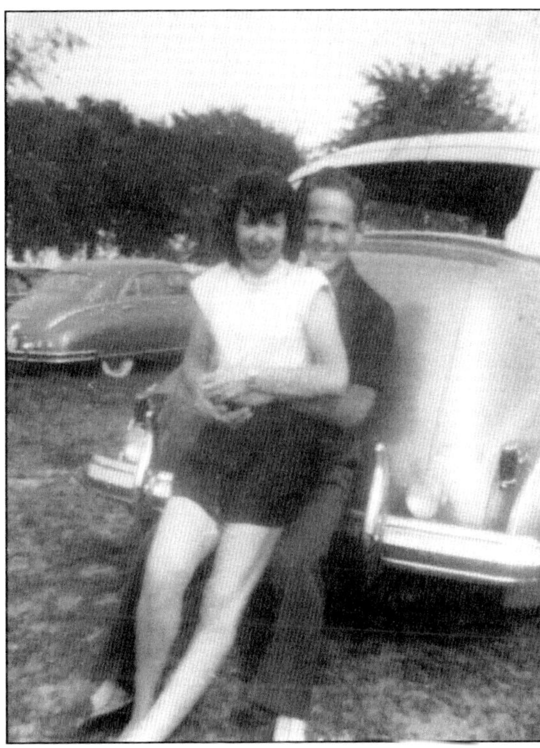

Brewster and Geraldine Paffendorf, married on October 8, 1950, are seen here enjoying an outing. Paffendorf had worked in the family furniture business with his father and took over when his father passed away. He upheld the outstanding reputation of the business, which he ran until his own death in 2010. (Courtesy of Jeri Paffendorf.)

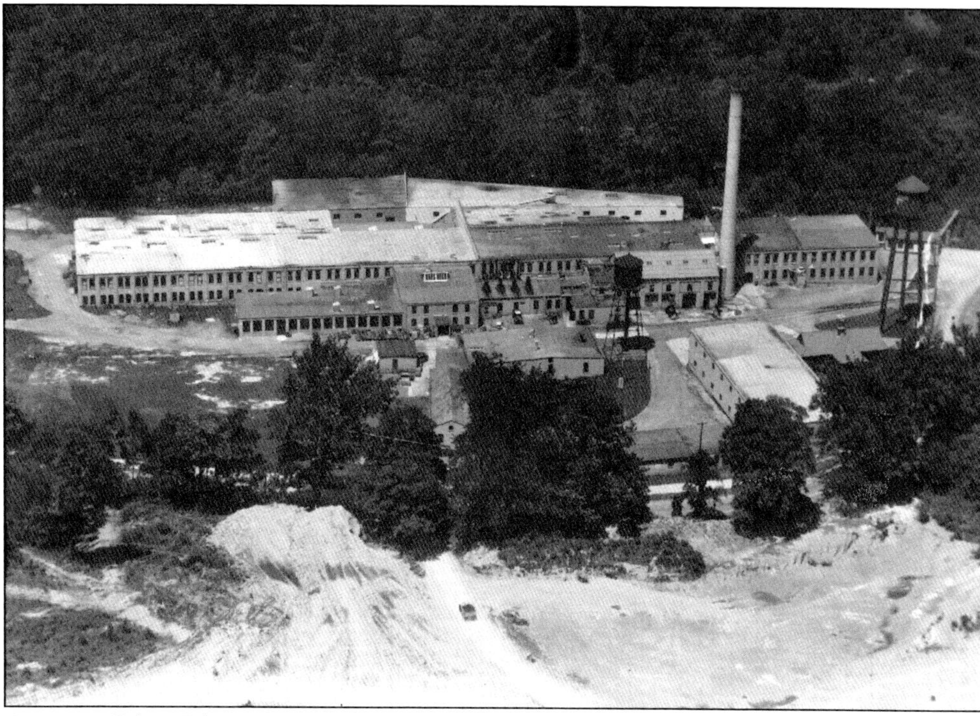

American Felt & Filter Company, a supplier of felt products, came into being through the merging of six specialized companies. For over 70 years, the Walsh Road–based company has employed people from the New Windsor area and beyond. (Courtesy of the Historical Society of Newburgh Bay and the Highlands; American Felt & Filter Company.)

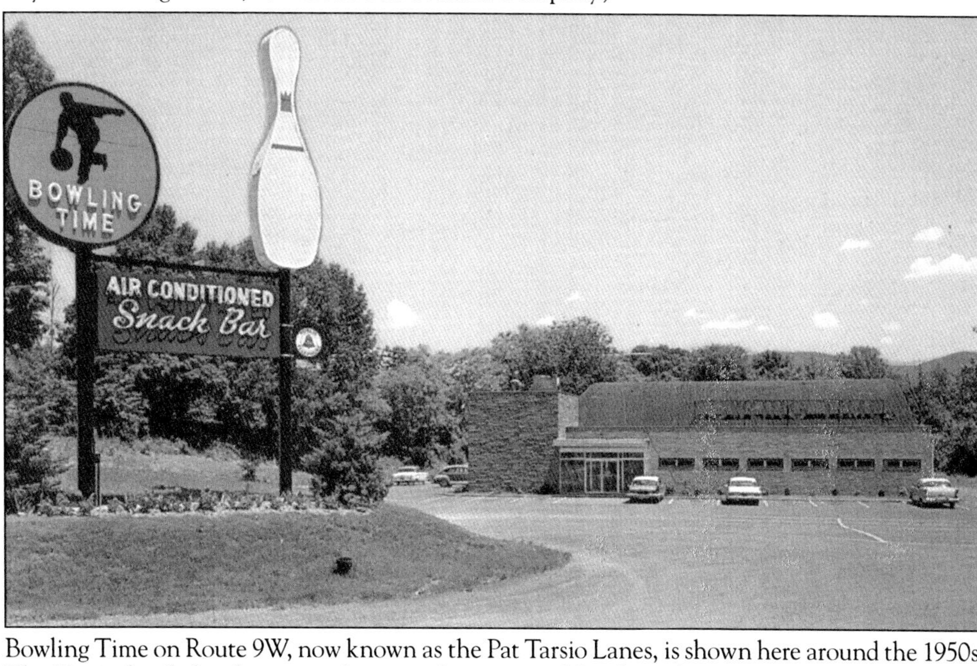

Bowling Time on Route 9W, now known as the Pat Tarsio Lanes, is shown here around the 1950s. The Tarsio family has long stayed true to their roots of family and community and continues to keep bowling a fun and affordable activity for all. (Courtesy of the Whitehill Collection.)

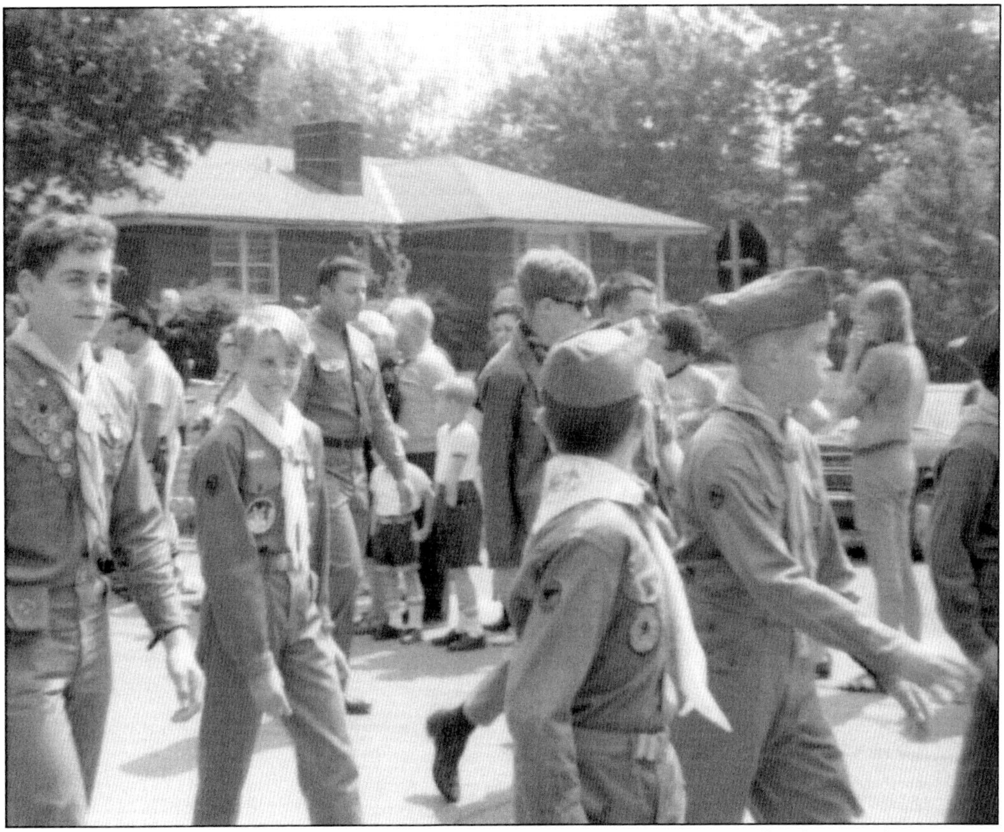

Shown to the far left is Bruce Williams in his Scout uniform. He was the first Eagle Scout in the New Windsor American Legion–sponsored Troop 15. To earn the prestigious award, a Scout must pass through six ranks, earn 21 merit badges, serve six months in a leadership position, perform a service project, participate in a conference, and complete a board of review. (Courtesy of Bruce Williams.)

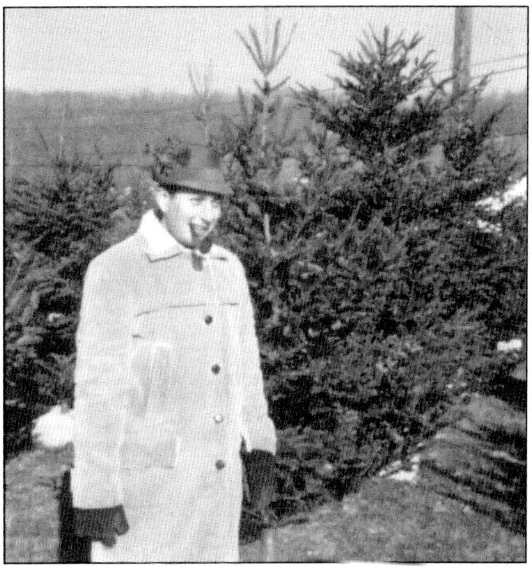

Dolph Schaeffer founded Pleasant Acres Nursery in 1927. When he married Mary Cornell (a member of the family that founded Cornell University) in 1935, the business was moved to the Cornell property. By 1970, the Schaeffers had died, and the business became family owned with Innis Williams, former Schaeffer Farm superintendent, as president and his son Bruce as vice president. Bruce Williams, shown here, was president from 1980 until the business closed in 2008. (Courtesy of Bruce Williams.)

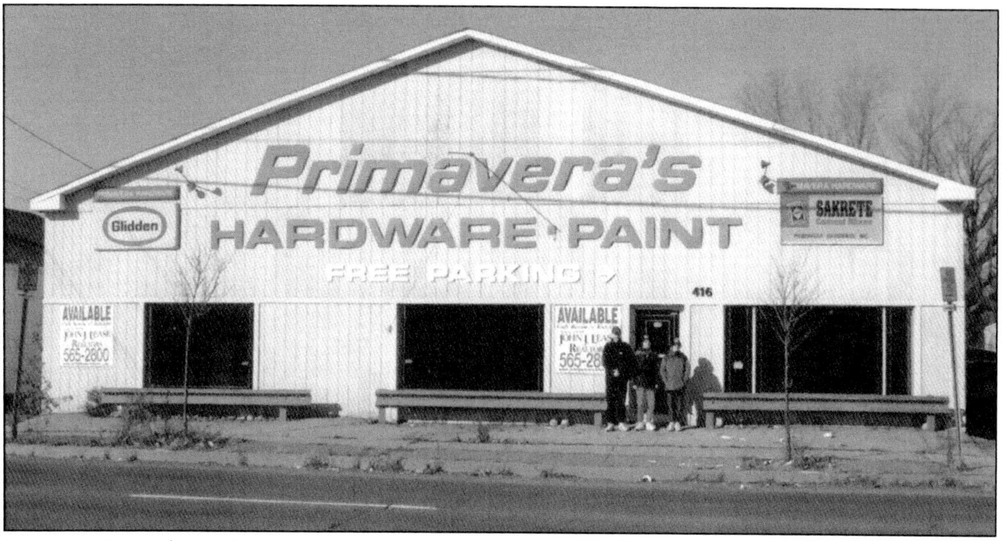

Primavera's Hardware & Paint Store, located on Windsor Highway, was a true family business, with three generations of Primaveras serving local needs. Joseph E. Primavera began the business in 1944 and was succeeded by Joseph A Primavera. Pictured here are Joseph C. Primavera and his sons. Originally housing a bakery, post office, hardware store, and paint store, the business continued to expand. It closed in 2006 as superstores moved in. (Courtesy of Joseph C. Primavera.)

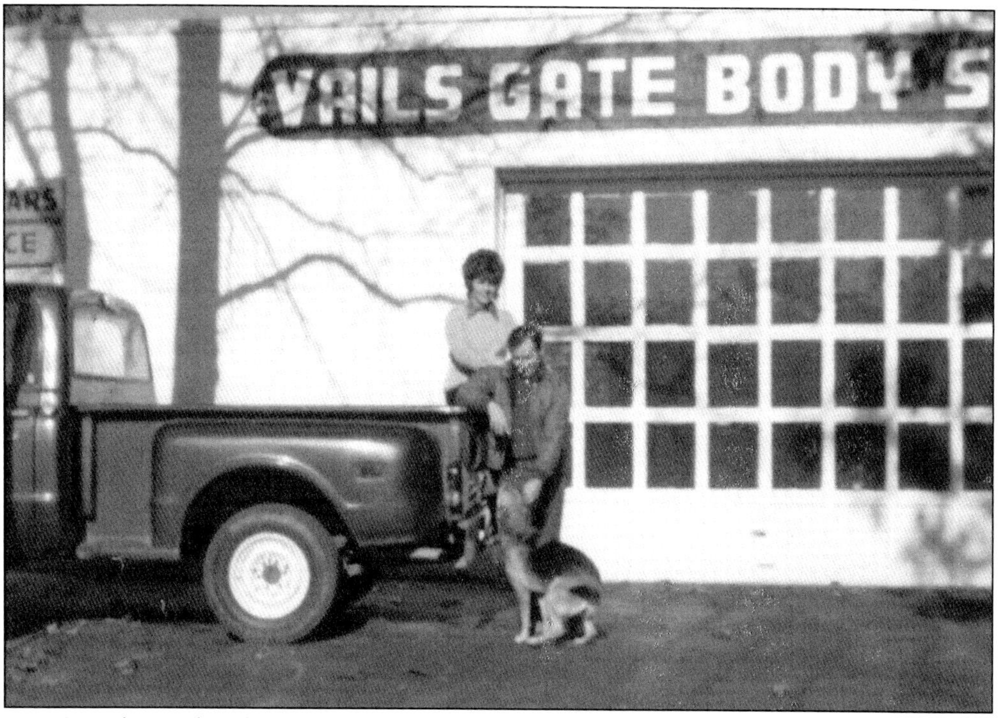

In 1953, Robert Babcock was working full-time for a body shop in Newburgh. During that time, he worked nights and weekends repairing cars on his own on the Paul Babcock Sr. Dairy Farm. In 1966, as the business grew, he opened his own shop on Temple Hill Road on the Vails Gate property where he and his wife, Catherine, lived. When they retired in 1975, their three sons took over the business, which is still in operation today. (Courtesy of the Robert Babcock family.)

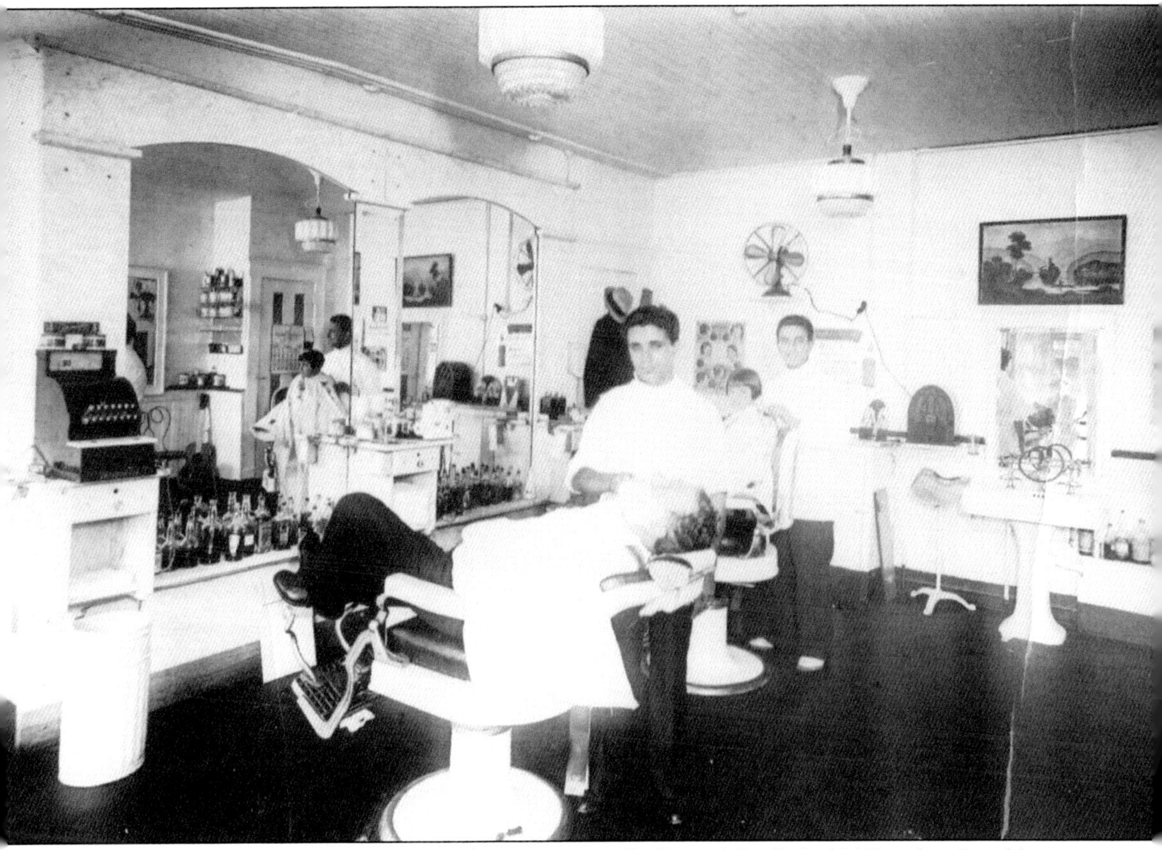

Guinness World Records proclaims Anthony Mancinelli (born March 2, 1911) to be the oldest professional barber still practicing as of May 2, 2012, at the age of 101 years, 2 months, and 26 days. He was born outside of Naples, Italy, and immigrated to Newburgh with his family when he was eight years old. Mancinelli's father was employed in a Newburgh Felt Mill and supported seven children on a weekly income of $25. After hanging around other barbershops, where he would clean up while watching the barbers work, Mancinelli began cutting hair himself when he was 12 years old. Mancinelli bought his first shop when he was 20 years old. Haircuts originally cost two bits, the equivalent of a quarter. Later, it was 25¢ for a haircut, 15¢ for a shave. Mancinelli recalls that he used to keep a bottle of leeches handy to treat customers' black eyes. (Courtesy of Anthony Mancinelli.)

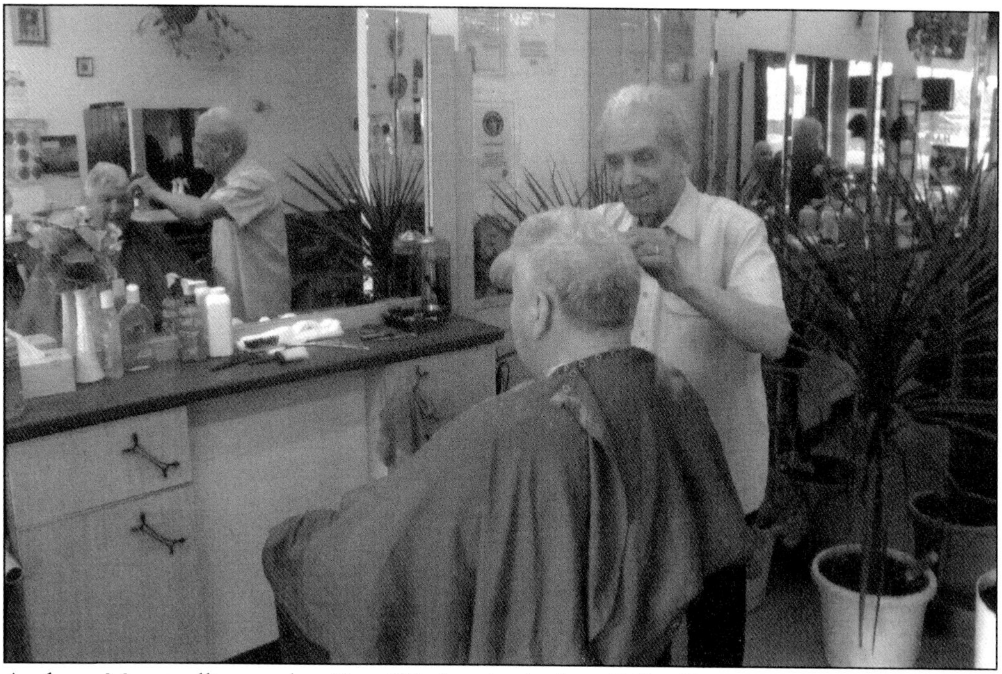

Anthony Mancinelli moved to New Windsor in the late 1960s. Here, he is cutting the hair of Michael Jaffe and talking about the old days. Mancinelli was married for 69 years until his wife, Carmella, passed in November 2004. He loves to dance, does not drink or smoke, and eats anything he wants. When people ask how he manages to stay so slim, he replies, "I eat pasta." When others respond, "Pasta? That makes you fat," he specifies, "I only eat thin spaghetti." He continues to live independently, drives his own car to work, and does not require glasses. Mancinelli, who turned 102 on March 2, 2013, has no plans to retire and hopes to continue with the distinction of being the oldest active professional barber passing out lollipops to children coming in for a haircut. (Both, courtesy of Anthony Mancinelli.)

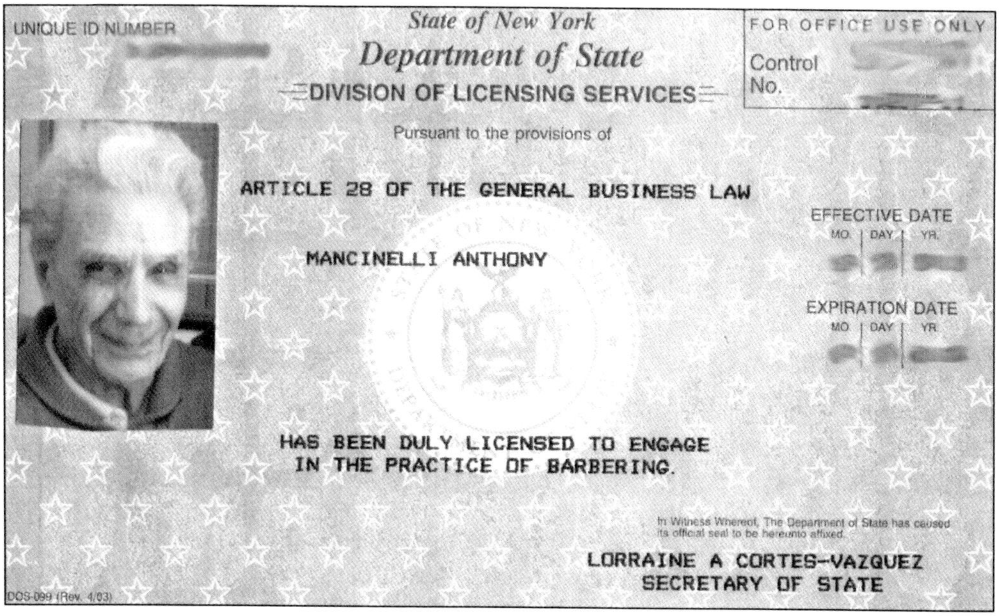

UNIQUE ID NUMBER

State of New York

Department of State

DIVISION OF LICENSING SERVICES

FOR OFFICE USE ONLY

Control No.

Pursuant to the provisions of

ARTICLE 28 OF THE GENERAL BUSINESS LAW

MANCINELLI ANTHONY

EFFECTIVE DATE
MO. | DAY | YR.

EXPIRATION DATE
MO. | DAY | YR.

HAS BEEN DULY LICENSED TO ENGAGE IN THE PRACTICE OF BARBERING.

In Witness Whereof, The Department of State has caused its official seal to be hereunto affixed.

LORRAINE A CORTES-VAZQUEZ
SECRETARY OF STATE

DOS-099 (Rev. 4/03)

Seven

People Come Together

As in any growing community, demand arose for organizations and clubs to allow people to come together for a common purpose. Many such groups developed over the years; some were cultural, civil, or political in nature, while others were oriented to residents of different ages. There was, and continues to be, something for everyone.

People young and old also came together to enjoy early games and activities, such as playing cards or dice, kicking the can down the road, or playing marbles, stickball, checkers, pickup sticks, and the like. Women gathered to quilt, knit, crochet, tat, and share conversation; men preferred darts or horseshoes. By 1850, baseball clubs had formed, including the Highlands of New Windsor and their archrivals, the Newburghs.

As people began living in larger groups, more structured clubs and organizations evolved. Scouting, 4-H clubs, and Little League were magnets for youth. The New Windsor Recreation Department was formed to provide parks, facilities, and fields in support of soccer, martial arts, yoga, tennis, softball, field hockey, and a host of other activities, including CPR courses, resident trips, and even a summer concert series. There is little doubt that such organizations and clubs will continue to grow and thrive.

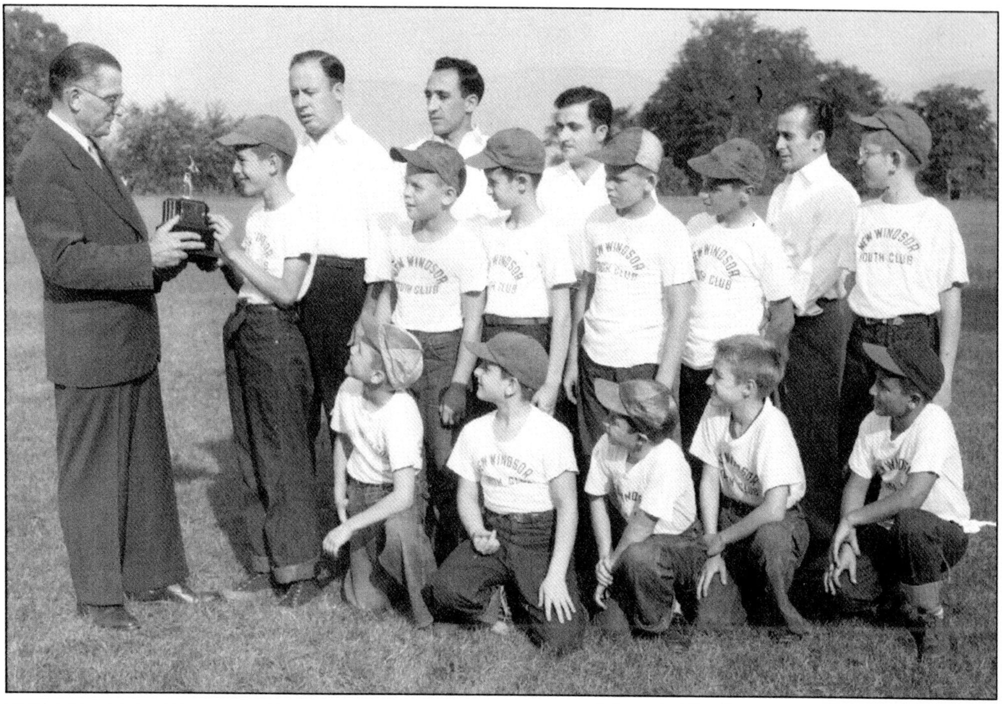

This 1951 photograph is of an early New Windsor Little League team at Starr Field. Pictured are, from left to right, (first row) unidentified, Michael Crudele, Kenneth Bento, Ronald Hotaling, and ? Russo; (second row) George Manuche, John Kavanaugh, William Dabroski, Alfred Crudele, John Dabroski, and two unidentified players; (third row) Salvatore DiTrocchio, Nicholas D'Egidio, and two unidentified members of the Crudele, family. (Courtesy of the Dabroski family.)

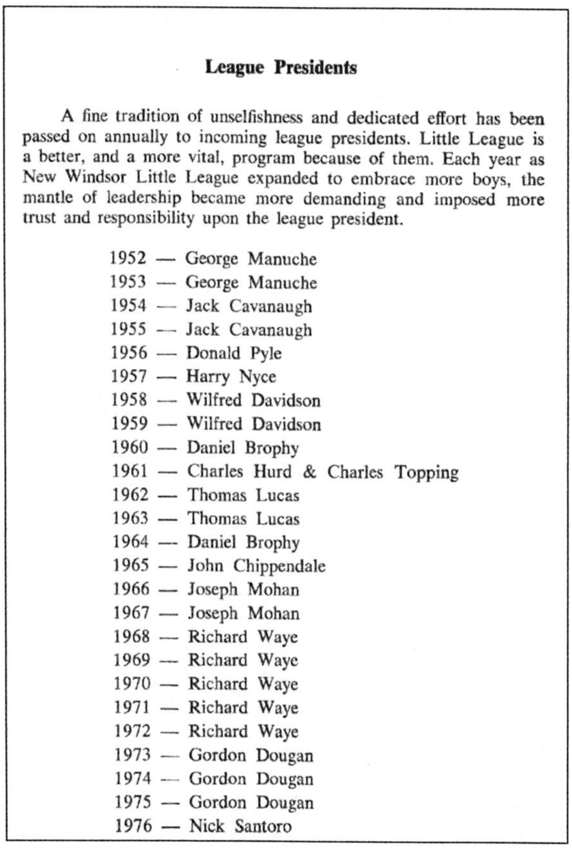

League Presidents

A fine tradition of unselfishness and dedicated effort has been passed on annually to incoming league presidents. Little League is a better, and a more vital, program because of them. Each year as New Windsor Little League expanded to embrace more boys, the mantle of leadership became more demanding and imposed more trust and responsibility upon the league president.

1952 — George Manuche
1953 — George Manuche
1954 — Jack Cavanaugh
1955 — Jack Cavanaugh
1956 — Donald Pyle
1957 — Harry Nyce
1958 — Wilfred Davidson
1959 — Wilfred Davidson
1960 — Daniel Brophy
1961 — Charles Hurd & Charles Topping
1962 — Thomas Lucas
1963 — Thomas Lucas
1964 — Daniel Brophy
1965 — John Chippendale
1966 — Joseph Mohan
1967 — Joseph Mohan
1968 — Richard Waye
1969 — Richard Waye
1970 — Richard Waye
1971 — Richard Waye
1972 — Richard Waye
1973 — Gordon Dougan
1974 — Gordon Dougan
1975 — Gordon Dougan
1976 — Nick Santoro

New Windsor Little League on Cedar Avenue touched many lives from its beginnings in 1951. Many supporters volunteered as league presidents, coaches, and fundraisers. As noted in the *1951–1976 25th Anniversary* booklet, the facility could also field teams in T-ball, minor, major, and senior leagues. Since the 1980s, the 12-acre complex has been known as the Ace of Diamonds. (Courtesy of the Dabroski family.)

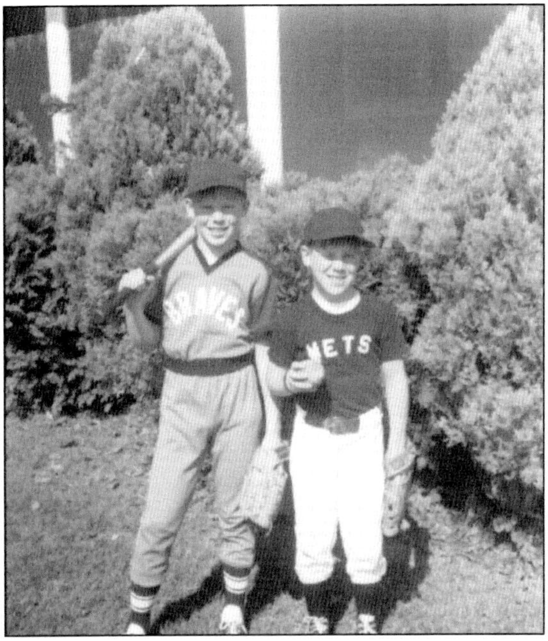

Brothers William (left) and Michael Dabroski don their uniforms to play for New Windsor Little League at Starr Field. In May 1976, William played for the Braves, while Michael played for the Mets. They are the grandsons of John and Lillian Dabroski and Edward and Thelma Stotesbury. (Courtesy of the Dabroski family.)

On August 20, 1981, the members of Operating Engineers Local 825 constructed three new fields, for which Little League vice president Emile Casale was most appreciative. Pictured here are, from left to right, operating engineer Ed Loeven, business agent John Fanning, lead engineer William Dabroski, Kenneth White Sr., and training director Neil Hughes. (Courtesy of the Dabroski family.)

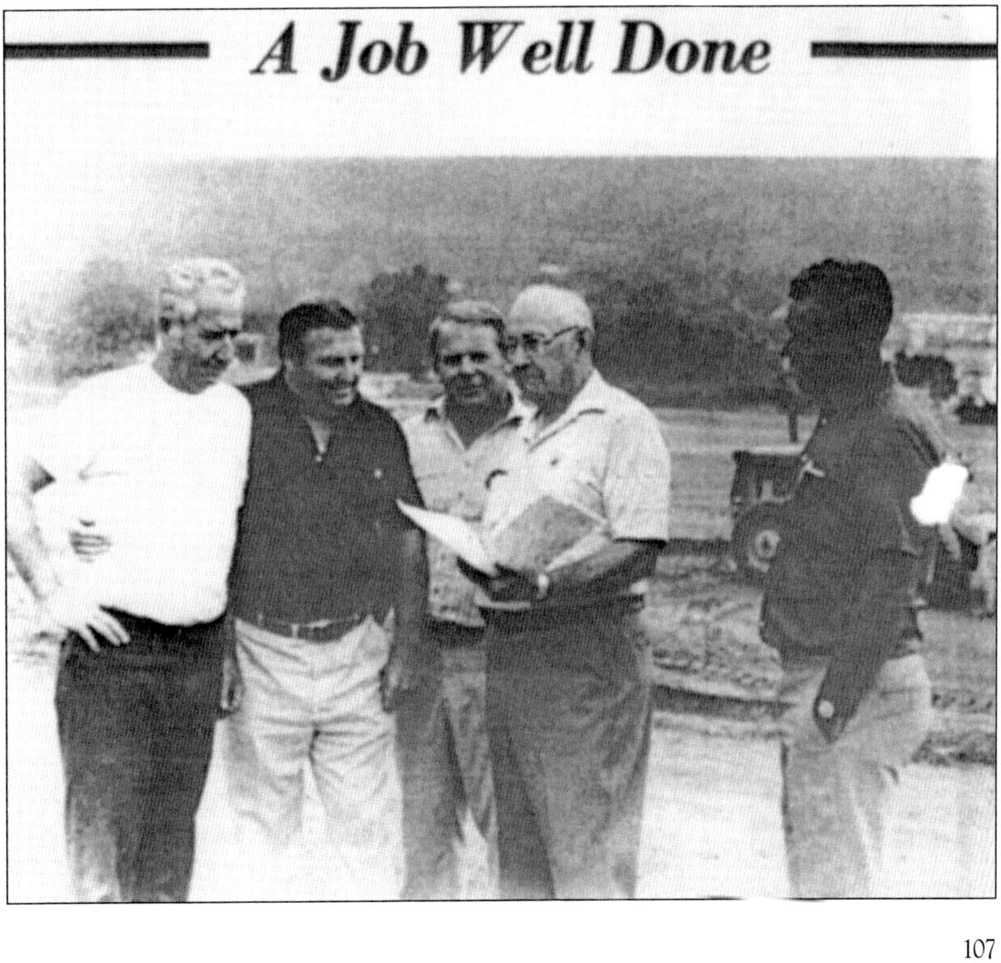

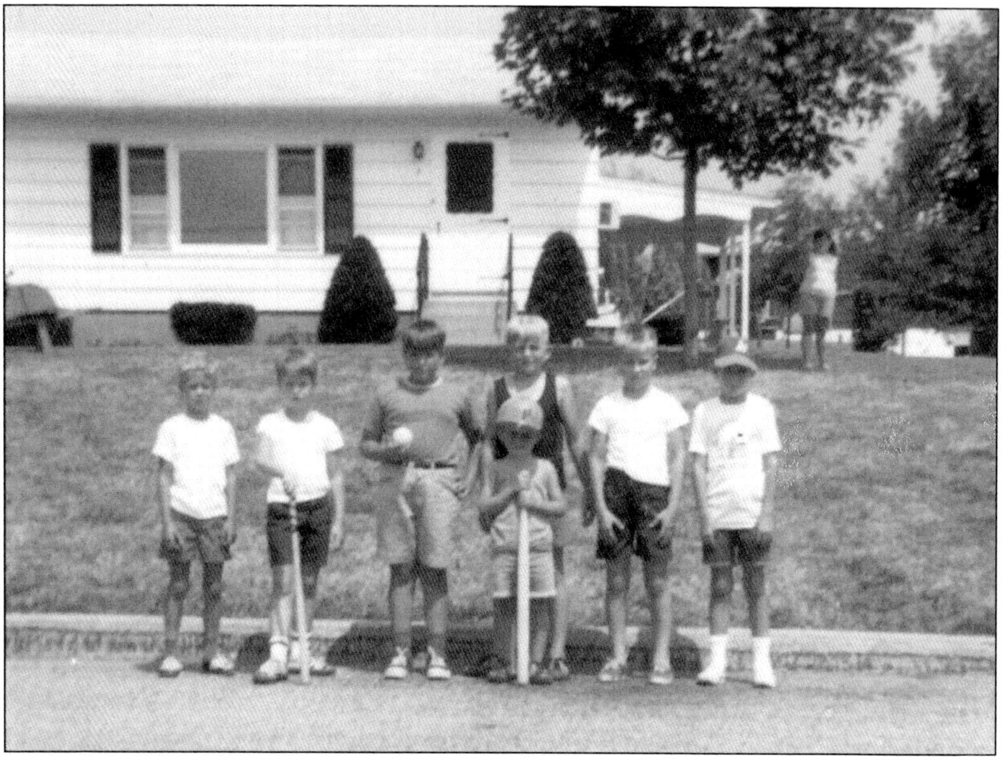

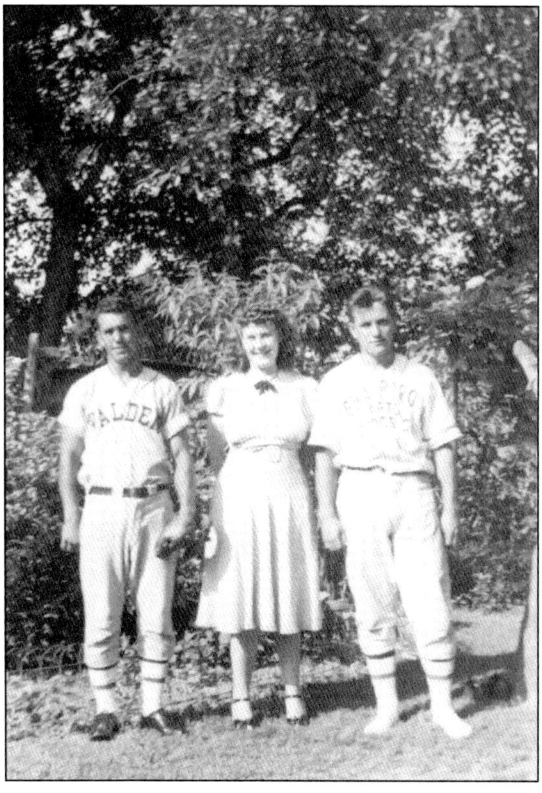

In the summer of 1970 and the four years that followed, the neighborhood boys of Willow Acres met every afternoon to play baseball on Valewood Drive. They are, from left to right, Kenneth Harris, Robert Cummings, Harry Lare, Robert Mauchline, Donald Mauchline (standing in front of his big brother), Glenn Seagren, and William Pullar. The plastic bat and whiffle balls were put to good use. (Courtesy of the Pullar family.)

Brothers and avid baseball players John (left) and William Gastka (pictured with an unidentified woman) proudly donned their baseball uniforms in the 1930s. Baseball was a very popular sport around New Windsor, with various businesses and towns sponsoring teams. New Windsor had had a baseball team since the mid-1800s, when Newburgh and New Windsor were stark rivals. (Courtesy of Irene Pullar.)

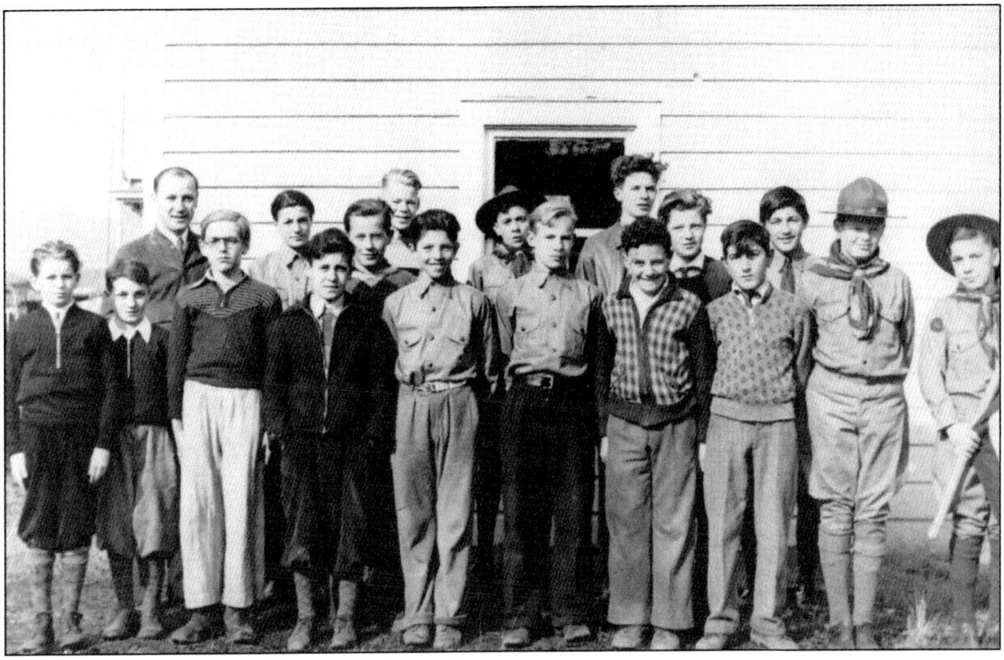

The first New Windsor Scout Troop 17 was formed in 1937. Pictured are, from left to right, (first row) Charles Edge, Thomas Yannone, Howard Bowen, Ernest Spignardo, James Ruscitti, Chester Sladeski, Frank Pennacehio, William Petro, Corby Simonson, and Joseph Antonelli; (second row) Scoutmaster and New Windsor School principal Robert Zachary, Gus Yannone, Clem Hacunda, Matthew Malensky, Archie Antonelli, Richard Simonson, Robert Maines, and John Petro. The Quassaick Fire Engine Company (now New Windsor Fire Department, Inc.) applied for a charter for Boy Scout Troop 17 in November 1941. When it was awarded March 31, 1943, John V. Lahey and Archie Antonelli became Scoutmaster and assistant Scoutmaster, respectively. Around 1942, the first Boy Scout cabin was built on property donated by Frank Orzechowski, who also helped with labor, materials, and equipment. (Both, courtesy of John T. Babcock Sr.)

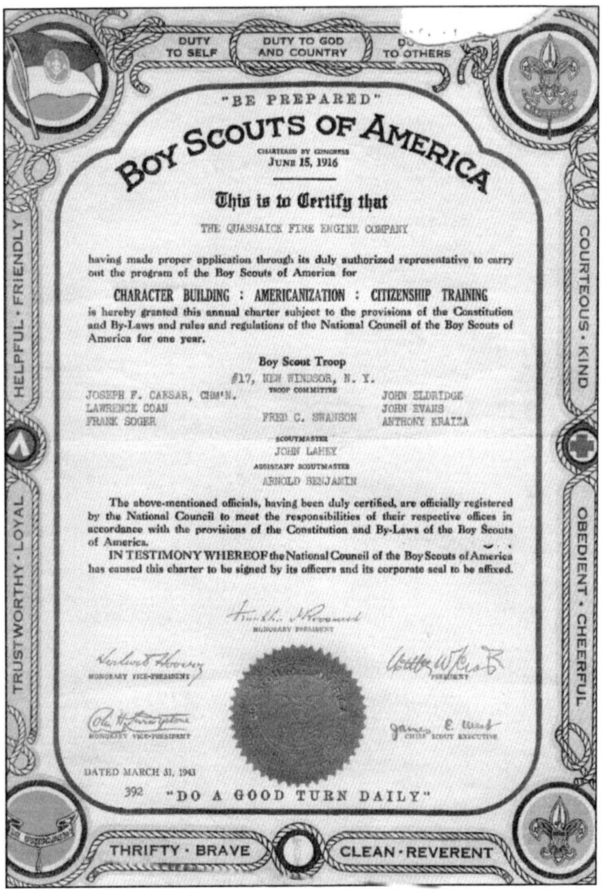

DUTY TO SELF — DUTY TO GOD AND COUNTRY — DU[TY] TO OTHERS

"BE PREPARED"

BOY SCOUTS OF AMERICA

CHARTERED BY CONGRESS
JUNE 15, 1916

This is to Certify that

THE QUASSAICK FIRE ENGINE COMPANY

having made proper application through its duly authorized representative to carry out the program of the Boy Scouts of America for

CHARACTER BUILDING : AMERICANIZATION : CITIZENSHIP TRAINING

is hereby granted this annual charter subject to the provisions of the Constitution and By-Laws and rules and regulations of the National Council of the Boy Scouts of America for one year.

Boy Scout Troop
#17, NEW WINDSOR, N. Y.

TROOP COMMITTEE

JOSEPH F. CAESAR, CHM'N.
LAWRENCE COAN
FRANK SOGER
FRED C. SWANSON
JOHN ELDRIDGE
JOHN EVANS
ANTHONY KRAIZA

SCOUTMASTER
JOHN LAHEY

ASSISTANT SCOUTMASTER
ARNOLD BENJAMIN

The above-mentioned officials, having been duly certified, are officially registered by the National Council to meet the responsibilities of their respective offices in accordance with the provisions of the Constitution and By-Laws of the Boy Scouts of America.

IN TESTIMONY WHEREOF the National Council of the Boy Scouts of America has caused this charter to be signed by its officers and its corporate seal to be affixed.

HONORARY PRESIDENT

HONORARY VICE-PRESIDENT — PRESIDENT

HONORARY VICE-PRESIDENT — CHIEF SCOUT EXECUTIVE

DATED MARCH 31, 1943

392 "DO A GOOD TURN DAILY"

HELPFUL · FRIENDLY — COURTEOUS · KIND — TRUSTWORTHY · LOYAL — OBEDIENT · CHEERFUL — THRIFTY · BRAVE — CLEAN · REVERENT

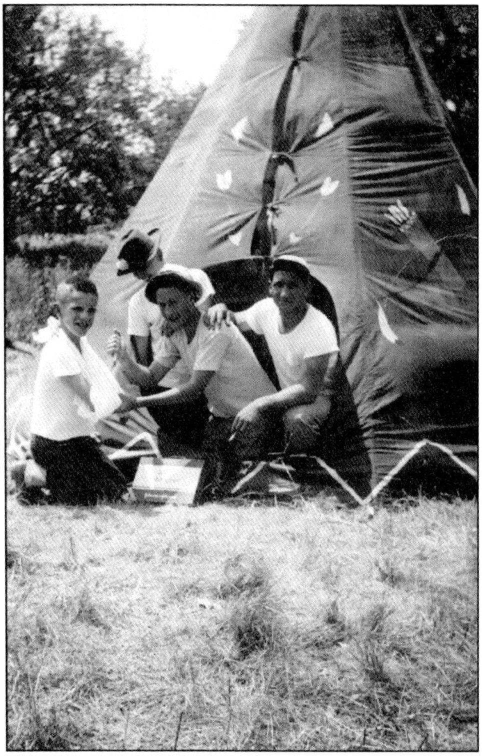

Shown at the 1952 camporee are, from left to right, Scouts Daniel Reilly, unidentified, William Laddick, and assistant Scoutmaster James Petro. They are pictured in front of the award-winning teepee made by James's brother John Petro and John's wife, Martha, at their Myrtle Avenue home in Clancyville. Martha did all the sewing of the canvas, and the Scout troop waterproofed it. In addition to their time, the Petros donated all the material. (Courtesy of Edward Stent Jr.)

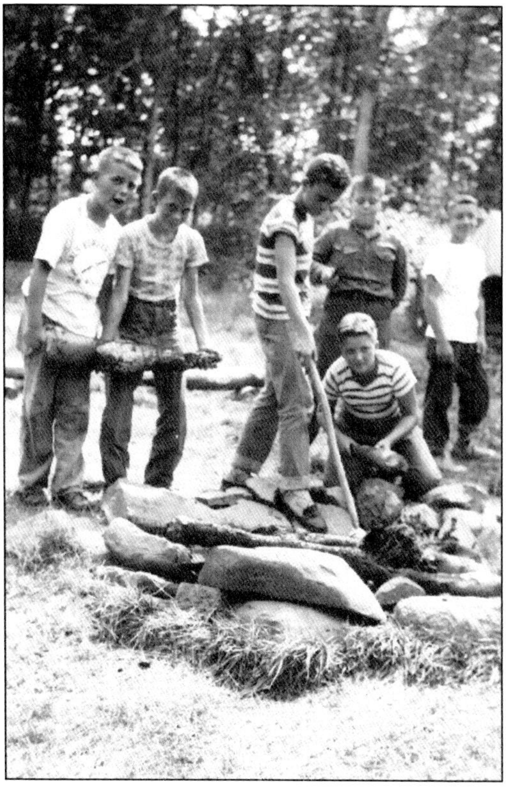

Boy Scout Troop 17 members learn how to safely build campfires at Beech Mountain Boy Scout Camp in Livingston Manor. Pictured here are, from left to right, Edward C. Stent Jr., Jerome Miller, John Scott, Matthew Herbison, Richard Tomashevski (crouching), and Lawrence Millard as they prepare for that night's bonfire lighting. The fireplace is designed so that it will contain the flames and prevent them from spreading into the woods. (Courtesy of Edward Stent Jr.)

The Boy Scout Troop 17 sign was built by Scouts with help from John Petro. Among those pictured here are Edward Coykendall, Michael Bucciarelli, Daniel Reilly, John Versusky Jr., John Scott, Robert Radulski, Edward Sloboda, Kirk McQuiston, John Dabroski, John Cavanaugh, Robert Lewis, Edward Babcock, Peter Ralph, John Petro, Edward Stent Jr., James Petro, William Laddick, Edward McDaniels, and James Pullar. The sign won the Horn of High Hiker award. (Courtesy of Edward Stent Jr.)

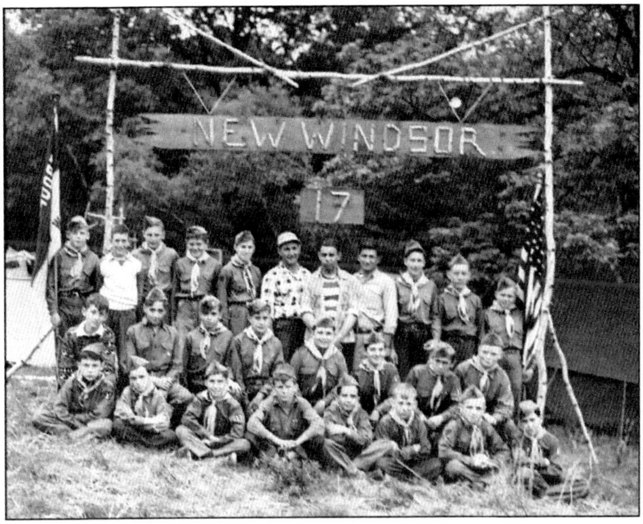

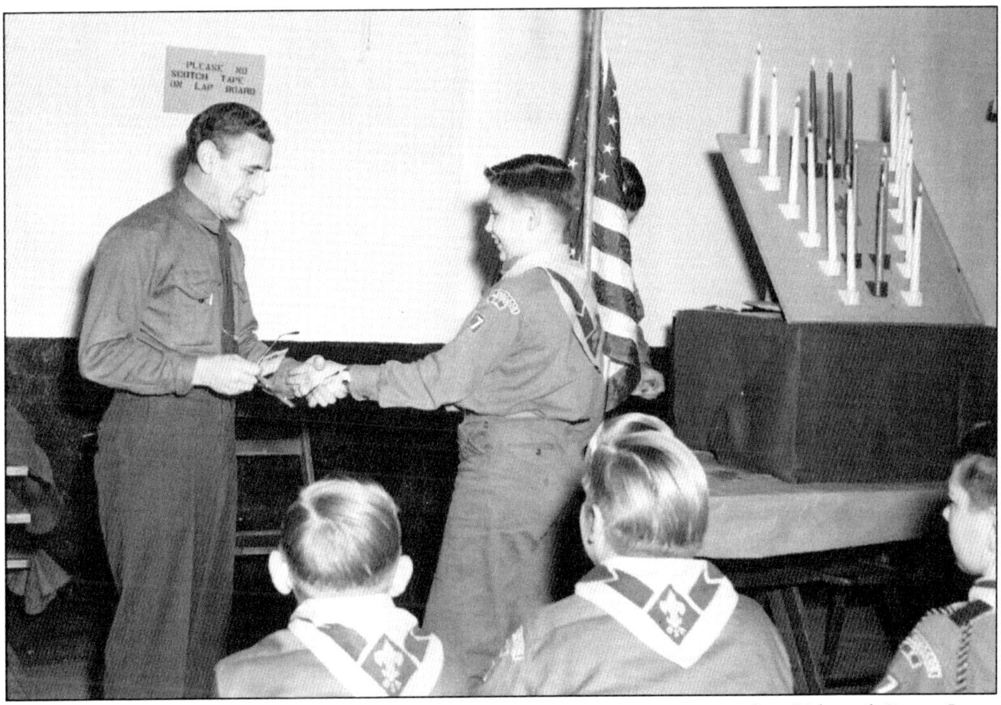

Boy Scout neighborhood commissioner Harry Katz presents an award to Edward Stent Jr. at Troop 17's 1956 Court of Honor. The Court of Honor, one of Scouting's most formal events, is a public ceremony recognizing achievement while providing other Scouts incentive to advance. The lighting of symbolically colored candles starts with gold, signifying Scouts' honor. (Courtesy of Edward Stent Jr.)

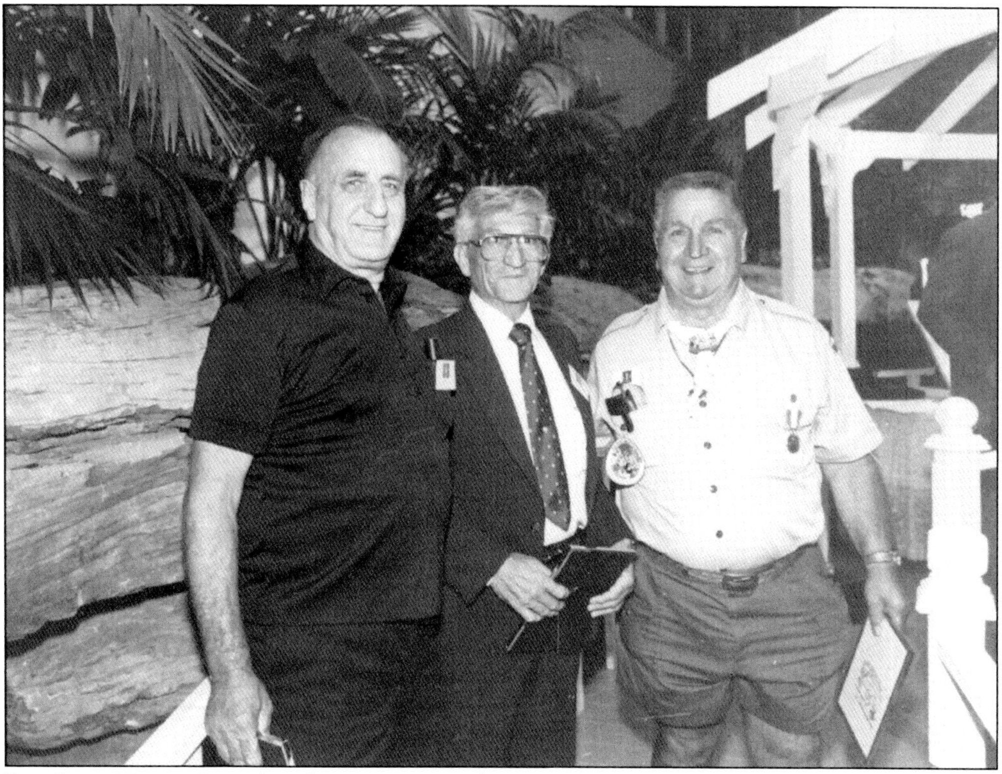

Boy Scout Troop 17 produced many Scouts who moved on to great success in their lives. They were fortunate to enjoy the support of many throughout the community. Pictured in 1993 at the troop's 50th-anniversary celebration are Frederick Thompson (left), James Petro (center), and Alfred Crudele. (Courtesy of John T. Babcock.)

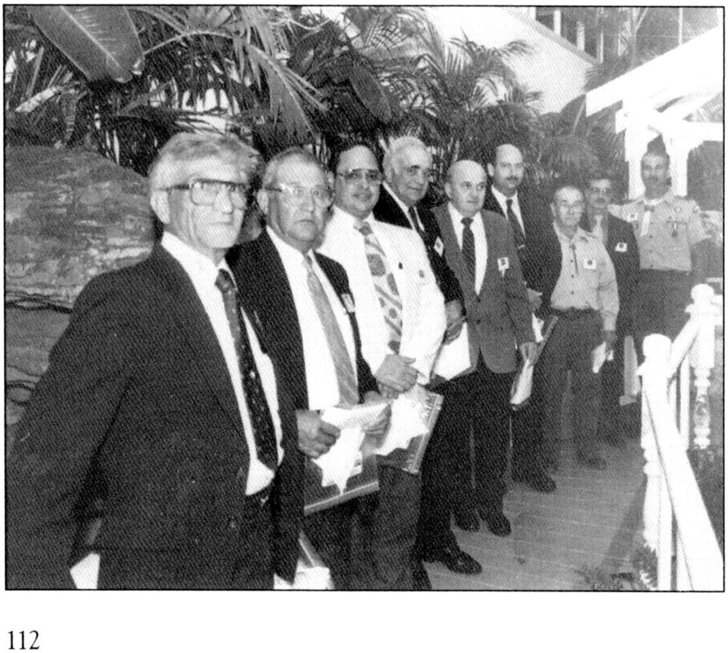

The New Windsor Fire Department had sponsored Boy Scout Troop 17 for 50 years as of September 1993. Attending the celebration in support of the Scouts are, from left to right, James Petro, John Petro, Michael Lugg, Archie Antonelli, William Babcock, unidentified, Richard McGrath, unidentified, and James Green. (Courtesy of John T. Babcock Sr.)

Eight

Over the Years

People moved into the area from cities, seeking life in the suburbs and countryside. At the time, trains and cars opened the door to expansion. A number of affluent people with businesses in New York City built mansions, many of which became resorts, bed-and-breakfasts, or schools, while others remained occupied by families. A few were sold, torn down, or lost to fire, at times becoming the footprints for newer buildings.

As the political world also evolved, the need to serve the country grew. Throughout the years, locals went off to serve in different branches of the military, and in times of peace, newly built homes filled with families that became involved in various aspects of the community. They went to church, attended schools, joined the firehouse, and participated in a number of other activities.

The New Windsor Police Department, which started in 1763 as a constabulary, is now a full-time public-service agency providing 24-hour law-enforcement coverage and emergency dispatching services. The department's shoulder patch contains depictions of historical events of the past, representing the principles and patriotism that are consistent with life in New Windsor.

Archie Stewart's field, originally used for growing crops, became an airport where West Point cadets were trained as pilots. It played a strategic military role and later evolved into an international airport.

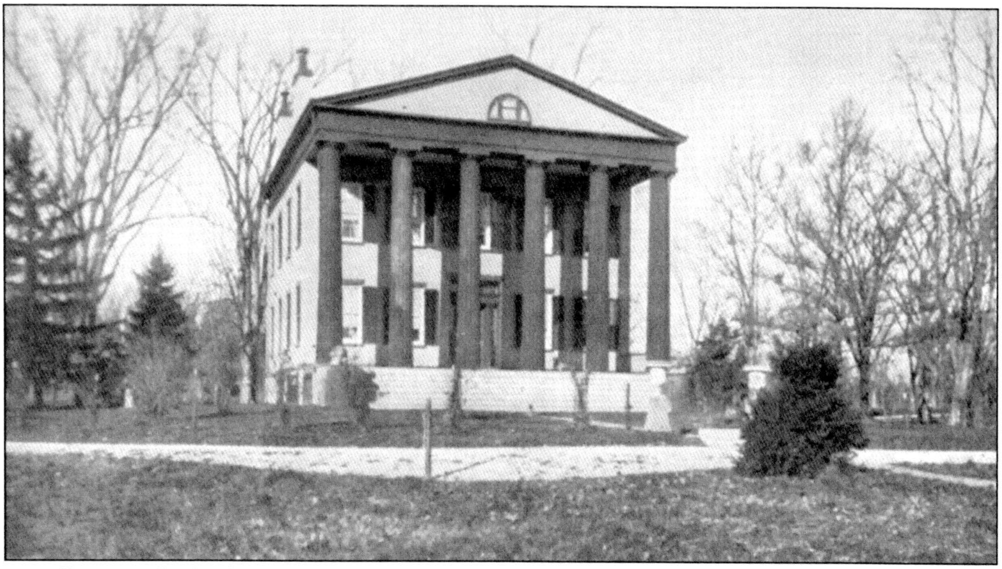

Woodburn Hall, also known as the Cooper-Hewitt Mansion, was built in 1840 at Plum Point for the Charles B. Miller family. During the 1890s, Miller kept a wolf named Bob, 96 Great Danes, a boar named Socrates, and two alligators named Jack and Jill that shared a fountain with a statue of the Greek god Hermes. Lucy Cooper-Hewitt bought the mansion in 1912. (Courtesy of the Dabroski family.)

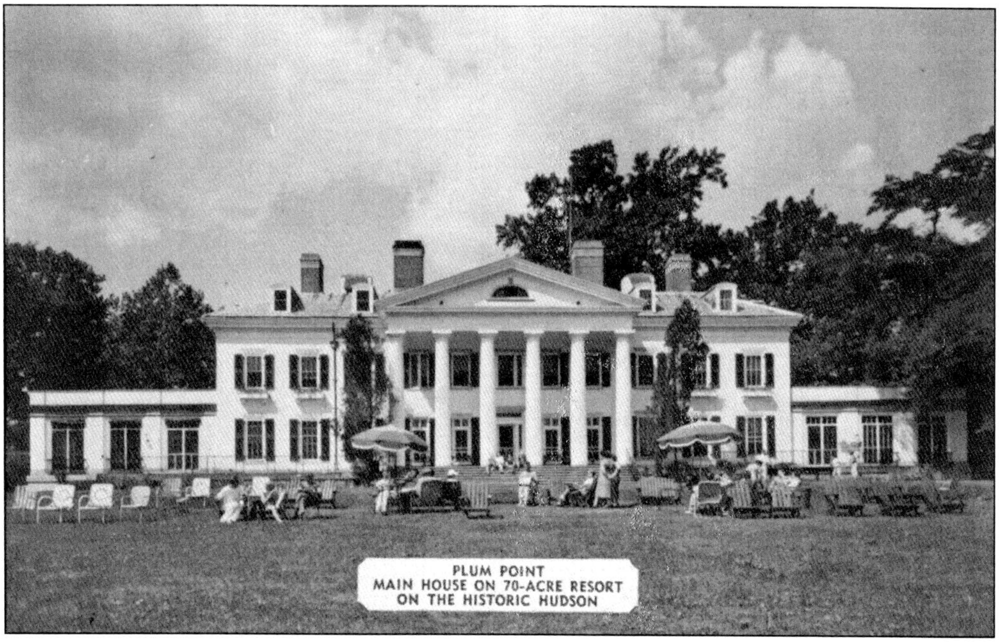

The Cooper-Hewitt Mansion was later converted into a resort called Plum Point. Pictured here around 1950, the resort overlooked the Hudson River and drew guests from New York City. There were rose gardens and a swimming pool, and the exquisite interior boasted a marble staircase. The building was sold to a boys' school, Oakwood Academy, in the early 1960s and subsequently deteriorated. (Courtesy of the Whitehill Collection.)

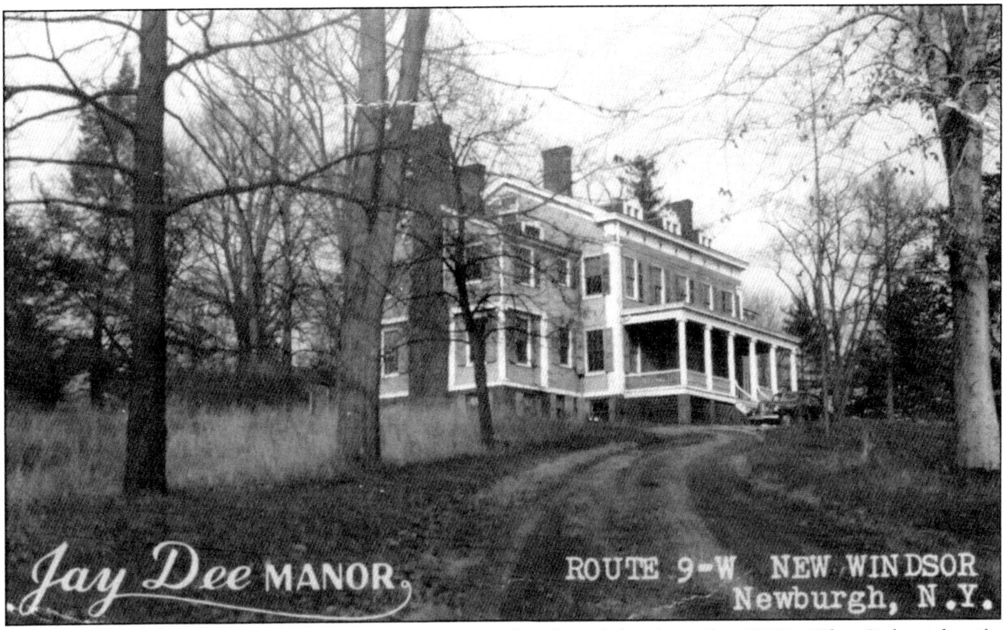

Jay Dee Manor on Route 9W was a most majestic landmark back in the 1940s. The Coloni family took possession of the property years ago and operated it as a funeral home, providing quality services to the community while maintaining the elegance of this mansion overlooking the Hudson River valley. Today, the mansion is closed and for sale. (Courtesy of the Whitehill Collection.)

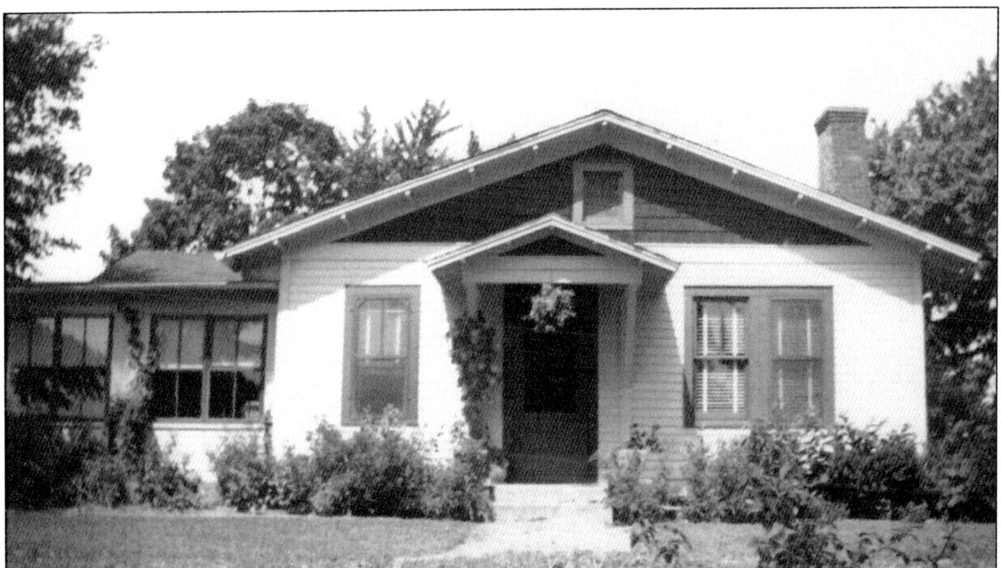

This house at 194 Quassaick Avenue, now Kayleen Drive, belongs to James Nugent. It was built in 1923 on the footprint of the J. Abner Harper (of *Harper's Bazaar Magazine*) mansion. The home, known as Ingleside, had burned down around the turn of the century. (Courtesy of Catherine Molloy Nugent.)

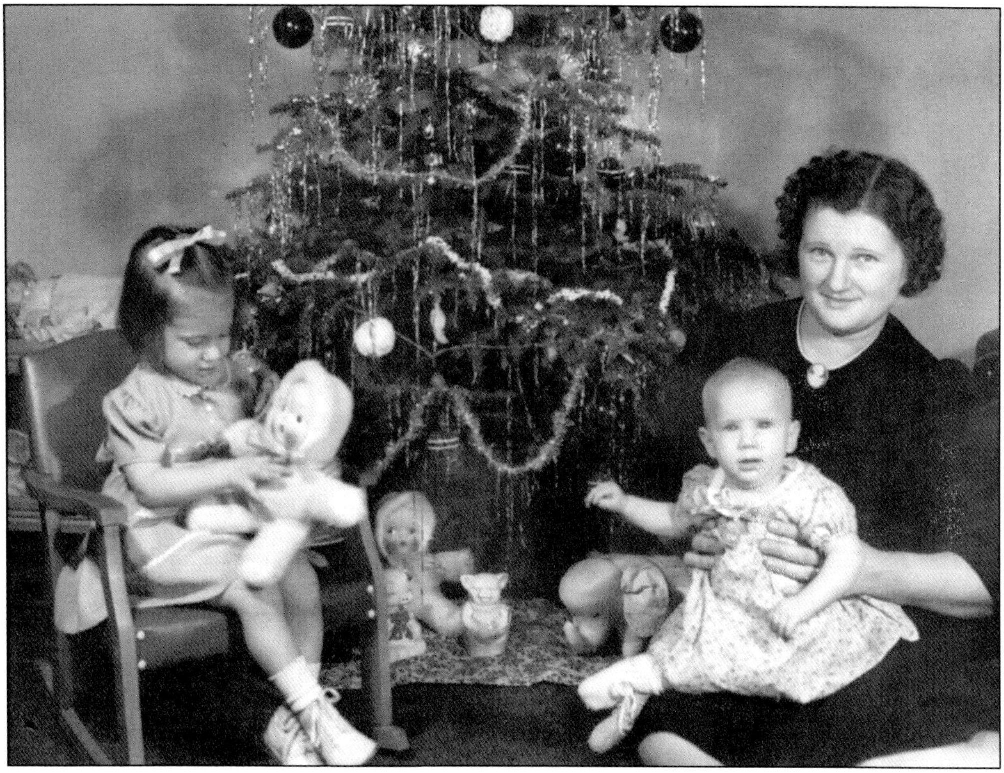

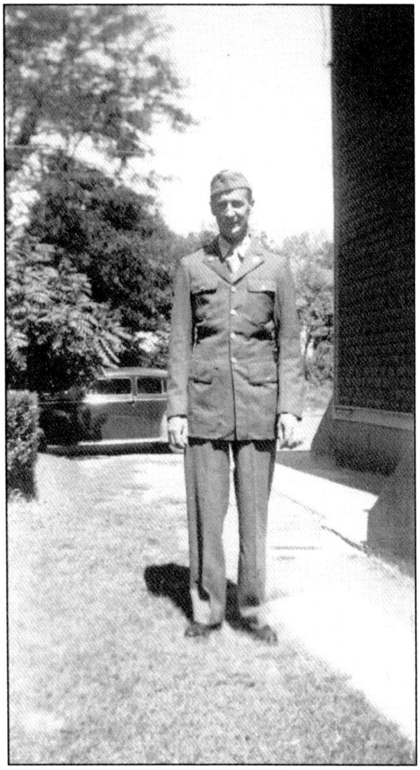

Josephine Raz Swanson is pictured on Christmas Day 1944 with daughters Joanne, age two, and Susan, age six months. The girls' father, Fred C. Swanson Jr., was not at home that Christmas and had been in basic training with the Army when Susan was born. It was an experience shared by many local families at that time. (Courtesy of Joanne Swanson Versusky.)

Fred C. Swanson Jr., seen here in uniform in 1944, fought in the Battle of the Bulge, an engagement in which the German army launched a counteroffensive with the intention of turning the tide of the war in Hitler's favor. Losses were high on both sides, but freedom won over tyranny, and Swanson survived to return to his family. (Courtesy of Joanne Swanson Versusky.)

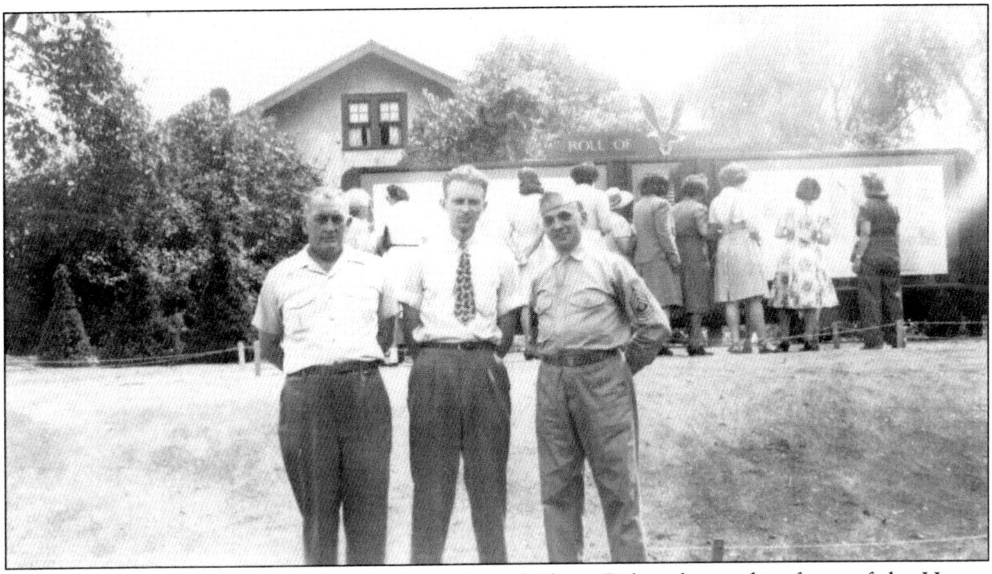

Harold Jett Sr. (right), Harold Jett Jr. (center), and Elmer Babcock stand in front of the Honor Roll Memorial at the corner of Routes 9W and 94 on Memorial Day, May 30, 1944. Annual services are still held at this site to honor veterans who served their country. (Courtesy of the Babcock family.)

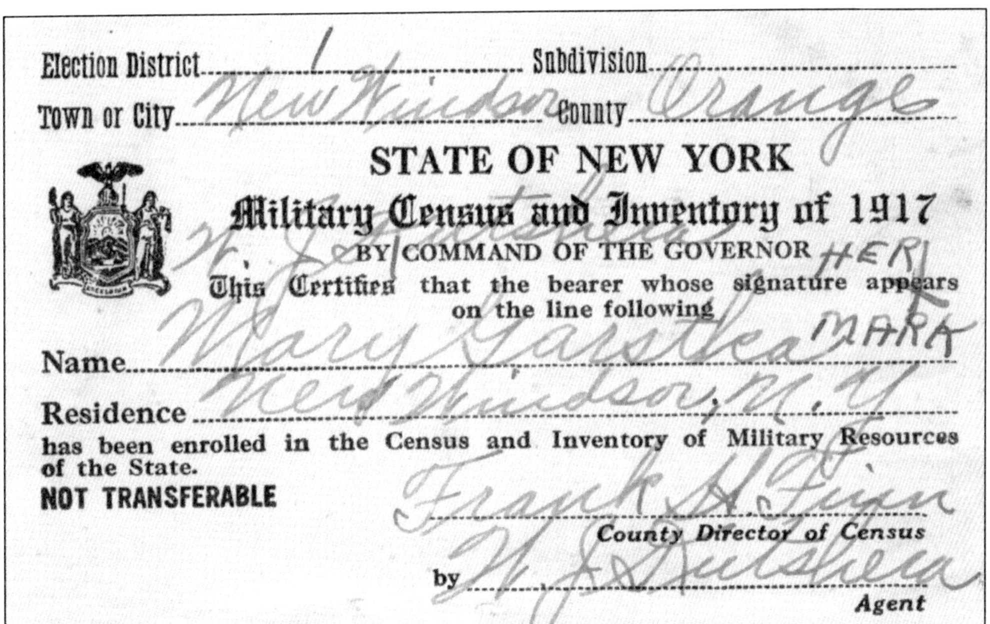

Election District 1 Subdivision

Town or City New Windsor County Orange

STATE OF NEW YORK

Military Census and Inventory of 1917

BY COMMAND OF THE GOVERNOR

This Certifies that the bearer whose signature appears on the line following

HER MARK

Name Mary Gastka

Residence New Windsor, N.Y.

has been enrolled in the Census and Inventory of Military Resources of the State.

NOT TRANSFERABLE

County Director of Census

by

Agent

In 1916 and 1917, New York governor Charles Whitman felt that the country would not be able to avoid active participation in a world war and should begin preparations. A census was taken to determine the number of people who were at the government's disposal. This 1917 card was for Mary Gastka, who could not write and marked her name with an X. (Courtesy of Irene Pullar.)

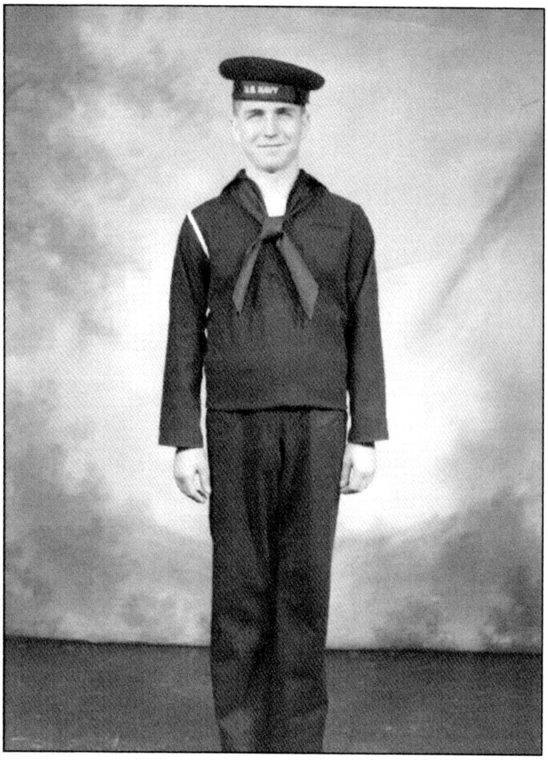

Alfred T. Crudele, born in 1924 to Michael and Rose Cimmorelli Crudele, was a Navy veteran of World War II, achieving the rank of signalman second class. He retired from IBM and was greatly respected for his support of and work with the New Windsor Boy Scout Troop 17. (Courtesy of the Crudele family.)

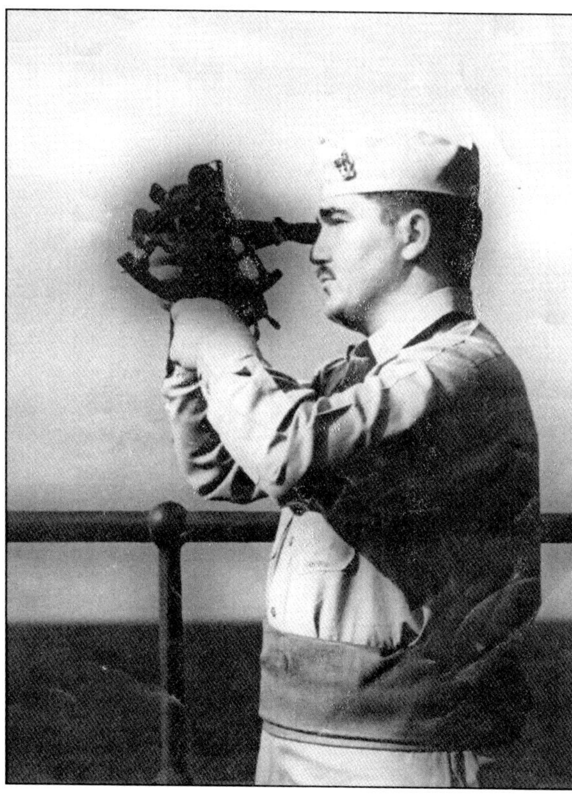

New Windsor native Arthur Crudele was born on March 9, 1918, and passed in 1984. He was another son of Michael and Rose Cimorelli Crudele and a career Navy serviceman. He was predeceased by three sisters—Dora, Olga, and Mary—and two brothers—Michael and Anthony. (Courtesy of the Crudele family.)

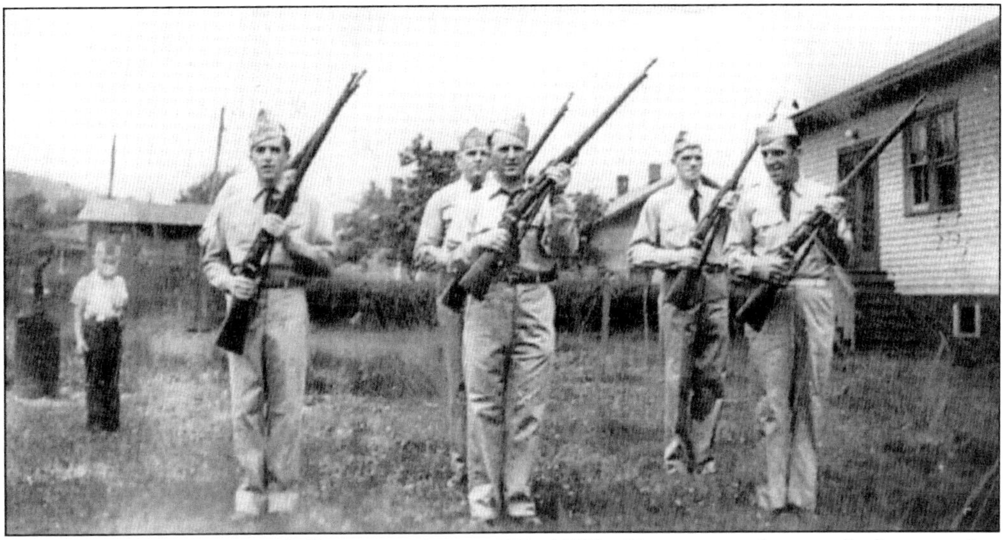

New Windsor had its own drill team made up of World War II veterans who marched in parades. Parades became a popular family outing, and these proud veterans, pictured in the late 1940s or early 1950s, are practicing for just such an event by Malinowski's Hall on Lawrence Avenue. They are, from left to right, (first row) John Mangi, unidentified, and Frank Zgrodek, (second row) unidentified, John Duda, and Charles Zgrodek. (Courtesy of Charles Zgrodek.)

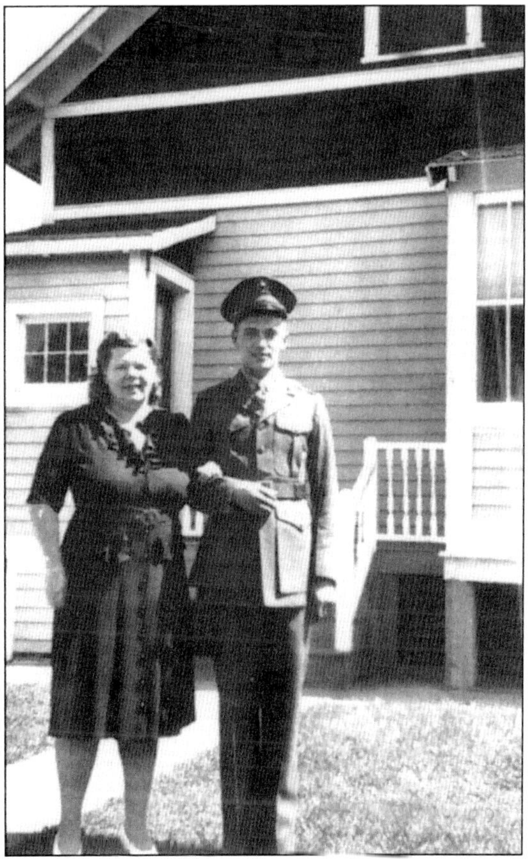

Marion Babcock stands with her son Robert, who is donning his military uniform, in William Weygant's yard on August 26, 1944. Robert was one of many members of the family to serve his country. (Courtesy of the Babcock family.)

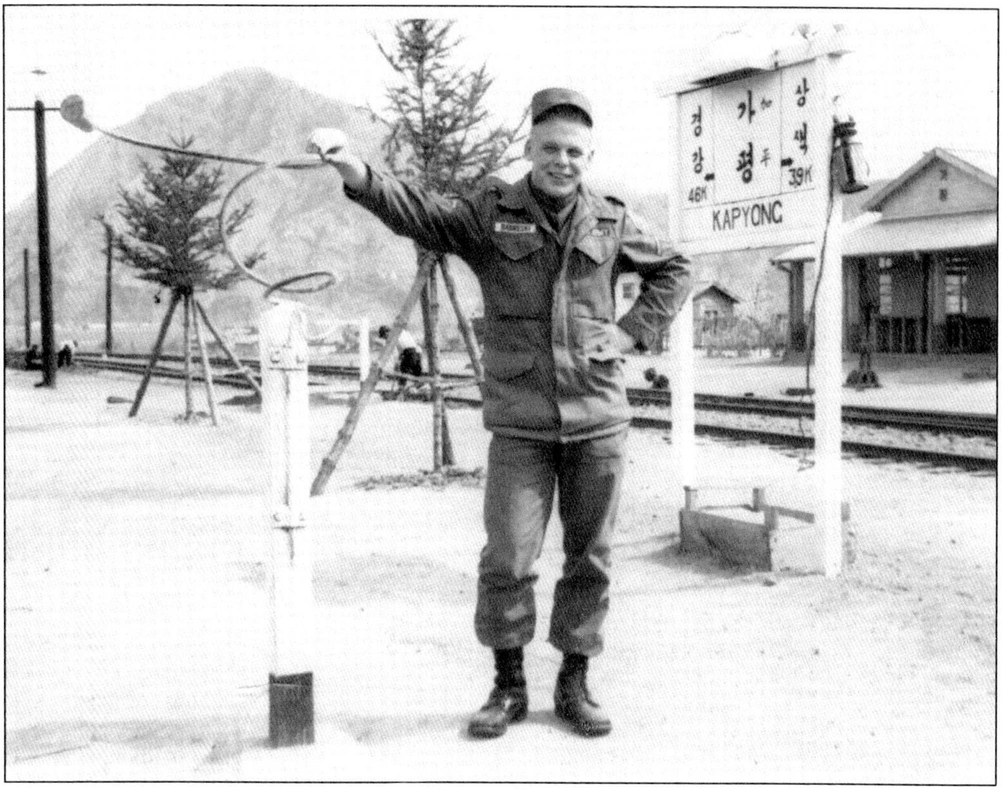

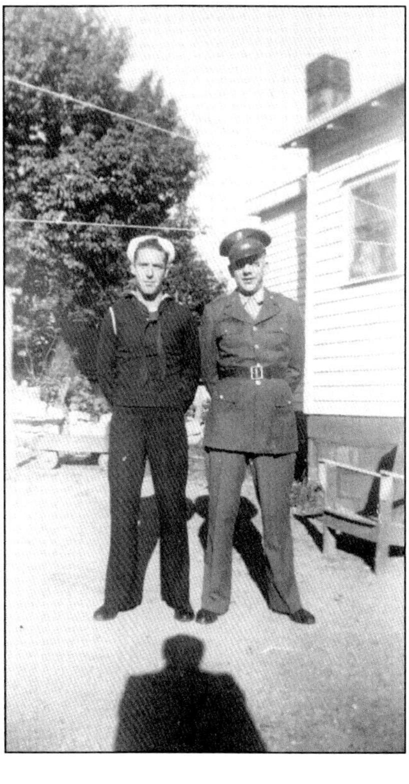

In April 1960, 19-year-old William Dabroski, like so many other young New Windsor men, was serving with the US Army in Korea. Describing this photograph, he wrote home, "A picture of me waiting to get mail off the train and guard it. See how bare the mountains are? That's just how Korea looks like all over." (Courtesy of the Dabroski family.)

Harold Connelly (left) and his brother-in-law, John Dabroski, were proud veterans of the Navy and Army, respectively. Here, they stand together at Rose Zamenick's house on Walsh Avenue in 1940. Many Clancyville/Ducktown men served their country in World War II. (Courtesy of the Dabroski family.)

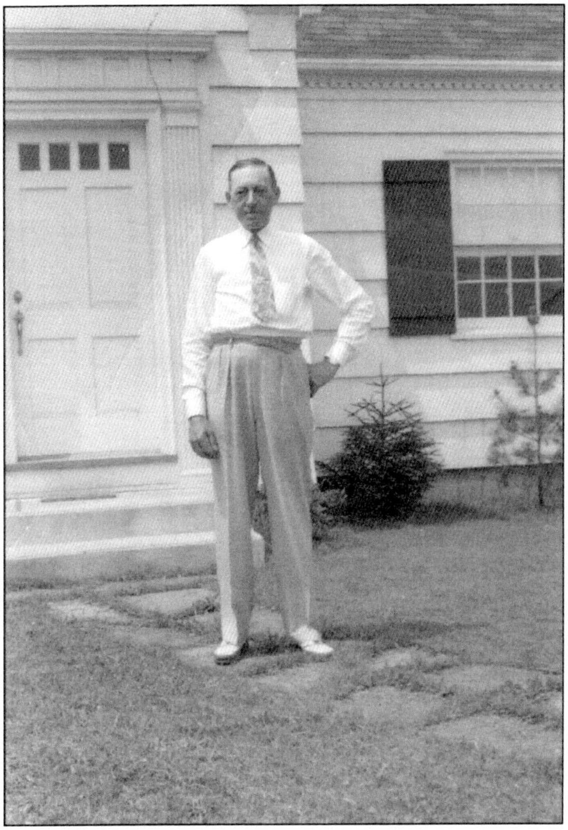

At right, Simon Gold, a 1940s real estate broker, stands before one of the Lacey Field model homes. Below, there were four different models from which to choose. The property was originally a part of the Lucas Estate. Lucas also owned the Hudson Valley Concrete Company. As veterans returned from World War II and times became better, quality housing was in demand. In earlier times, the Lacey Field site had been an airstrip where locals could take a plane ride in a Ford Tri-motor nicknamed "The Tin Goose." (Both, courtesy of the Historical Society of Newburgh Bay and the Highlands.)

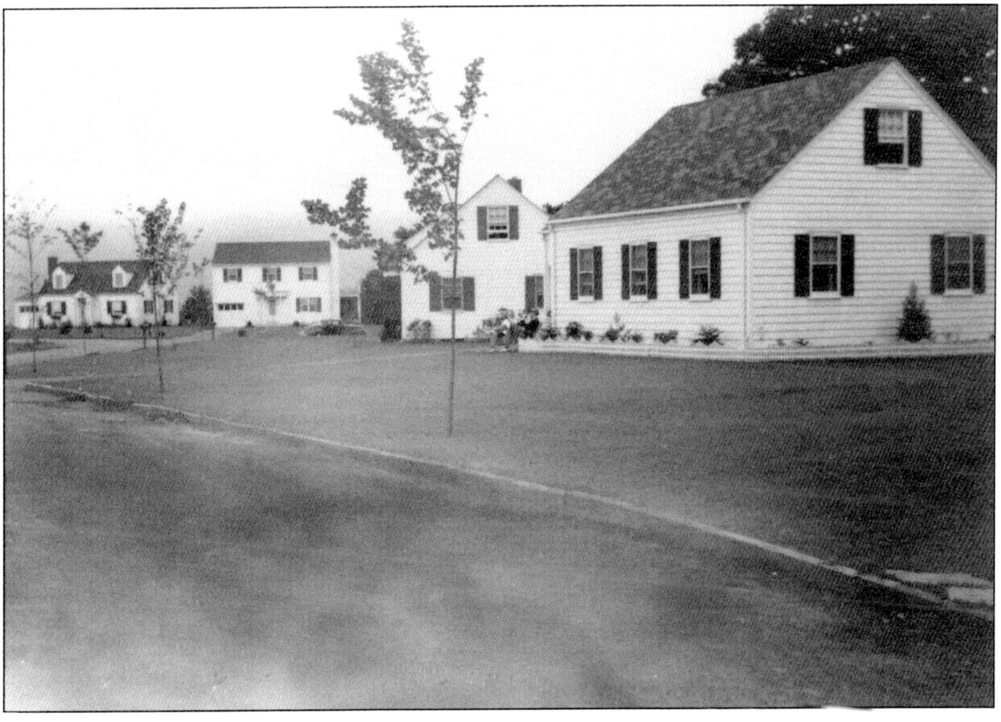

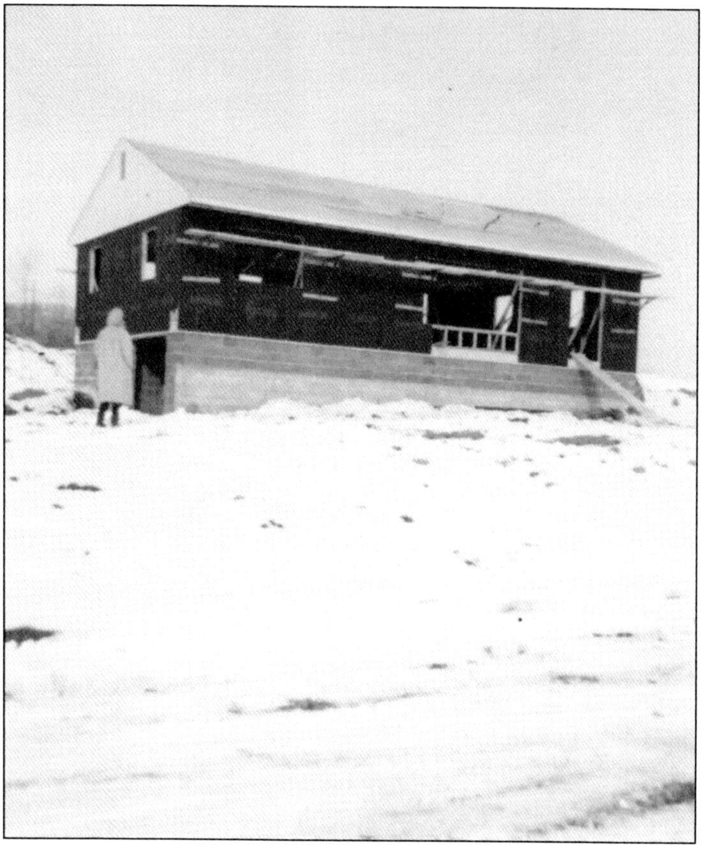

In 1952, brothers D. Bruce and Harvey B. Schoonmaker formed a partnership for the purpose of building homes. Using their own homes as models and a pickup truck as their office, they found a formula for success. The pair developed the 40-foot, basic-model rancher, which accounted for a substantial portion of their business, and built four furnished models on Route 94 in New Windsor. Their company was responsible for a large number of homes built between New Windsor and Vails Gate. Pictured here are examples of the basic style of house, both under construction and then finished. (Both, courtesy of the Pullar family.)

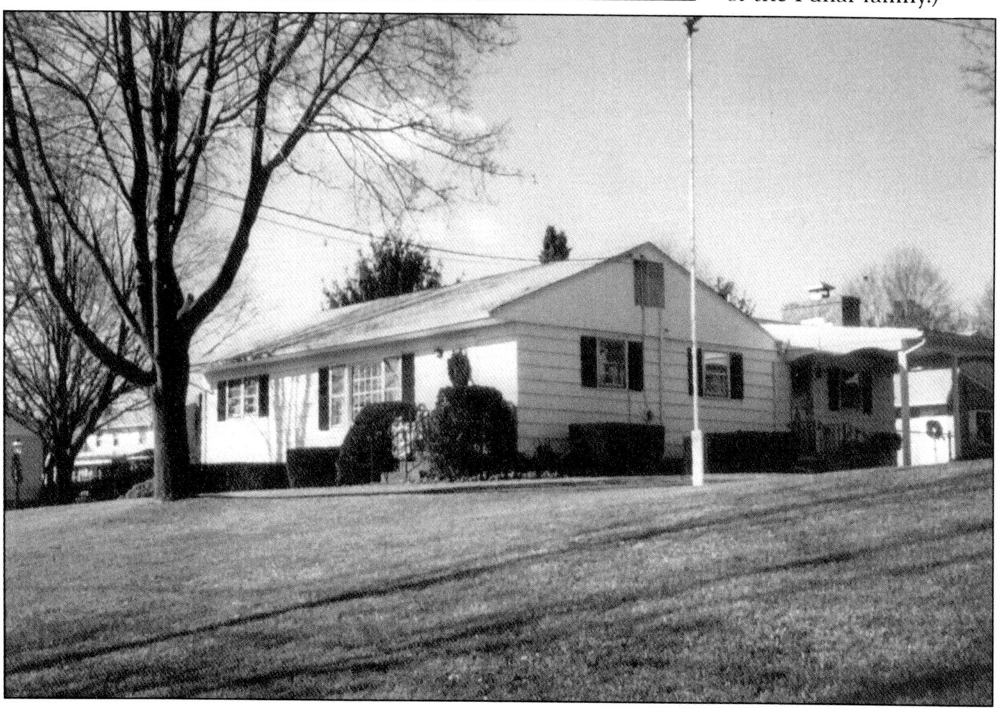

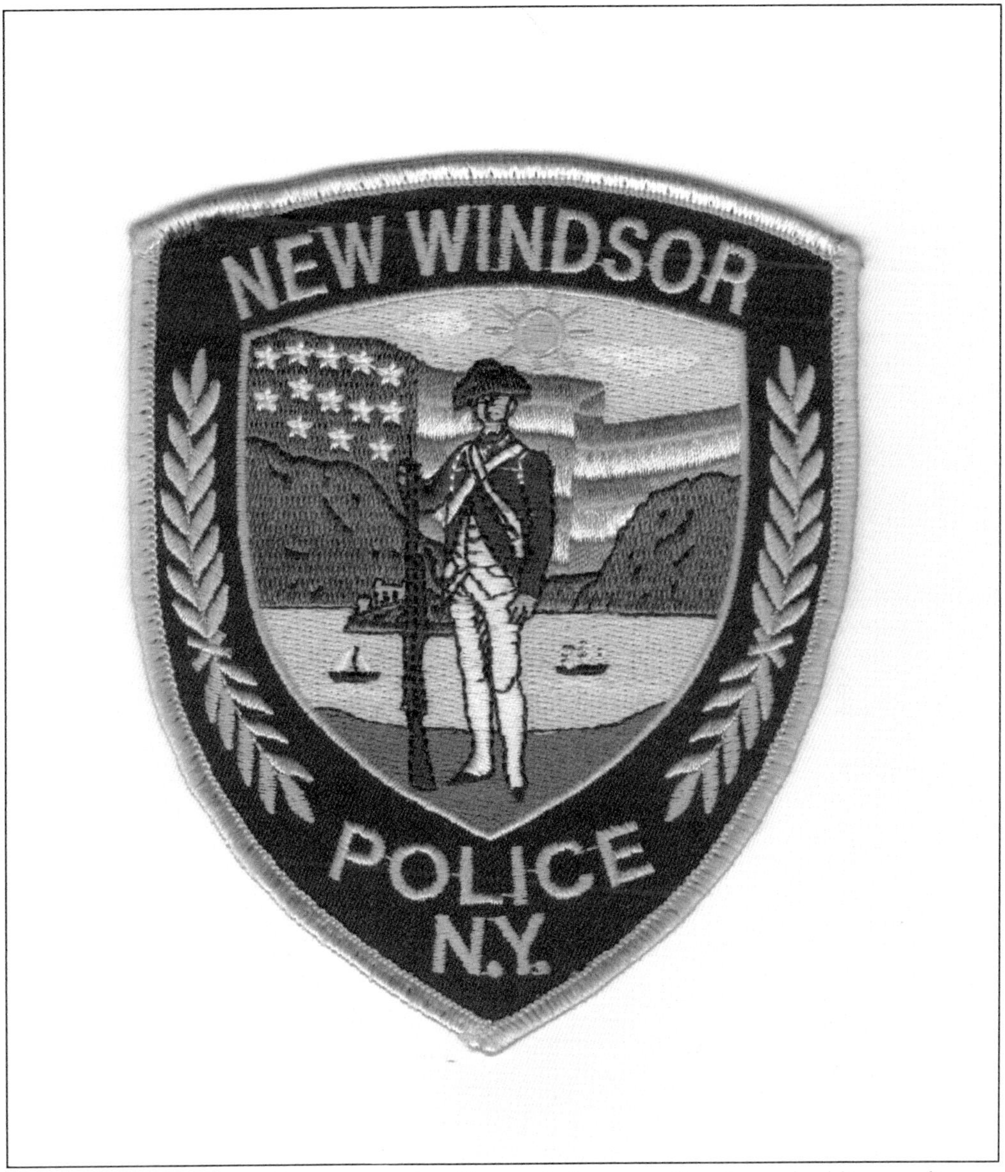

The New Windsor Police Department shoulder patch features a Continental soldier standing on the Hudson River shoreline with Breakneck Mountain on the left and Storm King Mountain on the right. The American flag, with its 13 stars representing the original colonies, is tucked behind the mountains. The rising sun represents freedom and the birth of a new nation, and the ships traversing the bay represent exploration and commerce. The shoulder patch embodies historical themes to include freedom, new democracy, exploration, commerce, pride, and peace. The Town of New Windsor Police Department began in 1763, shortly after the French and Indian War. In 1783, the cantonment was the site of a speech by George Washington. His words defined core values that set the foundation for the mission and purpose of the Town of New Windsor Police Department that continues to this day. (Courtesy of the Town of New Windsor Police Department.)

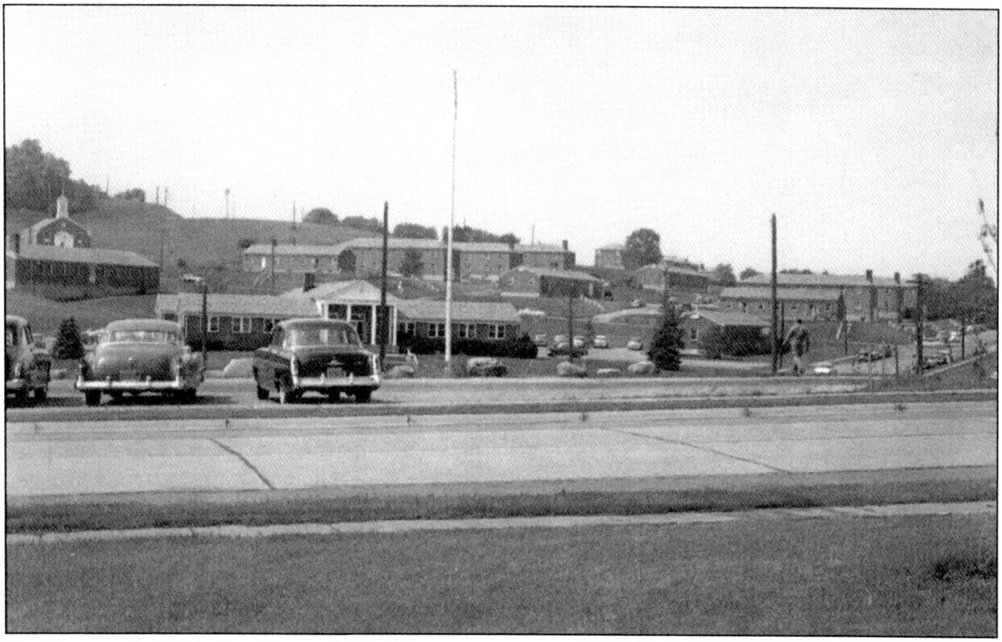

On January 1, 1948, the 21st and 22nd Reconnaissance Squadrons were activated at Stewart Air Force Base. Personnel and aircraft such as the RF-51D Mustangs were assigned. The group trained pilots and reserve airmen in fighter techniques, medium bombardment, and aerial reconnaissance. The 1970 drawdown of the renamed Aerospace Defense Command site resulted in civilian control once again. Visible in this image are the headquarters, barracks, and base chapel. (Courtesy of the Whitehill Collection.)

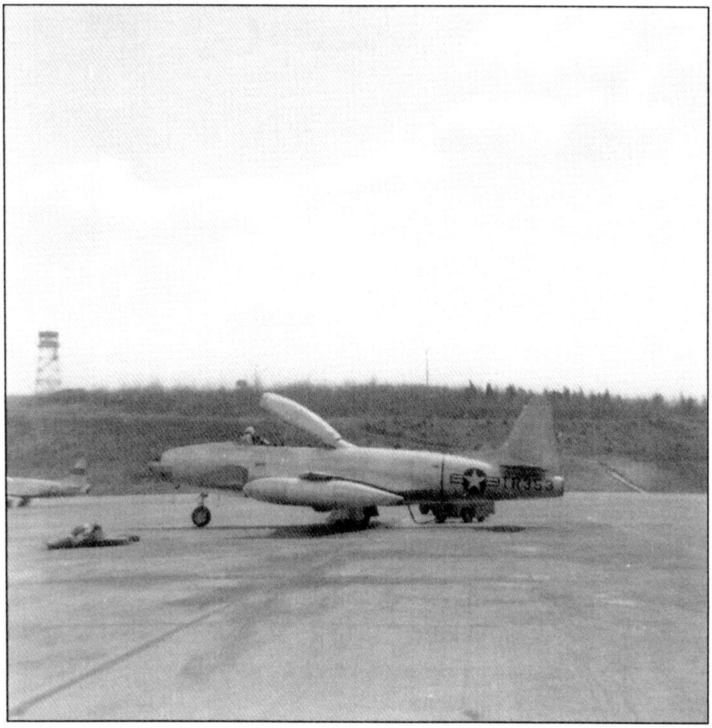

In 1953, the sights and sounds of planes like the Lockheed T-33, a training version of the P-80 Shooting Star, were commonplace in New Windsor. Stewart Air Force Base, with a main runway measuring 11,817 feet in length, was the most important East Coast command headquarters for the US Army Defense Region until 1972. (Courtesy of the Pullar family.)

Because of the proximity to the US Military Academy, Air Force One often landed at Stewart Field Air Force Base carrying passengers destined for West Point graduations or other important Hudson Valley events. Here, Pres. Dwight D. Eisenhower has landed at Stewart Field Air Force Base to speak at the academy's graduation ceremony in June 1960. (Courtesy of Marilyn Hearns.)

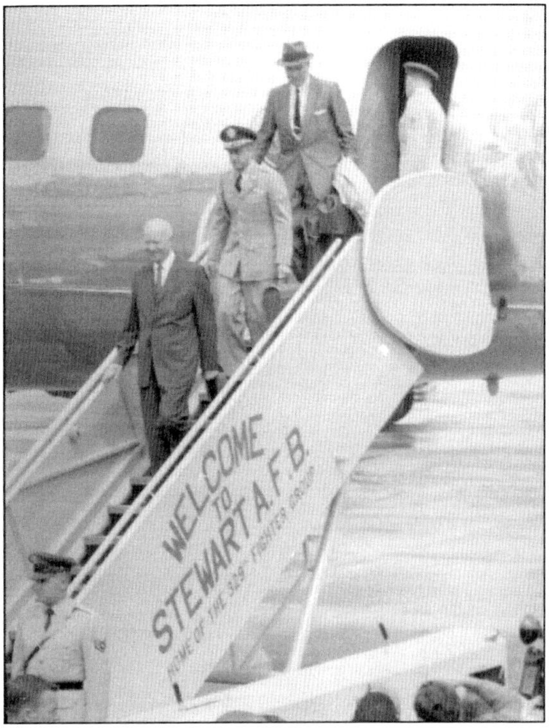

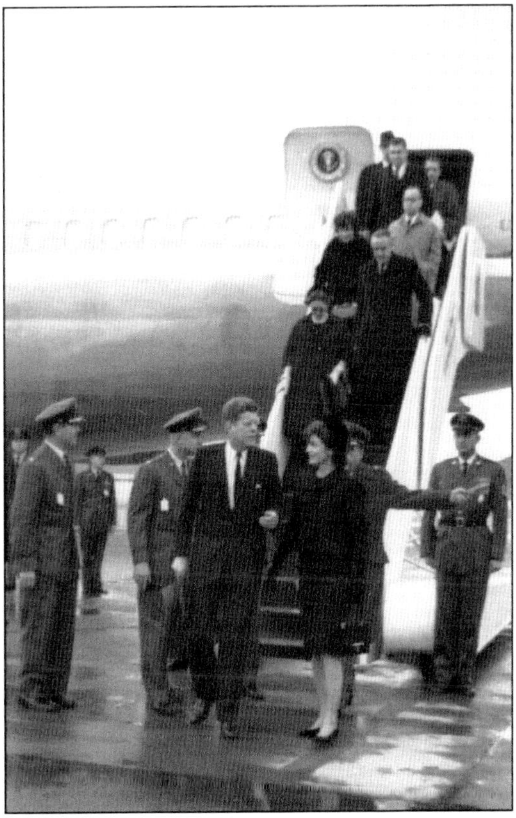

After Eleanor Roosevelt, the longest-serving first lady of the United States, died in November 1962, Pres. John F. Kennedy and First Lady Jacqueline Kennedy (forefront) land at Stewart Field Air Force Base on Air Force One to attend her funeral. Accompanying the Kennedys, and seen descending the ramp about halfway down on the right, is the former (48th) governor of New York, diplomat, and businessman W. Averell Harriman. (Courtesy of Marilyn Hearns.)

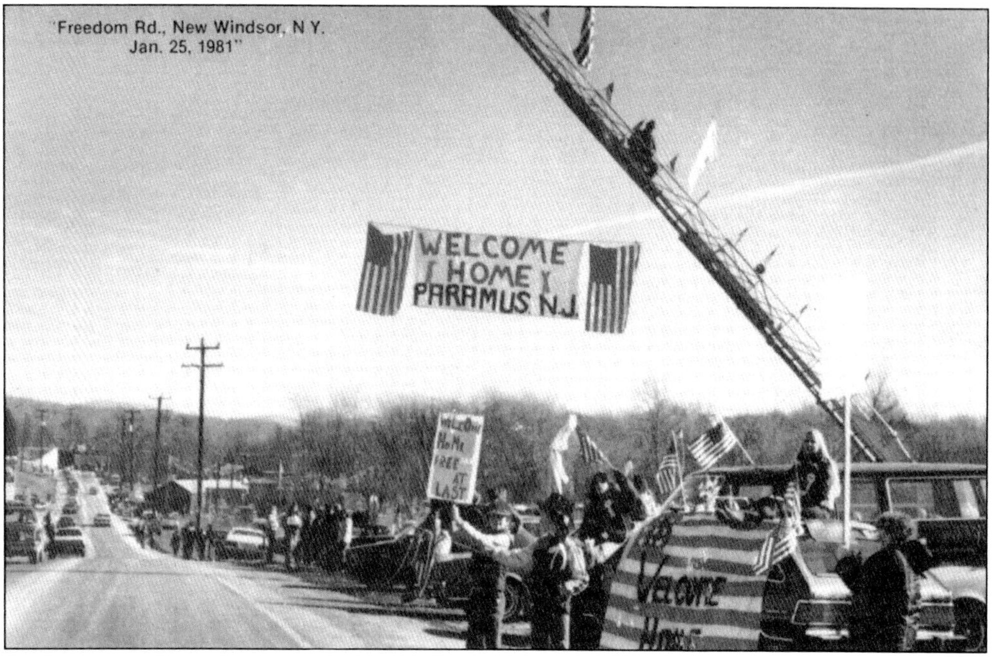

The Iran Hostage Crisis began on November 4, 1979, when hundreds of militant Islamic students broke into the US embassy in Tehran and took 52 occupants hostage. When the presidency passed from Jimmy Carter to Ronald Reagan on January 20, 1981, they were released. The hostages flew into Stewart International Airport and were greeted by some 200,000 loyal patriots who had lined up along Freedom Road to welcome them home. (Courtesy of the Dabroski family.)

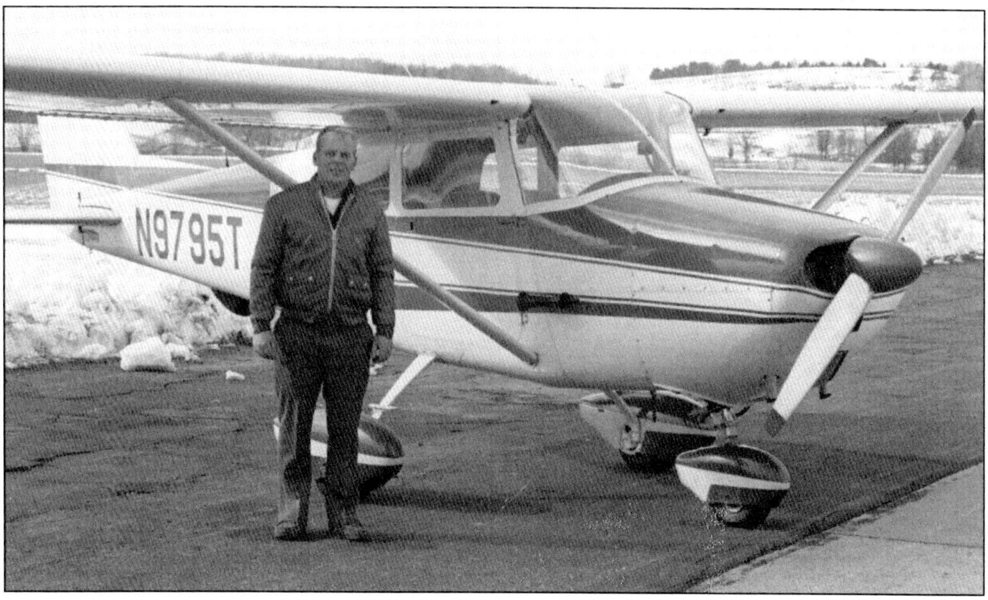

One of six children of John and Lillian Werner Dabroski, William Dabroski was born at his family's 66 Cedar Avenue home. An Army veteran, Dabroski enjoyed flying his 1960 172 Cessna airplane, which was based at Stewart Airport. He and his wife, Barbara Stotesbury Dabroski—both licensed pilots—and their two sons, William Jr. and Michael, flew many hours around the beautiful Hudson Valley area and as well as in Florida. (Courtesy of the Dabroski family.)

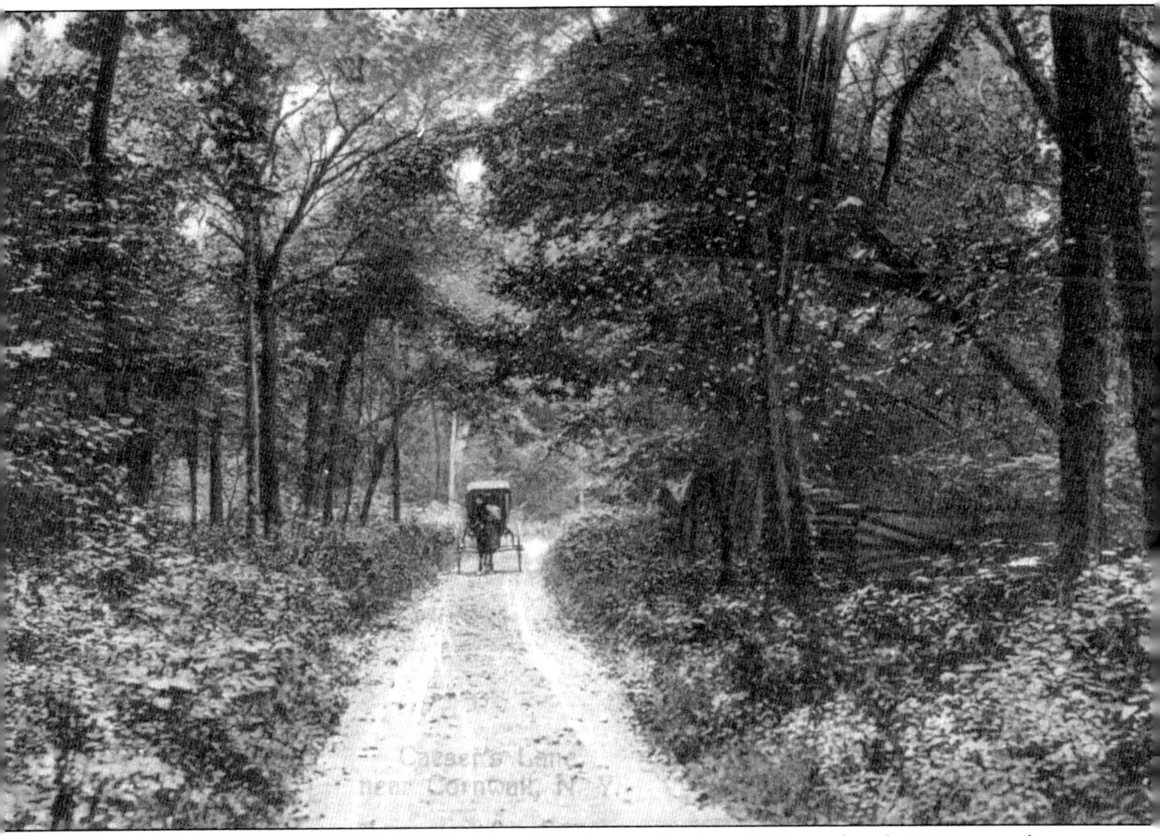

The primary mode of travel throughout New Windsor in the late 1800s and early 1900s was the horse and buggy. Caesars Lane, which stretched from the current-day Blooming Grove Turnpike to Route 9W, was a dirt road. It was the most convenient—and at times, even the most pleasant—route for those wanting to travel from town to town. As this horse and buggy approaches, perhaps the driver is thinking about the past he has left behind. One can only wonder whether he can imagine what the future will bring. (Courtesy of the Whitehill Collection.)